D1540036

Poverty from the Wealth of Nations

Also by M. Shahid Alam

GOVERNMENTS AND MARKETS IN ECONOMIC DEVELOPMENT STRATEGIES
Lessons from Korea, Taiwan and Japan

Poverty from the Wealth of Nations

Integration and Polarization in the Global Economy since 1760

M. Shahid Alam
Professor of Economics
Northeastern University
Boston
Massachusetts
USA

First published in Great Britain 2000 by
MACMILLAN PRESS LTD
Houndmills, Basingstoke, Hampshire RG21 6XS and London
Companies and representatives throughout the world

A catalogue record for this book is available from the British Library.

ISBN 0–333–77931–2

 First published in the United States of America 2000 by
ST. MARTIN'S PRESS, INC.,
Scholarly and Reference Division,
175 Fifth Avenue, New York, N.Y. 10010

ISBN 0–312–23018–4

Library of Congress Cataloging-in-Publication Data
Alam, M. Shahid (Mohammad Shahid), 1950–
Poverty from the wealth of nations : integration and polarization in the
global economy since 1760 / M. Shahid Alam.
p.   cm.
Includes bibliographical references and index.
ISBN 0–312–23018–4
1. Regional economic disparities—History.   2. Income distribution—History.
3. Capitalism—History.   4. International economic integration—History.   5.
Economic history—1750–1918.   6. Economic history—1918–   I. Title.

HC51 .A466   1999
337—dc21
99–046992

© M. Shahid Alam 2000

All rights reserved. No reproduction, copy or transmission of this publication may be made
without written permission.

No paragraph of this publication may be reproduced, copied or transmitted save with written
permission or in accordance with the provisions of the Copyright, Designs and Patents Act
1988, or under the terms of any licence permitting limited copying issued by the Copyright
Licensing Agency, 90 Tottenham Court Road, London W1P 0LP.

Any person who does any unauthorised act in relation to this publication may be liable to
criminal prosecution and civil claims for damages.

The author has asserted his right to be identified as the author of this work in accordance with
the Copyright, Designs and Patents Act 1988.

This book is printed on paper suitable for recycling and made from fully managed and sustained
forest sources.

10   9   8   7   6   5   4   3   2   1
09   08   07   06   05   04   03   02   01   00

Printed and bound in Great Britain by
Antony Rowe Ltd, Chippenham, Wiltshire

Dedicated to
My sons, Junaid and Noor,
And the memory of my parents

*'If any of you sees something evil, he should set it
right by his hand; if he is unable to do so, then by his tongue;
and if he is unable to do even that, then within his heart–but this
is the weakest form of faith.'*

*'There are indeed people who boast of their dead ancestors; but in
the sight of God they are more contemptible than the black beetle
that rolls a piece of dung with its nose.'*

Muhammad
(Asad 1993: 77, 31)

Contents

Tables

Abbreviations and Acronyms

AFR	AFR=1 for countries in Sub-Saharan Africa
AGECOL	Years between date of colonization and date of independence or 1960
COL	COL=1 for all countries that were *colonies* in 1950
DEN	Population density: a country's population divided by area
DEP	DEP=1 for all countries that were *dependencies* before 1950
GATT	General Agreement on Trade and Tariffs
GDP	Gross Domestic Product
ICP	International Comparison Project
IMF	International Monetary Fund
LEAD	LEAD=1 for Japan and countries in Western Europe
LITERACY	Percentage of adult population that is literate
NBER	National Bureau for Economic Research
NIC	NIC=1 for all newly independent countries that gained independence during 1940-50
OECD	Organization for Economic Cooperation and Development
OIL	OIL=1 for oil-rich countries
PCI	Per capita income (for per capita GDP)
POP	Population of country
QC	QC=1 for all countries that were quasi-colonies through most of the century leading up to the 1950s
QCC	Quasi-colonies *plus* colonies
SD	Sovereignty differential
SOV	SOV=1 for all countries that were independent in, or before, and had *sovereign* status thereafter
USAID	United States Agency for International Development
YSCHOOL	Average years of schooling in the labor force

Preface

*'To suggest social action for the public good to the City of London is
like discussing the* Origin of Species *with a bishop sixty years ago. The
first reaction is not intellectual, but moral. An orthodoxy is in question,
and the more persuasive the arguments the graver the offense.'*

J. M. Keynes (1926: 884-85)

In writing about the consequences of unequal power among states, using
the very tools that are used by economists, I very quickly discovered that
I was rowing in the wrong direction–against the mainstream in economics
and the social sciences more generally.

Over the past decade, I have worked on several empirical papers
which showed that the erosion of sovereignty had visibly adverse economic consequences for lagging countries in the period before 1950. All
other things remaining the same, the loss of sovereignty retarded industrialization, human capital formation and economic growth. All these papers
were rejected out of hand by the journals to which they were submitted,
with the exception of the first paper published by the *Cambridge Journal
of Economics*. Not one editor extended me the opportunity to respond to
the reviewer's comments. Nevertheless, after each rejection I revised the
papers–heeding the referees' comments, paring down the rhetoric, cen-
soring all offensive references to 'imperialism' and 'exploitation'–and
resubmitted them to another 'friendlier' journal. But the results were always the same–the referees and editors were not deceived. When it became clear that perseverance was not going to pay off, I decided I would
take another route and try my luck with book publishers. Predictably, they
offered a warmer welcome.

Perhaps, in my situation, I might be excused for thinking that it was
not my methods but my results that were 'wrong'. How could the quasi-
colonies and colonies (*QCC*) have been the worse for colonization? This
was no laughing matter. According to conventional wisdom, the colonial
governments were models of economic virtue: they were small, balanced
their budgets, kept their taxes low, protected property rights, permitted
free trade as well as free movement of capital and labor, and rarely assumed a direct interest in productive activities. How could the colonies
fail? They had everything the International Monetary Fund (*IMF*) wanted
for its clients. The claim that the colonies had put in a less than stellar

performance would not only upset economic orthodoxy. It also raised questions about another cherished belief–the 'civilizing mission' of the West. The colonies were where the West had the best chance of fulfilling its 'civilizing mission'. My results suggested that the mission had failed.

My skirmishing with economic journals carried some insights into why the social sciences have failed to give greater attention to the dynamics of unequal power in social relations. Unequal power has been pervasive through much of human history: between civilizations, nations, races, classes, sexes, age cohorts, and species. It is perhaps uncontroversial that the inequalities between civilizations, races and nations were never so great and pervasive as they have been since the industrial revolution. One would have supposed that this growing inequality of power would have been one of the central concerns of the social sciences during this period. It is doubtful if it was even of minor concern to mainstream economists.

This neglect is rooted in inequality itself. Over the past two hundred years, the social sciences were nearly always appropriated by the more powerful party in these relations of inequality. As a result, they could not hold up the mirror to the rich and powerful nations, and show them the damage and pain their power inflicted on weaker peoples. The rich and powerful would have none of this; they demanded a flattering self-image, as agents of civilization, modernizers, and carriers of light and truth. The social sciences rose to the occasion, collating appropriate 'facts' and floating theories that preserved the advantages of the rich and powerful and, at the same time, flattered their vanity. A few voices of dissent might still be heard because some men and women choose to follow their conscience. But more often these voices were suppressed by nationalism, racism, and religious bigotry.

What were the 'facts' and theories which the social sciences employed to justify and perpetuate Western hegemony? The 'facts' were simple. All non-Western societies were stuck in the past; they lacked the dialectics of change; they were despotisms rooted in the absence of private property; they had no systems of science, philosophy or accounting; they possessed no notions of freedom and rights; their religions preached fanaticism or taught them to be fatalists; and, always, they lacked energy and enterprise. The theories were mostly supplied by economists, who employed a battery of assumptions to demonstrate that all trading partners benefit from voluntary exchanges, a principle that was shown to be equally valid for exchanges between individuals, regions and nations. The dogma of free economic intercourse between nations was built upon this theory. It

won for the capital, skills and enterprises of advanced countries the right
to displace the capital, skills and enterprises of lagging countries.

Once these 'facts' and theories were in place, Western hegemony became an instrument of change, a necessary if painful step in the ad-
vancement of backward peoples. The white man assumed the burden of
governing these peoples because this was the only way they could be
introduced to the benefits of Western civilization. Colonialism was a
force for progress in the colonies. It replaced the Oriental despots with
the rule of law; placed private property on secure legal foundations; tore
down their previous isolationism; built roads and railways; freed them to
trade with the world, and benefit from capital inflows and the entry of
foreign skills and enterprises. The gains from colonization were incal-
culable. It is my impression that some of these ideas are still widely
held, by scholars and laymen alike–and deeply ingrained too.

These 'facts' and theories have come under fire in recent decades.
The challenge to the 'facts' began in the 1950s and has been gaining
ground ever since. It began with Needham's *Science and Civilization in
China* and Said's *Orientalism*, and continued to advance with Bernal's
Black Athena, Abu-Lughod's *Before European Hegemony*, Blaut's *The
Colonizer's Model of the World*, Amin's *Eurocentrism* and now Frank's
ReOrient and Goody's *The East in the West*. On the whole, these ad-
vances in scholarship have had a restraining influence on the Eurocen-
tric impulses in Western scholarship. That is not to say that defenders of
the true faith have been lacking. With his *Wealth and Poverty of Na-
tions*, Landes has now stepped into the fray as the chief defender of the
Eurocentric faith.

The challenge to the dogma of free trade came from two camps.
Starting in the late 1940s, several economists drew attention to market
failures which widened the disparities between advanced and lagging
countries, thus providing the economic rationale for policies of import
substitution that would sweep across the former colonies. There were
others who offered a more radical critique of global capitalism which led
to socialism and delinking from the world economy. The policies of import substitution went unchallenged for a while, but starting in the
1970s they called forth a neoliberal reaction, orchestrated by the advanced countries. By the 1990s, the Washington trio–United States government, *IMF* and World Bank–had re-established the dominance of the
old orthodoxy in policy making. Once again, the advanced countries
were busy creating a world economy that would brook no obstacles to
the free movement of their goods, services, capital, and corporations.

This is what makes it important that we review the impact of integration on polarization during the two centuries preceding the 1950s: the last time imperialism and free trade held sway over lagging countries in Asia and Africa. Once we recognize that integration between advanced and lagging countries widens the disparities between them, the Eurocentric thesis about the civilizing mission of imperialism is reversed. The countries which were forced to integrate had little to show by way of economic development. Those that were free to structure their integration did visibly better: they grew faster, achieved higher levels of industrialization, acquired a more educated labor force, and several of them nearly caught up with the advanced countries.

This thesis is developed at several levels. First, a review of the facts about disparities in chapter two shows that there was little to distinguish between now advanced and lagging countries around 1800, once we exclude a few outliers at both ends. A review of the trade statistics shows that Asia and Africa were rapidly integrated into the world economy, more rapidly than Latin America and the lagging countries in Europe; yet they were outpaced in growth by the latter. Integration did not lead to convergence. Chapter three surveys the theories on integration. We learn that the Smithian theory of the division of labor was quickly displaced by the Ricardian law of comparative advantage when the former would not support the dogma of free trade. However, lagging countries with industrial ambitions worked out their own theories of development with inspiration from Adam Smith. Drawing upon all these dissenting theories, chapter four develops a theory of integration *and* imperialism to show that in the two centuries before 1950 the evolution of global disparities was deeply conditioned by the loss of sovereignty. This takes us to the core of the book–chapters five and six–which develops a taxonomy of sovereignty and shows that economic policies and economic performance across the lagging countries varied systematically with sovereignty.

I have received encouragement and support from several sources in carrying this project to completion. My deepest thanks go to my graduate students, in my classes on development economics, for their forbearance as they endured a growing array of tables on sovereignty differentials. Amongst my colleagues, John Adams alone had the unique privilege of reading and commenting on all my unpublished papers. It was also his duty to commiserate with me and puzzle over their ill-starred encounters with reviewers and editors. I would also like to acknowledge my debt to Irma Adelman, Christopher Clague, Sandy Darity, Keith Griffin, G. K. Helleiner, Shahrukh Khan, Peter Kilby, David Landes, Jeffrey Nugent, Mancur Olson, Salim Rashid, and Robert Solow, who over the years have shown their graciousness in sending me their comments on papers that were eventually incorporated into this book. They assured me, without always agreeing with me, that I was not tilting against windmills.

Some of the material in this book has been published before, or is scheduled for publication. Parts of chapters one and seven have appeared before as a chapter, 'Does sovereignty matter for economic growth? An analysis of growth rates between 1870 and 1950', in John Adams and Francesco Pigliaru, eds., *Economic growth and change: National and regional patterns of convergence* (Cheltenham, UK: Edward Elgar, 1999). Chapter two of this book is based upon a paper, 'How rich was Europe around 1760 after all', which will appear in the *Review of Radical Political Economics*. I am grateful to Elgar and the *Review* for permission to reproduce this material in my book.

My personal debts are fewer but deeper. My thoughts turn in joy to my wife, Farzana, and my sons, Junaid and Noor, who have been my haven during my years of scholarly wanderlust. My thoughts also turn in sadness to my mother who departed to meet her Creator even as I finished this manuscript. Her prayers for me will remain my greatest solace.

I end with the prayer with which Al Biruni ended his book on India. 'We ask God to pardon us for every statement of ours which is not true. We ask Him to help us that we may adhere to what yields Him satisfaction. We ask Him to lead us to a proper insight into the nature of that which is false and idle, that we may sift it so as to distinguish the chaff from the wheat. All good comes from Him, and it is He who is clement towards His slaves. Praise be to God, the Lord of the worlds, and His blessings be upon the prophet Muhammad and his whole family (Sachau 1971: 246)!'

1

Introduction

'I contend that we are the finest race in the world and that the more of the world we inhabit the better it is for the human race.'

Cecil Rhodes, *Confession of Faith* (1877)[1]

'... the Indian Government, with every honest desire to its duty, is unable to secure the material welfare of the people, because it is not in touch with the people, does not accept the co-operation of the people, cannot by its constitution act in the interests of the people.'

Romesh Dutt (1901)

The asymmetric developments in the global economy during industrial epoch *I*–roughly the two hundred years ending in the 1950s–were a result not of unequal markets *per se*, but these dual asymmetries were shaped by two others, 'unequal races' and unequal states, whose seminal and enduring impact on the evolution of the global economy has not received the attention it deserves.[2]

The evolution of the global economy during industrial epoch *I* was defined by four stylized facts: (i) relentless polarization, (ii) international integration, (iii) spatial concentration of manufactures, and (iv) centralization of power. Once stated, these facts are a commonplace, and in one form or another they have formed the premises of every liberation movement over the past century. Yet orthodox theories of the global economy, as well as dissenting explanations, fail to account for one or more of these stylized facts. Orthodox theories admit only the second and third facts; their prediction that integration will lead to all round growth being at variance with the first. The dissenting writers incorporate the first, second and third facts, but exclude power from their analysis. Their narrative shows that growing disparities in the global economy were caused by international integration *per se*. They analyze the power *of* markets, but not the *powers* that shaped these markets. We advance their narrative by inserting power into the global economy: two manifestations of power, that of 'unequal races' and unequal states.

True, international integration *per se* was a force capable of compounding global inequalities during industrial epoch *I*. When commodity and capital markets in two unequal economies–one advanced and one lagging–are integrated, this sets up forces that concentrate manufactures, capital and technology in the advanced country, while the lagging country first loses ground in manufactures, and is later squeezed out of a growing array of primary goods.[3] The result is a global economic system wherein free exchanges between advanced and lagging countries continually enrich the former by marginalizing the latter. A well told story no doubt, but still, this is *Hamlet* without the Danish prince.

This vision of an integrated global economy is no doubt suggestive; but what it conceals is vital. It leaves out the states, both powerful and weak, without whom, for instance, the failure of integration in labor markets would be hard to explain. Once these political actors enter upon the world stage, the plot thickens, and the narrative becomes more nuanced. A collision between the advanced and lagging countries now becomes inevitable. The advanced countries seek to integrate the lagging countries, monopolize their markets, and appropriate their resources. In order to prevent these outcomes, the lagging countries seek to *structure*[4] their integration into the world economy, to distance themselves from the advanced countries. The advanced countries have the upper hand in this contest, but their imperialism is not without limits. Many lagging countries were converted into colonies and quasi-colonies, but quite a few also preserved their sovereignty. These sovereign lagging countries structured their integration and developed indigenous manufactures, capital, enterprises and technology. They grew, some of them rapidly, and a few even caught up with the advanced countries. Those that lost their sovereignty, often, also lost a lot more, including manufactures, indigenous enterprises and a chance to expand their capital and technology. Very few of them knew any growth at all.

Racism was intimately woven into this dynamic of polarization. Barred from membership in the 'family of sovereign nations', a whites-only club founded on cultural and racial distinctions, the non-Western states became fair game for ambitious Western powers. The military superiority of the advanced countries would be applied with enduring and, often, devastating consequences only against non-Western countries in Asia and Africa, all of whom were colonized or converted into 'open-door' countries before the close of the nineteenth century.[5] On the other hand, over the same period, the Ottoman domains in Eastern Europe and the Iberian colonies in the Americas moved firmly in the opposite direction, and most of them had graduated to full sovereignty before the close of the nineteenth century. The 'white' lagging countries were marked out for sovereignty because of their racial and cultural affinities to the great powers–not because they were better governed.

The global system created during the nineteenth century was enduring but not immutable. It entered into a new phase–industrial epoch *II*–in the 1950s, marked by a dispersion of manufacturing capacity to lagging countries. Two developments prepared the conditions for this reversal. Its proximate cause was the dramatic decentralization of power from advanced to lagging countries starting in the late 1940s, precipitated, in turn, by the cumulative effects of the two great wars, the Russian revolution of 1917, and the gathering storm of liberation movements in the colonies and quasi-colonies. This decentralization of power, when combined with the now large wage disparities between advanced and lagging countries, signaled the diffusion of manufactures to lagging countries. Once set in motion, this diffusion would become irreversible.

This decentralization of power, however, could not have lasted very long. After a quick recovery from the ravages of war, the advanced countries entered into a golden period of growth, which greatly increased their absolute lead over most lagging countries. Moreover, the threat of global communism, together with the risk of a nuclear war with the Soviets, had early on created a unity in the ranks of advanced countries never seen before. Once the combined resources of this resurgent capitalism were mobilized to combat the spread of communism, the Soviets did not have a prayer. Thus, notwithstanding several tactical advances, in Cuba, Vietnam, Afghanistan and parts of Africa, it was clear by the early 1980s that the policy of containment had the Soviets tied up in knots. Communism was now a spent force. Finally, the oil crises of the 1970s, together with the global recession of 1981, had placed the external payments of many lagging countries under serious strain, making them vulnerable to external pressures.

Taking the cue from these developments–and spurred by a growing industrial challenge from several lagging countries–the advanced countries went on the offensive in the 1980s. They initiated moves to *re*-centralize the power they had lost after the second great war: to close the window of opportunity that had opened up for lagging countries in the late 1940s. The International Monetary Fund, the World Bank and, later, the World Trade Organization went into action, stripping the lagging countries of their ability to structure their integration into the global economy. The lagging countries' honeymoon with sovereignty was nearly over towards the end of the 1990s. Industrial epoch *II* had now been joined by imperialism *II*.

A Theory of the Global Economy: 1760-1960

The Industrial Revolution inaugurated a new period in world history, an industrial epoch, which at first concentrated the world's manufactures in a small number of advanced countries, but is now, in its second phase, dispersing them to a growing number of lagging countries.

The evolution of the global economy in the first phase of the industrial epoch–roughly the two hundred years preceding the 1950s–was attended by growing disparities in development even as integration between the advanced and lagging countries continued to deepen. This paradox of inequality, the issue at the heart of this book, contradicts much of what we have been taught for more than two hundred years about international integration. Ever since Adam Smith (1776) formulated his critique of mercantilist policies, economists have believed that free markets, and their extension across national boundaries, offer the best chances for growth. Starting with David Ricardo (1817), generations of economists have worked to translate this vision into theories of the international economy that have remained unassailable in their eminence. In time, with a little mathematical teasing, economists pulled out theorems and lemmas about international trade whose rigor, at times, is only matched by their irrelevance. One of these theorems, the factor-price equalization theorem, proclaims that free trade alone may push all trading countries to the same absolute level of factor rewards.[6] Even in a world of nation states, each jealously guarding its frontiers against the movements of capital and labor, a dispensation of free trade promises to carry us to the Valhalla of absolute global equality.

In fact, so deeply impressed were the early economists by the putative gains from integration, they counted it perverse if any lagging country chose to erect barriers to the free movement of goods and capital. Not surprisingly, this perversity was not to be tolerated. Throughout the nineteenth century, Western arms worked overtime to bring the black sheep into the fold of the global economy. Some quickly saw the light and acquiesced to the opening of their markets, in order to avoid worse consequences. Many more had to be conquered and colonized for a more thorough makeover of their economies and institutions. This global 'social work' was, of course, well worth the trouble. Nearly always, a party of obstreperous traders waited in the wings, anxious to collect the rich dividends.

This vision of the global economy was deeply flawed. Starting in the sixteenth century, many countries were forcibly integrated into the global economy, their markets flung open to the free movement of goods, capital, labor and enterprises. Yet, these primary-producing economies languished while their exports multiplied, so that after decades, and sometimes centuries, of assimilation into the global economy, they had very little to show for their unqualified devotion to free markets. In contrast, lagging countries which were free and chose to resist the logic of international integration–to save, shore up and modernize their manufactures, enterprises and skills–continued to industrialize, to grow and to narrow their economic distance behind the advanced countries. Quaintly, free countries with unfree markets nearly always outperformed unfree countries with free markets.

This discrepancy between theory and facts was scarcely noticed by mainstream economists for nearly two hundred years. The failure of some two-thirds of mankind to derive any advantage from their incorporation into global markets did not surprise, much less disturb, anyone. This was part of the Darwinian struggle for survival to which many are called but few are chosen. This equanimity was breached only in the 1950s when a changing world order elevated the 'wretched of the earth' to the center stage of global conflicts. After a long regress into abstractions, a few economists were now constructing theories of global markets that did not flinch in the face of facts. Perhaps the two most notable contributions to this new theoretical literature came from Gunnar Myrdal (1957) and Hla Myint (1954). Global markets, they argued, set up disequalizing forces between advanced and lagging countries. An initial advantage, even a small one, can be compounded several times by the free play of market forces; conversely, those who are drafted into markets with handicaps get the short end of the bargain. Their arguments rested on the recognition of differences in the technologies of manufacturing and primary sectors *and* the presence of monopoly power that worked against lagging countries.

Writers of the dependency school in Latin America also blamed global markets for their backwardness. But they told a somewhat different story. Capitalist development failed in lagging countries because it was not homegrown: it was transplanted by foreign capitalists who used their monopoly power to siphon off surpluses from lagging countries. Much worse, the foreign capitalists found allies in the indigenous landowning classes, and together they perpetuated a social system based on primary production, inequities and repression. Some neo-Marxists offered a more esoteric explanation of underdevelopment. Trade between countries with unequal wages, they argued, results in the exchange of unequal amounts of labor, and it is this 'unequal exchange' that is at the root of underdevelopment. To free themselves from this unequal exchange, lagging countries would have to disengage themselves from the world economy.[7]

The unorthodox writers did not show nearly the same interest in *how* unequal power entered into the creation of the global economy. Sure, there is talk of imperialism, but this never becomes the central factor in their analyses. It is in vain that one looks for a comprehensive statement about how advanced countries deployed their superior power to disequalize the terms under which lagging countries were integrated into the global economy. These unequal relations appear as datum in their analysis or, at best, they are seen as products of market forces, not outcomes enforced by inequalities of power between advanced and lagging countries. In other words, imperialism–as the deployment of real force–rarely becomes a factor comparable in importance to market forces in the ordering of economic relations between advanced and lagging countries.

The central task of this book is to incorporate states–unequal states–into the analysis of the global economy during industrial epoch *I*. States enter ineluctably into the analysis of the global economy. Global markets were both shaped and superseded by the actions of states, so that we cannot understand how the global economy took shape, and how different countries were assigned different functions in this economy, without also examining the distribution of power amongst states–which countries had the power to shape and supersede market forces?

Although our interest in the global economy begins with the Industrial Revolution, a brief digression into its origins may be useful. The maritime ascendancy of Western nations, signaled by the voyages of 'discovery', produced results that were momentous for the evolution of the global economy. It led to the dominance of Western mercantile capital over the major circuits of international trade; conversely, it produced a retreat of mercantile capital based in other regions of the world. This growth in Western mercantile capital led to cumulative advances in shipping, financial markets, property rights and urbanization–developments which eventually produced, in countries where they were most advanced, the ascendancy of markets over states in the spheres of production and exchange. In time, these changes culminated in the Industrial Revolution–a stream of innovations in energy use, production technology and organization–which gave to advanced countries a growing comparative advantage in manufactures and placed manufactures in the driver's seat of the global economy.

The Industrial Revolution created another asymmetry. The military superiority that Europeans had enjoyed for two centuries on the high seas was extended to the land in the first decades of the nineteenth century. Even the most powerful Asian empires were now unable to match the superior arms, organization and fighting tactics of the great European powers. The die was now cast. The spread and consolidation of Western Europe's dominance was now mostly a matter of time and opportunity. The only remaining hindrances were distance, access and tropical diseases. Advances in steam navigation, telegraph and railways removed the first two; quinine and vaccinations took care of the third.[8]

Although the Industrial Revolution created the conditions for the emergence of a disequalizing global economy, the disparities between advanced and lagging countries were still quite small at the time. In 1760, or even as late as 1800, these disparities were within a range that was not uncommon by historical standards. Although estimates of these disparities vary, they were nearly always smaller than two to one, and upon excluding the polar cases, the differences often favored some of today's lagging countries. Similarly, notwithstanding the catalytic role it had played in the two preceding centuries, international trade was still a sideshow. Even as late as 1820, global trade amounted to a modest two percent of global output.[9] On the surface, the global economy had changed very little.

All this would change dramatically over the next century and a half. The eight decades preceding 1800 recorded a doubling of global trade; in the next eight decades it had expanded 13-fold, and in 1913 it was more than 43 times its level in 1800.[10] A global capital market, centered in London, had also been established, with the capacity for moving vast sums of capital between advanced and lagging countries. This dramatic acceleration in the integration of global markets produced sustained growth in the advanced countries but stagnation or worse in most lagging countries. In consequence, the income gap between them in 1950 had widened to more than five to one.[11] Contrary to the prediction of orthodox economists, the development gap between advanced and lagging countries was increasing even as their economies were being pulled together by global markets.

This paradox called for an explanation. Several self-serving ones were readily available. The natives were lazy, irrational, risk-averse, and generally unfit for taking advantage of the opportunities made available by market economies. The first serious explanations were offered by structural economists in the 1950s who rejected the Ricardian theory of trade because it did not recognize the strong asymmetries in technology between manufacturing and primary activities. Not only was manufacturing characterized by increasing returns to scale, it generated important externalities for primary activities, transportation, and labor and financial markets. In the presence of these asymmetries, integration would deepen

Table 1.1
Gains and Losses from Integration

	State	Capital	Land	Labor: Manufactures	Labor: Primary
Advanced Countries	Gain	Gain	Loss	Gain	Loss
Lagging Countries	Loss	Loss	Gain	Loss	Gain

the advanced country's comparative advantage in manufactures, reduce costs in primary activities, increase the efficiency of capital markets, and augment organizational skills. Conversely, this would displace manufactures, enterprises, capital and skills from lagging countries. Attracted by higher returns, savings too would gravitate towards advanced countries.[12] In a nutshell, this was the dynamics of *unequal* development.

This heterodox account of international integration tells less than half the story. Polarization was not caused by market forces *per se*–nor by market forces alone. The global economy was not a spontaneous order created by the free play of market forces; it had to be politically constructed and, often, this involved bitterly fought contests between states and, within countries, between classes. It was the relative power of states and classes–as mediated and modified by race, religion and ethnicity–which determined which lagging countries would be free to structure their integration into the global economy. In order to unveil the political construction of the global economy, we have to begin by examining the asymmetric impact of integration on states and classes in advanced and lagging countries.

These effects are summarized in table 1.1. Capital, manufacturing labor and the state gain–landowners and primary-sector labor lose–from integration in advanced countries.[13] Since capital and the state were already strong, this explains why the advanced countries gravitated towards greater integration, even though this transition was often delayed in deference to the interests of powerful landowners. While landowners used their power to prevent or delay the free import of food and raw materials which competed with their own products, they could do little else to slow down the expansion of manufactures. In general, manufacturing capital from advanced countries had little difficulty in mobilizing official support to gain free access to markets in lagging countries. Thus, well before they had adopted a policy of free trade for their own economies, the advanced countries were advocating and pushing for free trade in the lagging countries. It is not too difficult to see why the lagging countries did not generally agree with this policy.

The gains and losses from integration are reversed in the lagging countries. Capital, manufacturing labor and the state lose–landowners and primary-sector labor gain–from integration. Although landowners were the dominant class in many lagging countries, they still had to contend with the combined interests of the state, capital and labor. This contest could go either way, though most likely, the size, power and symbolic force of the state were the determining factors in this contest. Not surprisingly, at the beginning of the nineteenth century, we encounter a variety of solutions to this contest. Some countries chose to integrate their economies, others sought to structure their integration, and a few opted for complete isolation. A fourth group had no choices to make: as colonies, they had been integrated into their metropoles.

There never existed a strong *ex ante* complementarity of interests between advanced and lagging countries, even where the landowners had the upper hand in the lagging countries. The advanced countries sought unconditional access to the markets and resources of lagging countries, generally without any *quid pro quo*. It was unlikely that lagging countries would agree to these demands voluntarily. Even when the balance of their class forces leaned towards integration, they would move forward gingerly because there were industries they might want to protect for reasons of security and domestic politics; and almost certainly they would seek to protect indigenous enterprises, capital and skills from direct foreign competition. Moreover, at some later date, when political and economic conditions became more favorable to manufactures, they might want to reverse their present policy of integration. Lagging countries wanting to industrialize, or to isolate their economies from foreign contacts, would, of course, erect stronger barriers to deter entry into their markets. These conflicts were fundamental and defined the first and minimal task of imperialism: the use of force to open up the economies of lagging countries.

Imperialism had other aims too. The advanced countries would not be content with the gains that could be had on free markets; surely they had the power to take more. One way to do this was to keep rivals out of the lagging countries. Therefore, whenever they could, advanced countries would claim free *and* exclusive access to the markets and resources of lagging countries. But monopoly control carried them only as far as markets generally go; and they could go farther. The next step was direct expropriation: to use their superior power to capture the assets, lands, and mineral resources of lagging countries; to draft their labor for use on public works, plantations, and farms owned by settlers; to use their tax revenues for foreign conquests, to attract settlers, or guarantee minimum returns on foreign investments in infrastructure. While monopoly control over lagging countries tended to restrict integration, direct appropriation of their resources pulled in the opposite direction. Whenever the latter exerted the stronger effect, it would result in *hyper*-integration, that is, integration beyond what would be possible under free markets.

The logic of imperialism pointed inexorably in the direction of colonization: this would assure *exclusive* access to the lagging countries and direct expropriation of their resources. Over the course of the nineteenth century, with the growing military superiority of advanced countries, colonization for most lagging countries became a near certainty that could only be delayed by geography, diseases, distance, a determined resistance, or rivalry amongst advanced countries. Nevertheless, surveying the map of sovereignty in 1900 one finds that many lagging countries had escaped colonization or quasi-colonization.[14] With the solitary exception of Japan, all non-Western countries in Asia and Africa had by this date been reduced to colonies and quasi-colonies; on the other hand, the lagging countries in Europe and all the white settler states in the Americas, Africa and Oceania had retained their independence, or graduated to independence if they were colonies. Imperialism too admitted of limits—defined by racial, religious and ethnic affinities between advanced and lagging countries.

The classical economists maintained that colonialism was the *deus ex machina* that would bring civilization to the backward peoples of Asia and Africa. The superior rule of Europeans, together with free trade and a sprinkling of white settlers, would eventually elevate them into the ranks of civilized nations. This prognosis continued to command a loyal following even after the second great war in the guise of various modernization theories of development.[15] Only the neo-Marxists rejected this thesis, but their rejection did not go far enough. They argued that sovereignty in the periphery did not matter; advanced countries could always, or nearly always, threaten, cajole, or bribe their way around independent governments in lagging countries. We do not agree. Sovereignty did matter! Countries which had it would grow faster than countries which did not. The logic of it is simple. Colonization of lagging countries led, *via* forced integration, to the loss of manufactures, a shrinking comparative advantage in primary production, and the displacement of indigenous capital, skills and enterprises; it also led to monopolization and direct appropriation of their resources. Only sovereign lagging countries—free to structure their integration into the world economy—could avoid or minimize the adverse consequences of integration. *Ergo*, loss of sovereignty retarded economic growth.

Sovereignty and Polarization: Empirical Results

Our empirical investigations reveal a strong and systematic connection during industrial epoch *I* between sovereignty, on the one hand, and economic policies, structural economic parameters, and long run growth rates across lagging countries.

The predictions of our theory of the global economy, at each of these levels, are unambiguous. In the long run, sovereign countries will structure their international relations to develop manufactures and indigenous capital, enterprises and technological capabilities; they will impose at the outset, or gradually, policies that regulate the entry of imports and foreign capital, labor and enterprises. On the other hand, the quasi-colonies and colonies will implement policies which facilitate the free entry of imports and foreign factors; the establishment of foreign monopolies over their markets; and direct expropriation of their resources. These asymmetries ensure that loss of sovereignty will produce lower levels of industrialization, lower levels of productivity in the subsistence sector, lower levels of human capital, lower rates of taxation and public expenditure and, finally, lower growth rates of per capita income.

Nearly all these hypotheses can be tested once we have a taxonomy of sovereignty. This follows directly from our definition of sovereignty as the power of indigenous factors–including capital, land and labor–to *structure* their relations with global markets. Three criteria are employed in judging the sovereignty of a lagging country: whether it had an indigenous government; whether it was subject to 'open-door' treaties limiting its policy autonomy; and whether foreign capital had a dominant presence in its economy. This leads to a four-fold taxonomy of sovereignty. In decreasing order, these four categories are sovereign countries, dependencies, quasi-colonies and colonies. [16]

The definitions of these categories are transparent, ensuring that ambiguities about where a country belongs in the four-fold taxonomy are minimal. Colonies are governed by expatriates appointed *by* and *from* an advanced country; this ensures that colonial governments are accountable almost exclusively *to* an advanced country. Quasi-colonies are modestly better off. They have indigenous governments, but their ability to structure their international relations is severely limited by 'open-door' treaties. They are forced to limit their tariffs to very low levels, to permit free entry of capital and enterprises from treaty countries, and exempt citizens of treaty countries from local taxes and local courts. Dependencies have indigenous governments whose ability to structure their international relations is often constrained by the dominant presence of foreign capital. [17]

In the long run, they are in a stronger position than the quasi-colonies because their ability to formulate policies is not subject to limits enforced by treaties. Sovereign countries rank highest; they have indigenous governments that are free from 'open-door' treaties and are not visibly constrained by foreign capital.

The validity of the four basic sovereignty categories is first tested with reference to economic policies. A review of economic policies in lagging countries in the century before the 1950s shows that resistance to integration was directly correlated with sovereignty.[18] Sovereign countries and, to a lesser degree, dependencies employed a variety of policies that favored domestic manufactures and indigenous capital, enterprises and skills.[19] Not only did the colonies and quasi-colonies generally fail to support domestic manufactures and indigenous factors, they often enforced policies which discriminated against indigenous capital, enterprises, labor and skills. A lot of this discrimination was informal, the result of racial preferences, but often it was also enforced by 'open-door' treaties and colonial laws.

Correlations between sovereignty, on the one hand, and growth and structural parameters across lagging countries are easily estimated once we have a taxonomy of sovereignty. It involves estimating a reduced-form equation: $Y = \alpha + \beta U + \delta V + \varepsilon$, where the dependent variable, Y, represents growth rates of per capita income or one of several structural parameters in lagging countries, U is the set of economic and social determinants of Y, V is a set of variables relating to sovereignty and ε is a normally distributed error term. In every case, V includes a set of dummy variables measuring different levels of sovereignty. Sovereignty differentials in any dependent variable, Y, are given by the coefficients of the sovereignty dummies. Thus, if colonies are the base category, the estimated coefficient for sovereign countries ($SOV=1$ for all sovereign countries) measures the differential in Y between sovereign countries and colonies, everything else held constant.

In order to address concerns about the sensitivity of our results on sovereignty differentials to the taxonomy of sovereignty, we estimated these differentials for several alternative taxonomies. These alternative taxonomies are derived by successively merging the intermediate categories in the five-fold taxonomy into two polar categories.[20] Thus, the category comprising sovereign countries is expanded successively to include dependencies, quasi-colonies and newly independent countries (*NIC*); alternatively, the category of colonies is expanded to include *NIC*, quasi-colonies and dependencies. Taken together, these taxonomies permit us to make ten different comparisons between polar categories; these polar

Table 1.2
Complete Set of Binary Comparisons

Group I	Group II
SOV	COL
	COL-NIC
	COL-NIC-QC
	COL-NIC-QC-DEP
SOV-DEP	COL
	COL-NIC
	COL-NIC-QC
SOV-DEP-QC	COL
	COL-NIC
SOV-DEP-QC-NIC	COL

categories are set out in table 1.2.[21] We expect that sovereignty differentials for any category relative to colonies (or any other base category) will decrease as we expand the scope of the first category. Alternatively, a similar decline in sovereignty differentials is expected for an expansion in the scope of the base category.

This methodology was employed to estimate sovereignty differentials in growth rates of per capita income, export orientation, industrialization, and three measures of human capital. Nearly always, these estimates yielded sovereignty differentials that were positive (negative, for export orientation), statistically significant and quantitatively large. Further statistical analysis showed that these results were robust to variations in the taxonomy of sovereignty, changes in sample size and specifications, and corrections for simultaneity biases.

Export orientation in 1960 varied inversely with sovereignty. Export orientation was measured as the ratio of exports to gross domestic product; the independent variables included the sovereignty dummies, population density (proxy for resource endowments), population (proxy for size of economy), the square of population, a dummy variable for Western countries and Japan, and another dummy variable for oil surplus countries.[22] The regression results showed that in 1960 sovereign countries, dependencies, quasi-colonies and *NIC* were not as export oriented as the colonies. Interestingly, the higher levels of export orientation in the colonies varied directly with the age of the colony. A hundred years of colonization generally added five percentage *points* to the export ratio.

The results showed a strong positive correlation between sovereignty and industrialization, measured as the share of manufactures in national output.[23] The sovereignty differentials in industrialization between sovereign countries and the colonies was 11.9 percentage points in 1960, compared to an average industrialization of 8.6 percent for all the colonies in our sample. The basic thrust of this result did not change when we introduced a dummy variable to control for the presence of Sub-Saharan countries, disaggregated the sample into large and small countries, or employed alternative taxonomies of sovereignty.[24]

We found strong evidence of large sovereignty differentials in three measures of human capital: adult literacy rates in 1960 and average years of schooling in the labor force in 1960 and 1965.[25] The sovereignty differential in literacy rates between sovereign countries and the colonies was 62.6 percentage points; this would have to be adjusted downwards by eight to ten percentage points for every hundred years of colonial rule. The corresponding differential in average years of schooling in 1960 was 4 years; similar results were obtained for an alternative measure of schooling in 1965. Most likely, sovereignty differentials in the more specialized skills were even larger, since colonies systematically excluded natives from the best, most skilled jobs.

Finally, sovereignty differentials in growth rates of per capita income were estimated for the period 1900 to 1950, with controls for initial per capita income, adult literacy rates, and a dummy variable for countries in Europe.[26] These estimates yielded a sovereignty differential of 1.59 percentage points between sovereign countries and a composite category consisting of quasi-colonies and colonies (QCC); the corresponding differential between dependencies and QCC was 0.64 percentage points. Both differentials were statistically significant at the one percent level. Similar results were obtained for two alternative taxonomies derived by merging sovereign countries with dependencies or, alternatively, by merging dependencies with QCC. Further, the differentials became larger as the sample of lagging countries was made more restrictive.[27]

Correlation or Causation?

The presence of a strong inverse relation between colonization, on the one hand, and growth rates of per capita income, industrialization and human capital formation during industrial epoch *I*, can be unsettling for two reasons.

It undermines the claims of *mission civilizatrice*. Where was the civilizing mission if the colonies–where, unarguably, this mission was at its best–performed much worse than sovereign countries that had not been touched by the civilizing mission? Surely, if the classical ideal of *laissez faire* was realized anywhere, it would have to be in the colonies; while the sovereign countries openly flouted its dictates. Yet, the diligent acolytes of classical economics stayed back with failing grades while the dropouts graduated at the head of the class! There are of course other ways to skin a cat. True believers in the white man's burden and orthodox theory might tell other stories–contrary stories–to dismiss the observed correlations between economic backwardness and loss of sovereignty. They might argue that only the most backward countries lost their sovereignty: this, because economic backwardness made a country vulnerable to conquest. Thus, since the most backward countries were chosen for colonization, it is not surprising that their backwardness persisted *after* colonization. This syllogism is faulty in both its premises, although casting doubt on the first premise should be sufficient to establish a *non sequitur*.

The first premise stems from unfamiliarity with the nature and history of colonies. Colonization depended on a lot more than a country's backwardness and, hence, its ability to defend itself. First, it is not clear, *a priori*, why backwardness *per se* should mark out a country for colonization. After all, a country's value as a colony depends on the richness of its resources and markets; and backwardness *per se* does not signal the presence of rich resources or large markets. In some cases, a country might have invited colonization because it was perceived by one or more advanced countries as a potential economic or military rival; but here too, backwardness could not have been the source of this rivalry.[28] Finally, colonies were acquired for their strategic value. However, such strategic value had a lot more to do with a country's *location* rather than its backwardness.

Could it be, the skeptics will persist, that although unattractive as colonies, the backward countries offered the most vulnerable military targets, and this is what led to their colonization. Such an easy equation between backwardness and vulnerability will not stand up to scrutiny. In several cases, a country's best defenses against colonization consisted of barriers erected by nature, including landlocked isolation, impenetrable mountains, a desert terrain, remoteness from the bases of great powers, and diseases without cures: all of them conditions that would commonly be regarded as *causes* of backwardness.[29] Amongst other factors that might deter colonization one might include a country's great expanse, large population, a tradition of militancy, the presence of fierce tribes, or easy access to superior firearms. Once again, some of these factors may also have served to keep a country backward. Backwardness, it would appear, may actually have helped to *deter* colonization.

The presumption that colonies were easy military targets must also be rejected on empirical grounds. The evidence presented in chapter five shows that throughout the nineteenth century, the European powers and United States used armed coercion against Latin American countries, even the largest ones, frequently, at will, and without any effective resistance. On the other hand, the Algerians resisted the French invasion for four decades, and nearly a hundred thousand French men died before the resistance was finally broken. Later, when the Europeans invaded Africa, the African resistance often lasted for decades, even though the Europeans had the advantage of rapid-firing Gatlings and Maxims.

Military factors alone did not determine which countries would be colonized. Latin America and Europe's lagging countries were not less vulnerable to colonization than countries in Asia and Africa. Yet, during the nineteenth century, not a single country in Europe or Latin America was colonized, and many that were colonies gained their independence. On the other hand, all the countries in Asia and Africa, with the exception of Japan, eventually lost their sovereignty. How could it be that even the smallest, most backward countries in Latin America or Europe retained their independence, while larger, more powerful states and empires in Asia and Africa were unable to resist colonization?

The construction and deconstruction of sovereignty during the nineteenth century did not depend on power alone. The great powers did not conduct their affairs in a social vacuum. They were members of a Western 'family of nations' bound together by racial, religious and historical affinities, and sharing common norms regarding statehood, civilization and sovereignty. Non-Western states and societies were not admitted into this charmed circle since they had no racial, religious, or historical affinities with Europe. This exclusion had some radical implications. It automatically certified them as uncivilized, savages, barbarians, or heathens, and, in Strang's (1996) formulation, 'delegitimated' their sovereignty: thus exposing them to unprovoked wars, slaughter, slavery and colonization by Western states. On the other hand, the lagging countries in Europe and white settler countries in the Americas, Africa and Oceania belonged to the Western 'family of nations', and this nearly always protected them from the same depredations.

The second premise of the syllogism—that later backwardness of colonies is explained by their initial backwardness—fares no better on closer examination. That backwardness may sometimes be self-perpetuating, is a thesis that must be taken seriously, but its relevance to most of the colonies is doubtful. When backwardness persists over long periods, this is because the economic, political and social institutions that underpin and reinforce this condition, form an interlocking complex that will not unravel without some powerful external shocks. It is hard to imagine that the trauma of colonization had failed to administer these shocks, even though colonial rulers overthrew indigenous systems of power and land tenure; displaced indigenous populations; forcibly incorporated the colonies into global markets; completed the domination of their commerce, mining and plantations by foreign enterprises; imposed alien languages and systems of education; and, in many cases, introduced alien religions. Is it likely that the original causes of backwardness in the colonies survived the shock of so many transmutations in their fundamental structures and institutions? If anything did survive, this privileged position might belong to systems of family life, some elusive but ineradicable aspects of their culture, some irremovable skein of thought, some perverse deities who obstructed progress by their deadening hold on the minds of benighted worshippers.

But this thesis of an enduring cultural drag on growth in the colonies and quasi-colonies will not wash. First, consider the radical contrast in the growth experience of *QCC* (quasi-colonies and colonies) before and after their de-colonization. The *QCC* experienced a dramatic acceleration in growth rates in the four decades after 1950; their weighted average annual growth rate jumped up from -0.08 percent between 1900 and 1950 to 2.96 percent between 1950 and 1992. These results were confirmed when we estimated sovereignty differentials for growth rates between 1950 and 1992, still using the original sample of lagging countries, with controls for initial levels of per capita income, adult literacy rates in 1950–or 1965 when data for 1950 were missing–and location in Europe. The sovereignty differentials between sovereign countries and *QCC* were negative and statistically insignificant at the ten percent level. The estimates of the corresponding sovereignty differentials for dependencies had even larger negative values and were statistically significant at the one percent level. After regaining their sovereignty during the 1940s, the *QCC* had chalked up a growth record that was superior to that of dependencies *and* sovereign countries even after we control for initial per capita income, adult literacy rates and membership in Europe.

This quantum leap in the growth of *QCC* after 1950 defies explanation if we insist that growth, before this date, was retarded by some elusive but enduring cultural obstacles. It will not do to claim that the institutional incubus which had hung over colonies before 1950 and had resisted the deft touch of the civilizing mission, had suddenly, and conveniently, ended its vigil after this date. The fundamental change that *did* occur around this date was the weakening of imperialism generally and, more specifically, the dismantling of colonialism. Around this time, the *QCC* in our sample regained a substantial degree of sovereign control over their policies and lost no time in implementing policies that supported the growth of industrialization and indigenous capital, skills and enterprises. Could these interventionist policies have been responsible for the dramatic acceleration in the growth rates of former quasi-colonies and colonies in the four decades after 1950, just as they were responsible for the rapid growth of sovereign countries in the decades before 1950?

Africa's cultural legacy is being blamed once again for her recent economic troubles. This is not warranted by the evidence. Africa was not alone in suffering sharp economic reversals starting in the 1980s. The oil crises of 1974 and 1979, the slowdown in the global economy since 1973, and the adverse movements in relative prices for many primary commodities, took a heavy toll in much of Latin America as well. Not even the Middle East and North Africa, which gained so much from the oil boom of the 1970s, were exempt from these global trends. If Africa's troubles went deeper and have lasted longer, this is largely due to the region's greater dependence on primary exports, a colonial legacy that African countries could not have reversed in a short period of two decades following decolonization.[30]

Africa's colonial legacy was troublesome in other ways. While it is true that state structures in large parts of Africa were still in a formative stage in the nineteenth century, colonization abrogated all indigenous political movements and contests–already gathering momentum–that would have carried many of them towards modern, bureaucratized and more stable state structures. Worse, by imposing borders that paid no regard to ethnic or geographic boundaries, colonialism greatly magnified the burden of state formation that would fall upon the indigenous governments that succeeded them. This has led to a great deal of internal strife that continues to explode to this day.

Africa's troubles were also compounded by the high levels of state control and state-ownership that emerged after independence, although colonial governments made no small contribution to this development with the creation of state-marketing boards during the war years. This *dirigisme* was not inspired by any African traditions of socialism; it had more immediate political and economic antecedents. The near absence at independence of an indigenous capitalist class in Africa virtually locked the newly independent countries into a program of state ownership and dirigiste policies; this was the only way open to Africans intent on wresting control of their economy from foreign companies and expatriates. The consequences of a heavily interventionist state would be more unfortunate in Africa than in Egypt or India. This is because Africans had not been prepared–because of their near complete exclusion from responsible positions in colonial governments–to handle this great expansion in the powers of government. The result was a great deal of waste, corruption, ethnic conflict and wars. One must also contend with the fact that the decolonization of French West Africa was more pretended than real. Paris continued to call the shots in this region.

Industrial Epoch *II*

The 1950s marked the beginning of industrial epoch *II* which reversed the earlier trend towards concentration of the world's manufactures in a small number of advanced countries.[31] The conditions for this reversal were immanent in the contradictions of the global economy.

The economic conditions for this reversal were created by the process of polarization itself. We have argued that the cumulative processes which underlay the concentration of manufactures also produced a growing wage gap between advanced and lagging countries. Wages in the most advanced countries began to rise in earnest towards the middle of the nineteenth century once their labor surpluses were drawn down and industrial labor learned to organize itself. At the same time, productivity growth in the labor-intensive manufactures tapered off during the second half of the nineteenth century as the first wave of industrial innovations reached maturity, making it easier for some lagging countries to adapt these technologies to their own conditions. Thus it was that India and Japan, even under conditions of free trade, began to set up their own textile industries towards the end of the nineteenth century. Imperialism, while it ruled the roost, sought to delay this shift in comparative advantage to lagging countries.

But imperialism too was plagued with contradictions. Since advanced countries sought exclusive control over markets and resources in lagging countries, rivalries between them were inevitable. These rivalries were contained as long as Britain's industrial dominance sustained its hegemonic role in the global economy. When new industrial powers– such as United States, Germany and Japan–emerged to challenge Britain's industrial preeminence and hegemony, a period of instability followed that would lead eventually to two great wars during the first half of this century. Devastating as these wars were for many of the advanced countries, they opened windows of opportunity for the lagging countries. Ineluctably, and in stages, the two wars forced the advanced countries to decentralize their power. The first war freed the quasi-colonies from their worst disabilities, while the second war led to the dismantling of colonial empires.

Industrial epoch *II* was inaugurated by this second more massive devolution of power which unfolded rapidly after the second great war. Most lagging countries employed their new found sovereignty to try to break out of the narrow specializations imposed on them by the international division of labor; they implemented economic and social policies to promote manufactures and to nurture a class of indigenous capitalists. The result was the emergence in many lagging countries of an industrial sector which first displaced imported consumer goods and gradually moved into the production of intermediate and capital goods. This dispersion of manufactures was pregnant with ramifications. All too soon, it would inject a new dynamic into the global economy. A clear notice of these changes was first served during the 1970s when manufactures from lagging countries, with the advantage of lower wages and rapidly improving skills, began to penetrate markets in advanced countries. The industrial genie in lagging countries was now out of the bottle.

This was also the cue for the revival of imperialism. Conditions for such a resurgence had improved dramatically since the 1950s. After a quick recovery and two decades of unprecedented growth, the advanced countries presented a solid front under the hegemony of United States. On the other hand, following the open split between Soviet Union and China in 1962, the communist movements in lagging countries were divided and less menacing. Minor reverses apart, the global efforts to contain communism had been a huge success. By the 1980s, the advanced countries were ready to begin the task of crafting a new imperialism. The aim of this new imperialism was not to reverse the dispersion of manufactures that was underway, but to delay its progress and to capture the markets and investment opportunities it was creating in lagging countries. As this new imperialism has unfolded, lagging countries have come under growing external pressures to liberalize their trade policies, capital accounts and financial markets; to privatize their industries; adopt the labor and environmental standards of advanced countries; enforce intellectual property rights; prosecute trade in counterfeit products; and eliminate preferences for domestic suppliers in state procurements. Imperialism *II* looked eerily like its predecessor.

But there are differences too. Since direct colonization is not an available option, imperialism *II* has been forced to find new instruments of coercion. Unlike imperialism *I*, which relied heavily on gunboats, its successor operates primarily through markets and multilateral agencies. This is only a minor limitation since advanced countries can exercise considerable leverage over lagging countries by controlling access to international loans, direct foreign investments and advanced technologies. This leverage has grown dramatically in recent years because of two factors. Since the 1980s, the growing debt burden of many lagging countries has forced them to trade their sovereignty for debt rescheduling. The more serious blow to lagging countries came from the demise of Soviet Union. The advanced countries lost no time in signaling the new re-centralization of power this had created. This message was delivered with stunning clarity by the Allied forces during the Gulf War. Imperialism *II* would now have a field day.

It is our reading that imperialism *II* has greatly narrowed the window of opportunity that had opened up in the aftermath of the second great war. The dispersion of manufactures to lagging countries that began in the 1950s is likely to continue but not–as in Taiwan, Korea and Japan– under the aegis of indigenous capital. The creation of cores of indigenous industrial capital in a new tier of lagging countries will face growing difficulties. More and more, capital from advanced countries will seek to ensure that lagging countries are converted into global production platforms, with minimal indigenous participation in the ownership and control of what they produce. These developments are troubling. Since production platforms are constituted to sell cheap labor and infrastructure, and attract foreign investments with promise of low taxes, lagging countries will compete for this right by erecting regimes that keep taxes low and labor cheap and disorganized. Is this the primrose path that leads to prosperity, democracy and civil liberties?

Notes

1 Cited in Gong (1984: 52).
2 The industrial epoch may be dated from the 1750s with the growing application of inanimate sources of energy to manufacturing production–first water power, then coal and oil. In its first phase that lasted for roughly two hundred years, the industrial epoch led to a growing concentration of manufactures in a small number of advanced countries. The industrial epoch entered into its second phase, starting in the 1950s, when the tendency towards concentration of manufactures was reversed. See table 7.1.
3 'Advanced' and 'lagging' are relative terms; they are defined with respect to the development of a country's markets, in particular the markets for capital, labor and land.
4 This is a central concept in our analysis. A country can *structure* its integration into the world economy if it has the power to decide when, how fast and how far to integrate; what markets to integrate; and with whom to integrate.

5 Japan was no exception. It was forced to sign 'open-door' treaties with several Western powers starting in 1850, but gained full tariff autonomy in 1915.
6 Samuelson (1948).
7 Amin (1990).
8 Headrick (1981).
9 Maddison (1995: 227, 239).
10 Rostow (1978: 669).
11 Bairoch (1981: 9).
12 The absence of spillovers from a dynamic manufacturing sector slowed down technical progress in the primary sector of lagging countries. Also, they were unable to benefit from technical progress in the agricultural sector of advanced countries because of differences in their ecology and plant varieties.
13 The state is defined in terms of three functions: governance, production and defense; and three overlapping interests: those of its personnel, the dominant classes and security of the country. In addition, three classes are defined, depending on whether their primary source of income is land (primary production), capital (manufacturing and commerce) or labor.
14 The term quasi-colonies is used for the 'open-door' countries which retained an indigenous government but surrendered control over trade, foreign investments, expatriates, and, often, fiscal matters, to advanced countries.
15 For a recent valiant attempt to revive Marx's original vision of imperialism, see Warren (1973, 1980).
16 In addition, a fifth category, newly independent countries (*NIC*), was created to account for colonies that had gained their independence between 1940 and 1950. In 1960, the *NIC* were ranked below former quasi-colonies and above colonies. A list of the countries belonging to different categories is presented in table 2 in the appendix.
17 Foreign capital includes only direct foreign investments, not portfolio investments or foreign loans.
18 See chapter five.
19 The interventionist policies employed by sovereign countries included tariffs, overvalued exchange rates, debt repudiations, public enterprises, tax-breaks, state procurements, state schools and training centers, and low-interest loans to industries.
20 The five categories include: sovereign countries, dependencies, quasi-colonies, colonies and newly independent countries (*NIC*).
21 Sovereignty differentials are not reported for intermediate categories because of the small number of observations available for these categories.
22 For this and subsequent exercises, the sample of lagging countries includes countries which had a per capita income in 1900 that was less than 50 percent of the US per capita income in 1900.
23 1960 was the earliest year for which data on national accounts were available for a large number of lagging countries. The control variables in these exercises included per capita income, population, the squares of these terms, the

age of colonies, population density, a dummy variable for Western countries and Japan, and a dummy variable for oil-surplus countries.

24 Small countries are those with populations of less than 5 million in 1960.

25 These estimates allow for several control variables, including per capita income, square of per capita income, population density, percent Muslims and Christians in total population, interactive dummy variables for percent Muslims and Christians in colonies, a dummy variable for countries with initially high levels of human capital, and a dummy variable for oil-surplus countries.

26 The sample of observations for these estimations consisted of all countries with a per capita income equal to or less than 66 percent of US per capita income in 1900.

27 The sample of lagging countries was successively restricted to countries with a per capita income in 1900 less than 50 percent *and* less than 40 percent of the US per capita income.

28 Egypt's bid for independence would be frustrated twice, in 1840 and 1882, not because she was destined to remain backward, but because she showed signs of moving forward: and a strong, sovereign and industrialized Egypt would be a serious threat to European ambitions in the Arab East.

29 More recently, it was backward Vietnam and Afghanistan which defeated invading Western armies, whereas the more advanced countries of Eastern Europe threw off their foreign yoke only when Soviet Union collapsed internally.

30 Between 1980 and 1991, the terms of trade loss for Africa (excluding Nigeria and other oil exporters) was equivalent to as much as one-quarter of aggregate GDP in 1980; the losses for Asia and Latin America were 12 and 14 percent respectively (Maizels 1994: 12-13).

31 Between 1953 and 1980, the share of the five largest industrial countries–United States, Germany, France, Britain and Soviet Union–in world manufacturing output declined from 72.9 to 58.9 percent (Bairoch 1982: 302-3).

2

Integration and Polarization
since 1760

*'There is, unfortunately, a kind of alchemy about figures which
transforms the most dubious materials into something pure and precious; hence the price of working with historical statistics is eternal
vigilance.'*

Thomas Carlyle (1980: 64-65)

Our search for the causes of global inequalities during industrial epoch *I*
will be greatly advanced if questions about the timing of these inequalities, as well as their relationship to international integration, can be re-
solved at the outset.

How great were the disparities between now advanced and lagging
countries at about the time of the Industrial Revolution? If all the now
advanced countries had a lead of six to one–or even four to one–over
lagging countries in 1760, as some have claimed, we must look for causes
of global disparities in factors specific to the advanced countries before
this period. This argument loses much of its force if, as we show, only some of
the now advanced countries enjoyed an early lead over lagging countries
and, besides, this lead was never very large. If an early lead was not necessary for later growth, this redirects our search towards causes that operated *during* industrial epoch *I* to advance growth in some lagging countries and to retard it in others. We think that these causes are to be found
in the way these countries related to the global economy: *whether* they
were free or not to structure these relations, and this depended on their
sovereignty.

The first tentative evidence in support of our thesis comes from a negative
connection between success in integration and the failure to grow during industrial epoch *I*. Starting from very modest levels, international trade expanded very rapidly over the period 1800 to 1913. The lagging countries
in Asia, Africa and the Americas had a more than proportionate share in
this expansion of global trade; and Asia and Africa integrated faster than
any other region over the seven decades ending in 1950, so that by the
end of this period several of them had export ratios comparable to the
highest in the world.[1] What this means is that attempts to pin the poorer

24

growth record of Asia and Africa on any failure to integrate will simply not wash; lagging countries with the most open economies also had the worst growth record. Could it be that the orthodox economists were after all wrong about international integration: that too much of a good thing could be bad for the economy? At any rate, this is a suggestion that we take very seriously.

Disparities in Per Capita Income Around 1760

A review of the literature on historical comparisons of per capita income suggests that around 1760 disparities between now advanced and lagging countries were quite small and, once polar cases are excluded, probably nonexistent.

National income accounts for most countries do not go very far back; few countries were maintaining these accounts before 1950. Where then do we get the numbers for making historical comparisons of per capita income dating back to the nineteenth century? The short answer to this question is that these numbers have to be reconstructed. This is not an exercise for the squeamish. It takes a great deal of hard work, and strong faith in ones assumptions, to reconstruct national income accounts from government surveys and reports, data on tax collections, records of industry associations and observations of curious contemporaries. But this is not all. To make comparisons of per capita income, we also need data on population levels, and these too are produced with similar exertions of detective work and ingenuity.

Once this work has been completed the comparisons can begin. The method adopted is that of 'backward projections', and this proceeds in two steps. The starting point is a benchmark comparison of per capita income across countries that uses dollar exchange rates (this is what nearly all the early writers did) or purchasing power parities. Next, these benchmark estimates of per capita income are projected backward–using growth rates of per capita income–to derive comparable estimates of per capita income for earlier years. There now exist several such estimates of per capita income for many countries going back to the nineteenth century, and for some going even further back. Impressive as these exercises are, one should never lose sight of the speculative methods on which they are so often based. In describing his own estimates of per capita income for Britain prior to the mid-nineteenth century, Crafts (1985: 9) cautions that these numbers must be treated as 'controlled conjectures rather than definitive evidence'.

Nearly all the early comparisons of per capita income in the eighteenth and nineteenth centuries supported the thesis that Europe had a strong lead quite early on over today's lagging countries.[2] Kuznets (1954: 144) gave the seal of his authority to this view in an early paper which concluded that 'per capita incomes in underdeveloped countries today are from about one-sixth to one-third of the per capita income of the developed countries a century ago [in the 1850s]'. Although he is aware of the downward bias in these estimates stemming from the reliance on exchange rate conversions, this does not deter Kuznets from taking his estimates seriously. Without further ado, and even though Britain and France in the 1850s were well past their pre-industrial phase, he concludes even more strongly that 'the pre-industrial level [of per capita income] in the developed countries was several times that of most underdeveloped countries today'.[3]

Similar assessments may be found in at least two other sources. Also using exchange rate conversions, Zimmerman (1962: 35), another early authority on national income accounting, showed that 'Northwest Europe' in 1860 had a per capita income of $230 compared to $50 in the Far East, $48 in Southeast Asia and $44 in China, all expressed in 1952-54 US dollars. North America had a much bigger lead with a per capita income of $420 in 1860. Another estimate of the same ilk may be found in Landes (1969: 13). Starting from Deane's (1965: 7) estimate of a per capita income of £12.5 for England and Wales in the 1750s, he multiplied this by a factor of eight (instead of six as suggested by Deane) to obtain a per capita income of £100 in 1960 prices. By this reckoning, Britain had a lead of at least four to one over India in the 1760s.[4]

One might have thought that specialists in the economic history of lagging countries, with more intimate knowledge of their economic conditions, would have known better. But they too could not resist the thrall of Eurocentrism: it felt good to make Europe look better. Lockwood (1954: 3), for many years the leading Western authority on the economic history of Japan, declared that 'Japan as recently as the early nineteenth century remained in a state of economic development hardly more advanced than that of Western Europe in the late Middle Ages'. An expert on the economic history of India, Morris (1967: 610), made an identical assessment of the lag between India and Europe. 'It is much more likely that in the eighteenth century India had achieved a technology that was at about the production levels of late medieval Europe.' It would appear that for centuries Europe had been steadily moving ahead, while the rest of the world was stuck in the mud.

The large historical disparities revealed by the early use of backward projections were mostly an illusion–a result of their reliance on exchange rate conversions in the benchmark comparisons. It is now well understood that market exchange rates are not likely to reproduce purchasing power parities between currencies. Generally, exchange rates undervalue the currencies of poor countries relative to those of rich countries, a problem that worsens as the income gap between them increases. As a result, when exchange rates between countries at opposite ends of the income scale are used for conversion to a common currency–precisely what was done in the early benchmark comparisons–this is likely to produce a serious understatement of the per capita income of the poor countries. Conversely, when purchasing power parities are substituted for exchange rates in the benchmark comparisons, the early disparities begin to narrow considerably. Several of these estimates based on purchasing power parities are reviewed here.[5]

Clark (1957) made two sets of international comparisons, one for the rich and another for the poor countries.[6] The comparisons for the rich countries employed an international unit (IU) of currency with the average purchasing power of a US dollar over 1925 to 1934. Using Clark's benchmark comparisons for 1950, backward projections yield per capita incomes in 1820 of 154 in Britain, 112 in France, 77 in Italy, 73 in Brazil and Japan, and 62 in Finland; all expressed in IUs.[7] These results give Britain a lead of roughly two to one over the last four countries, although France's lead over the same countries is quite a bit smaller. Brazil and Japan are in the same league as Italy but ahead of Finland. Some additional comparisons can be made, using per capita incomes measured in Oriental Units (OUs) with purchasing power equal to the Indian rupee in 1948-1949. Once again, starting from Clark's (1957: 58-9) benchmark comparisons for 1950, backward projections yield a per capita income in 1913 of 303 for Turkey, and in 1820 a per capita income of 171 for India, 269 for Italy, 327 for Finland and 385 for Ireland; all expressed in OUs.[8] No one thinks that Turkey experienced much growth in the century preceding 1913, so that in the early decades of the nineteenth century she would be in the same league as Italy and Finland. On the assumption that India's per capita income declined by a fourth between 1760 and 1820, this would raise her per capita income to 227 in 1760, not far behind Italy's.

The assumption of a decline in India's per capita income between 1760 and 1820 requires some explanation. This was a period when much of India was subjected to repeated wars as the British, the French and successor states to the Mughal Empire fought each other for control over India's trade and revenues. These wars were attended by serious disruptions in trade, the decay of irrigation works, destruction of indigenous elites, peasant dislocations and desertions, pillaging by bands of soldiers from defeated armies, and the terrible famine of 1769-70 which destroyed a fourth of Bengal's population.[9] It is difficult to imagine that all this did not exact a heavy toll on India's productive potential. Bairoch (1991: 27) believes that India's per capita income around 1750 was 'probably at least a third higher than around 1830'.[10]

The first complete set of historical comparisons of per capita income between now advanced and lagging countries, based on purchasing power parity conversions, was provided by Bairoch (1981). At the aggregate level, his estimates give the palm to lagging countries, reversing by a slight margin the Kuznets-Zimmerman-Landes position on historical disparities. In 1750, the 'developed' countries had a per capita income of $182, compared to $188 in the Third World, both expressed in 1960 US dollars and prices.[11] Western Europe, with a per capita income of $190, was barely ahead of the Third World, while the Third World had a slim lead of 1.14 over Eastern Europe. Only the 'most developed' countries, with a per capita income of $230, had a small but clear lead of 1.22 over the Third World, 1.27 over Asian market economies, and 1.10 over China; and a larger lead of 1.77 over Africa.[12] Only Latin America had a slight lead of 1.07 over the 'most developed' countries. Thus, if we exclude the 'most developed' countries and Africa from the comparisons, the lagging countries had a modest lead over the 'developed' countries.

These results did not find favor with Maddison (1983: 29), who presented alternative estimates which he claims are 'much closer to the Landes-Kuznets conclusion than those of Bairoch'.[13] However, this assessment is not supported by his own results. Maddison (1983: 30) shows that in 1760 Britain and France had a per capita income of $233 and $198 at 1965 US factor cost, while India, China, Mexico and Brazil had a per capita income of $123, $118, $112 and $97.[14] It follows that in 1760 Britain had a lead of 1.89 over India, 1.97 over China, 2.08 over Mexico, and 2.40 over Brazil. France had a smaller lead, at 1.61 over India, 1.68 over China, 1.77 over Mexico, and 2.04 over Brazil. If we assume that India's per capita income declined by a third between 1760 and 1820, then UK's lead in 1760 reduces to 1.42, while France is only modestly ahead with a margin of 1.21. It is a stretch to claim that these results are closer to Kuznets' (1954: 145), who concluded that per capita incomes in developed countries *before* the Industrial Revolution were 'several times that of most underdeveloped countries *today* (italics added)'. On the other hand, Bairoch's (1981: 8) estimates yield a gap of 1.22 between his 'most developed' countries and the Third World. Maddison *is* nearer to Bairoch than he is to Kuznets!

Nevertheless, important differences between Maddison (1983) and Bairoch (1981) remain to be explained. In part, these differences are due to the higher growth rates Maddison uses in his backward projections for lagging countries. Maddison (1983: 30) assigns an annual growth rate of 0.8 percent to China between 1820 and 1980, whereas Bairoch (1981: 14) uses an annual growth rate of 0.28 percent between 1800 and 1977. If Maddison had used Bairoch's growth rate, his backward projections would yield a per capita income of $265 for China in 1820 at 1965 US factor cost. This is somewhat higher than France's per capita income of $254 in 1820 and lags only modestly behind Britain's per capita income of $312 in 1820. Similarly, Maddison (1983: 30) assumes an annual growth rate of 1.62 percent for Brazil between 1820 and 1980 and 0.98 percent for Mexico between 1803 and 1980. Bairoch (1981: 14) assumes a significantly lower annual growth rate of 0.6 percent between 1800 and 1977 for Latin America.[15] Once again, the use of Bairoch's growth rate would substantially reduce Maddison's gap between Britain, on the one hand, and Brazil and Mexico.

Maddison's (1983:31) benchmark comparisons too are less favorable to lagging countries. His 'correction coefficient' for India is 1.96 compared to 2.80 in Bairoch (1981: 4).[16] Had Maddison used Bairoch's correction coefficient, his estimate of India's per capita income in 1820 would be $176 (not $123) in 1965 US factor costs. Even on the assumption that India's per capita income remained unchanged between 1760 and 1820, this would give France only a modest lead of 1.13 over India in 1760. Similarly, had Maddison used Bairoch's correction coefficient for Mexico (1.60 instead of 0.91), Mexico's per capita income in 1760 (assumed to be the same as in 1803) would be $197, virtually the same as France's. Maddison (1983: 32) acknowledges that if he had used 'the Kravis-Heston-Summers estimates [of per capita income] at American prices ... [his] 1760 position would be virtually as Bairoch claims'.[17]

This raises questions about which of the two benchmark comparisons is more accurate. Maddison (1983: 36-37) argues that Bairoch's (1981) benchmark comparisons overstate per capita incomes in lagging countries because they are based on final expenditure categories.[18] These comparisons ignore quality differentials in consumption arising from the different proportions of distributive services expended upon a unit of consumption: they follow the rule that a potato is a potato regardless of where, when or in what quantities it is purchased. Since the proportion of distributive services is generally lower in lagging than in advanced countries, Maddison (1983: 37) concludes that their neglect in expenditure-based comparisons overstates per capita incomes in the lagging countries. Kravis (1986:

22-23) acknowledges this criticism but maintains that the bias this introduces is quite small. The share of services in lagging countries would have to be zero in order to explain all the differences between the Maddison and ICP estimates.

There is a second source of differences in the two benchmark comparisons; they make different assumptions about productivity in 'comparison-resistant' services, including the services of medical personnel, teachers and civil servants. Kravis *et al.* (1982) assume that productivity levels for teachers and civil servants are roughly comparable in advanced and lagging countries, although medical personnel are assumed to be on average only half as productive as their counterparts in advanced countries. Maddison (1983: 36) thinks that these assumptions overstate productivity in lagging countries; he assumes that medical personnel, teachers and civil servants in lagging countries are on average only about one-third as productive as their counterparts in advanced countries. It is difficult to agree with this assessment. For standard medical services, it makes more sense to assume that doctors, nurses, and medical technicians have the same productivity in lagging and advanced countries. Similarly, where teaching effectiveness does not depend on the use of classroom equipment–not very common at the time these comparisons were made–one can assume comparable productivity for teachers in advanced and lagging countries. A more plausible case can be made for a productivity gap in the services of civil servants, due primarily to over-staffing in lagging countries. Following these assessments, we would reduce the productivity estimates in Kravis *et al.* (1982) for civil servants in some lagging countries while raising their estimates for the health and education sectors.[19] It is likely that these opposite corrections will just wash out.

A closer examination of Maddison's (1983) correction coefficients for individual countries also reveals some troubling anomalies. Balassa (1964) and Samuelson (1964) have shown that prices of services across countries are likely to be inversely correlated with per capita income: a prediction that can be verified by almost any international traveler without the aid of *t*-statistics.[20] However, Maddison's (1983) correction coefficients do not always conform to this pattern. It strains credulity to learn that two countries at opposite ends of the income range, United States and Ghana, had nearly identical price levels in 1965; or that Mexico, a middle-income country, had a price level some nine percent above that of United States; or that Ghana, Peru, Colombia and Mexico had higher price levels than Japan or Italy. This would only be possible if the currencies in these lagging countries were highly overvalued, possibly by a hundred percent or more above their market values. Currency overvaluations of this magnitude were not common in 1965.[21]

In his most recent historical comparisons of per capita income, Maddison (1995) abandons the production approach used in his earlier paper in favor of comparisons based on expenditure categories.[22] These estimates give Britain a lead of 1.73 over Mexico, 1.86 over Japan, 1.96 over Brazil, 2.14 over Indonesia, 1.86 over India and Bangladesh, and 2.51 over China. France has a smaller advantage of 1.25 over Mexico, 1.35 over India, and 1.82 over China.[23] These disparities are only modestly below those in Maddison (1983); the gap for China is wider. This is at first surprising since the correction coefficients employed in the new estimates are larger than before. But this is nearly offset by use of lower growth rates in the backward projections for Britain and France. The average annual growth rates in Maddison (1983: 30) for Britain and France between 1820 and 1980 are 1.31 and 1.62 percent; these are replaced by 1.24 percent and 1.57 percent in Maddison (1995: 194-197). Had Maddison (1995) used his earlier growth rates, this would reduce Britain's lead over India from 1.86 to 1.66, and France's lead over India would be pared down from 1.35 to 1.25.

The growth rates Maddison (1995:24) uses in his backward projections for India, China, and Brazil are still too high.[24] Thus, he assumes that India's per capita income rose by 18 percent between 1820 and 1900. This is not rapid growth even by the standards of nineteenth century; nevertheless, this is hard to reconcile with Bairoch's (1991: 3) estimate of a decline of 83 percent in India's per capita industrial output over the same period.[25] This would have reduced India's per capita income by 16.6 percent, on the assumption that manufactures accounted for 20 percent of her national output in 1830.[26] It is unlikely that this could have been offset by an expansion in primary exports, since India's merchandise exports stood at 2.5 percent of the national output in 1870.[27] A similar point could be made regarding China. Maddison's (1995) assumption of a constant per capita income for China between 1820 and 1870 is hard to reconcile with the violent history of this period. A series of devastating rebellions racked much of China during the 1850s and 1860s; the Taiping rebellion alone is estimated to have killed more than 30 million people.[28] Further, between 1870 and 1900 China is assumed to have grown at the rate of 0.73 percent per annum. This outdoes Italy's record of 0.58 percent for the same period!

Crafts' (1984) historical comparisons are easily extended to the lagging countries in his benchmark comparisons, yielding results similar to Bairoch's. When combined with growth rates from Maddison (1995: 24),

Craft's benchmark comparisons yield per capita incomes in 1820 of $250 for Brazil, $260 for Mexico, $241 for Pakistan and $172 for Bangladesh, all in 1970 US dollars and prices; compare this to British per capita income of $399 in 1760 and $333 in 1700.[29] On the assumption that per capita income in the lagging countries remained unchanged between 1760 and 1820, Britain has a lead of 1.53 over Mexico, 1.60 over Brazil, 1.66 over Pakistan, and 2.30 over Bangladesh. The per capita income for Bangladesh in 1820 is implausibly low. According to Bayly (1988: 51), Bengal was 'almost certainly the wealthiest province of Mughal India' and proved 'an extraordinary prize' for the British. Assuming, as we did for India, that per capita income declined by a fourth between 1760 and 1820, this would give a 1760 per capita income of $229 in Bangladesh, reducing Britain's lead in 1760 to 1.74.[30] With a per capita income of $294 in 1781-90, France had a much narrower lead over these countries.[31]

To sum up, historical comparisons of disparities in per capita income have produced two classes of estimates. All the earlier estimates, based on exchange rate conversions, record per capita incomes in now advanced countries around 1760 that were three to six times greater than in lagging countries (not including Sub-Saharan Africa). Comparisons based on purchasing power parity conversions reveal much smaller early disparities. Around 1760, the gap between the first cohort of advanced countries (Britain, USA and France) and the lagging countries (not including Sub-Saharan Africa) were nearly always less than two to one. Most likely, these gaps were smaller for several important lagging countries, such as India, Pakistan, Bangladesh and China, if we recognize, with Bairoch (1981), that they suffered a decline in per capita income between 1750 and 1900. Significantly, the income gaps between the now advanced countries around 1760 were as large, and sometimes larger.

Alternative Comparisons

The evaluation of early disparities between now advanced and lagging countries is pursued in terms of several alternative correlates of development, *viz.* wages, agricultural productivity, manufacturing output per capita, urbanization and anthropometric measurements. These alternative comparisons confirm that the early disparities were small or non-existent.

Although limited, the historical evidence indicates that wages in India and Egypt were comparable to those in the now advanced countries.[32]

Contrary to views first circulated by careless and jaundiced European travelers, Parthasarathi (1998) has shown that workers in South India in the eighteenth century were neither poor nor oppressed compared to their counterparts in Britain. Comparisons of the purchasing power of wages, measured in their grain equivalents, show that Indian wages in textiles (weaving and spinning) and agriculture were at least equal to those in Britain, and, when annualized, Indian wages were most likely higher. These wage comparisons, however, tell only half the story. Parthasarathi shows that Indian workers were better organized; they worked in tight labor markets with lower levels of unemployment; they possessed superior contractual rights and could shift the risk of market fluctuations to merchants; they also did not have to contend with a state which intervened on behalf of the employers.[33] In a similar exercise, using data on wages and their grain-equivalents, Batou (1991: 189) has shown that Egypt had a per capita income of $232 in 1800 compared to $240 for France. Is it likely that historical comparisons using contemporary data might yield similarly favorable comparisons for other lagging countries?

Agricultural productivity in now advanced and lagging countries were roughly the same during the nineteenth century. Clark (1957: 253-277) has provided estimates of gross agricultural output per male worker in IUs for the richer countries and OUs (both defined earlier) for the poorer countries; estimates for some countries are available in both units, thus permitting conversion into IUs.[34] Measured in IUs, agricultural productivity in France was 78 in 1815-18, 70 in Ireland in 1837, 139 in Sweden in 1861-65, and 172 in Spain in 1906-10. Using the method of backward projections–with growth rates of per capita income as proxies for growth rates of agricultural productivity–the comparable figures were 70 for India in 1820, 109 for Pakistan in 1820, 153 for Egypt in 1900, 85 for Thailand in 1870, and 133 for Brazil in 1820. Most likely, these figures are underestimates, since agricultural productivity could not have grown as fast as per capita income. By these rough calculations, Brazil and Pakistan in 1820 were ahead of France and Ireland, and India was at par with Ireland.

These results are corroborated by Bairoch's (1975) caloric measures of agricultural productivity.[35] In 1909-13, the weighted averages of agricultural productivity for Asia (not including China), Africa and Latin America (not including Argentina) were 5.1, 6.9 and 7.2. On the assumption that their agricultural productivity had remained unchanged over the nineteenth century, the indices for Asia and Africa would be comparable to those for several European countries: 7.5 for Germany in 1840, 7.0 for France in 1810, 6.5 for Sweden in 1810, and 4.0 for Italy in 1840. Only Britain, with a productivity index of 14.0 in 1810, was distinctly ahead of the lagging and advanced countries.

Similarly, the most advanced countries in 1750 had only a modest lead over the lagging countries in manufacturing output per capita. According to Bairoch's estimates (1991: 3), the indices for per capita manufacturing output were 8 in China, 7 in India, 6 in Brazil and 6 in Mexico, compared to 10 in Britain, 9 in France, 9 in Belgium and 4 in United States; these indices are computed on a base of 100 assigned to per capita manufacturing output in Britain in 1900. Over the next fifty years, Britain acquired a commanding lead, with her index of per capita manufacturing output at 16, but most European countries were still at or below 8, comparable to the levels for China and India.

Historical disparities in living standards may also be examined in terms of urbanization rates.[36] Counting population centers of 5000 or more as urban, Bairoch (1988: 459) has shown that China, with a rate of urbanization between 11 and 14 percent, was slightly more urbanized than Europe at the beginning of the sixteenth century, but this ratio declined steadily over the next three centuries.[37] In 1700, the urbanization rate was 14-19 percent for Italy, 11-15 percent for England, 8-11 percent for Germany, and 4-7 percent for Russia. Amongst Asian countries of comparable size, Japan had an urbanization rate of 11-14 percent in 1700; and surely one could find regions within India with populations of 6-12 million in 1700 with urbanization rates between 15 and 20 percent.[38] Once again, comparing entities of similar size, the urbanization ratio in India was 11-13 percent in 1700, compared to 12.3 percent for Europe (minus Russia).[39] A hundred years later, the advanced countries had an urbanization ratio of 10 percent, compared to 9 percent for all (market-oriented) lagging countries.[40] The levels of urbanization in Iran and Turkey in 1900 were in the range of 12-15 and 15-18 percent respectively.[41]

Finally, we turn to historical comparisons based on anthropometric evidence. Over long periods, measures of height (or chest circumference) across different human populations are correlated with the state of nutrition and health, which, in turn, are influenced by wages, income distribution, conditions of work, and incidence of diseases. These considerations have persuaded some to argue that anthropometric indicators provide more comprehensive measures of living standards than real wages.[42] At the least, we would insist that these measures provide a useful alternative to wages and per capita income, as measures of the quality of life. Although anthropometrics is still in its infancy, especially with respect to populations in lagging countries, an examination of the limited evidence suggests that anthropometric indicators for populations in now advanced and lagging countries were quite similar historically.

The evidence from Southeast Asia indicates that average heights in this region during the seventeenth century were the same as in Europe. After sifting through observations of early European visitors, data collected by British missions in Thailand and Cochin China (Southern Vietnam) in 1821, and measurements based on skeletal remains from a cemetery in Luzon, Reid (1988: 48), concludes that 'on average Southeast Asians of the seventeenth century were as tall as Europeans, but that a discrepancy appeared as European nutritional levels began to improve about 1800'. Again, after surveying accounts left by foreign visitors, court diaries and parish registers, Reid (1988: 50) finds that 'Southeast Asians lived longer than Renaissance Europeans'.

On the basis of more solid evidence, we can conclude that Indians on an average were as tall as populations in several now advanced countries in the late nineteenth and early twentieth centuries. The data on average heights of Indians comes from two sources. Ganguly (1979) has assembled this data from 14 states for 60 population groups in the late nineteenth century; he shows that the average height of 36 groups with data at the district level was 64.22 inches, and 24 groups with state level data had an average height of 64.54 inches. In addition, we have measures on the average height of indentured Indian workers in the Fiji. The average height of all male recruits, ages 16 to 40, arriving in the Fiji between 1903 and 1913 was 63.8 inches, and the average height for all male North Indian recruits born in the 1840s and 1850s was 63.86 inches.[43] It does not appear that there was any upward bias in these measures arising from the manner in which the indentured workers were selected: the recruiters emphasized chest circumference as the main indicator of physical fitness.[44] Even at this late date, the Indians stood nearly as tall as populations of conscripts in several European countries. The average height of these conscripts was 63.86 inches in Italy (1874-76), 64.56 inches in Belgium (1834), 64.44 inches in Spain (1860-93), 64.33 inches in Portugal (1899 or 1911), and 64.37 inches in Switzerland (1884-86).[45] Thus, with a century or more of improvements in living standards behind them, the European conscripts in late nineteenth century were not much taller than Indian workers who, most likely, were worse off than their grandparents.

Evolution of Disparities: 1800 to 1950

Although disparities in per capita income between now advanced and lagging countries were small around 1760 or 1800, this would change dramatically over the next century and a half.

First, consider the evidence on overall disparities. Bairoch's (1981) estimates show that the advanced countries, starting with only a slight edge over lagging countries in 1800, had outpaced the latter by three to one 1900 and 5.2 to one in 1950.[46] This gap was created by an acceleration in the growth rates of advanced countries accompanied by a modest decline in the per capita income of lagging countries. A closer look at the evolution of disparities in table 2.1 reveals a more varied picture. Latin America was ahead of Britain in 1800, but fell behind till the gap in 1913 was 1.85 to one; the region grew faster over the next fifty years so that the gap had narrowed to 1.42 in 1950. Eastern Europe was modestly behind Britain in 1800, and fell back steadily until the gap had widened to 1.79 in 1950. Asia started off with a modest lag, but fell back rapidly over each of the three successive periods, till the lag had widened to 5.92 to one in 1950. Starting with a bigger lag, Africa too fell behind rapidly, so that in 1950 the lag had widened to 5.76 to one. Thus, between 1800 and 1950, the lagging countries had sorted themselves into two distinct classes, in terms of their lag behind Britain. Latin America and Eastern Europe fell somewhat behind Britain; the gap for Africa and Asia had widened to a chasm.

The polarization in per capita manufacturing output was more dramatic. In 1800, the disparity in manufacturing output per capita between advanced and lagging countries was of the order of 1.3 to one. This gap had increased to four to one in 1860, 27.5 to one in 1913, remained unchanged at this level in 1953, but had narrowed to 20 to one in 1980. The corresponding disparities in per capita incomes were 1.9 to one in 1860, 3.5 to one in 1913, and 5.2 to one in 1950.[47]

There was a slower increase in the gap in agricultural productivity between advanced and lagging countries. The advanced and lagging countries in 1800 had roughly the same levels of agricultural productivity (calculated in millions of direct calories per male worker in agriculture). More than a hundred years later, in 1910, the advanced countries had established a lead of to 2.8 to one.[48] This was quite modest compared to the productivity gap in manufacturing. Clearly, manufacturing was by far the more dynamic of the two sectors during most of industrial epoch *I*.

The International Economy Around 1800

The volume of global trade around 1800 was still small relative to the size of the global economy, with nearly three-fifths of this trade concentrated in Western Europe.

World trade (exports plus imports) constituted slightly more than two percent of the world output in 1820 when both are calculated in 1900

Table 2.1
Disparities between Britain and Lagging Countries: 1800 to 1950

Regions	1800	1860	1913	1950
Latin America	0.81	1.25	1.85	1.42
Eastern Europe	1.12	1.40	1.60	1.79
Asia	1.10	1.98	3.64	5.92
Africa	1.52	2.49	4.66	5.76

The ratios are PCI in Britain over PCI in the regions

international dollars. When evaluated in the current prices of each country, this proportion was higher at just under three percent in 1800.[49] In either case, it is clear that the relative volume of world trade was still quite small in the early nineteenth century. This global picture, however, conceals important regional differences. In 1800, 59 percent of world trade originated in Western Europe, 17 percent from the rest of Europe, six percent from North America and 18 percent from the rest of the world.[50] This concentration of trade in Western Europe produced very high ratios of exports to output in some countries. In the early nineteenth century, Germany had an export ratio of 28 percent, Britain 20 percent, and France 16 percent.[51] Not surprisingly, the levels of exports per capita, measured in current dollars, also varied greatly across different regions. In 1830, per capita exports were $7.6 in Britain, $3.2 in France, $3.6 in Germany, $5.2 in France, $5.3 in North America, and $5.1 in Latin America; the per capita exports for Asia and Africa were $0.2.[52] Thus, international trade was already very important to Latin America, North America and the advanced economies of Western Europe.

The patterns of specialization that would dominate world trade during industrial epoch *I* were already well-established in the Atlantic economy at the beginning of the industrial epoch *I*. Manufactures accounted for 81 percent of Britain's total exports at the end of the seventeenth century, 86 percent in 1772-74 and 87 percent in 1830-39. Conversely, foodstuffs and raw materials comprised 68 percent of Britain's imports at the end of the seventeenth century, 83 percent in 1772-74, and 94 percent in 1830-39.[53] On the other hand, Latin America's exports consisted almost entirely of primary products, including precious metals, sugar, tobacco and coffee. United States occupied an intermediate position. In 1821, foods and raw materials accounted for 65.3 percent of her exports, while 34.6 percent consisted of processed foods, semi-manufactures and finished manufactures.[54]

International Integration: 1800 to 1950

The movement towards the creation of a global economy accelerated dramatically in the first decades of the nineteenth century, reached a peak in 1913, fell back somewhat over the next three decades, but has since exceeded its earlier peak. The economies of Asia and Africa were rapidly integrated into the global economy during this period.

The expansion in global trade during the nineteenth century was phenomenal. The volume of global trade expanded 13-fold during the first eight decades of the nineteenth century, compared to a two-fold increase in the preceding eight decades. In 1913 global trade was more than 43 times its level in 1800, declined between 1914 and 1945, but rose dramatically thereafter, so that in 1970 it was at 213 times its level in 1800.[55] According to an alternative computation, the volume of world trade in 1970 was 199 times its level in 1820.[56] Since world output had not grown nearly as fast, all this translated into a steep rise in the ratio of world trade to output. The export ratio, with exports and output estimated in 1990 international dollars, rose more than eight-fold between 1820 and 1913, rising from 1.04 percent in 1820 to 8.67 percent in 1913, fell back to 6.99 percent in 1950, and climbed again to 10.47 percent in 1970.[57] These export ratios are significantly higher when both exports and gross domestic product are computed in the domestic prices of each country.[58]

The lagging countries held on to their share of global exports over the nineteenth century, but increased this share over the next half century.[59] Over the nineteenth century, this share fluctuated around 20 percent, but increased from 16 to 31 percent between 1900 to 1950.[60] At the same time, the share of lagging countries in world output declined rapidly throughout this period; they contributed 74 percent of world output in 1800, but this declined to 38 percent in 1900 and 27 percent in 1950.[61] Taken together, these two tendencies ensured that the export ratios of lagging countries rose continuously over the century and a half between 1800 and 1950. In addition, the export ratios for lagging countries were increasing faster than in the advanced countries. The growth of export ratios for lagging countries was fastest during the first half of the twentieth century.[62]

An examination of the regional shares in world exports suggests that export ratios in Asia and Africa were rising more rapidly than in Latin America during the nineteenth century. Africa increased its share of world trade from under 1 percent to 1 percent between 1840 and 1900, Asia's share declined from 12 to 9 percent over the same period, South America's share remained constant over this period, and Central America's share fell from 5 percent in 1840 to 2 percent in 1860 and was still at this level in 1900.[63] Combined with much slower output growth in Asia and Africa than in Latin America during this period, these numbers imply that export ratios in Africa and Asia were rising faster than in Latin America. This trend became more pronounced over the next half century. Between 1900 and 1953, total exports increased by a factor of 13 in Africa, 8.5 in Middle East, 3.9 in Asia and 4.7 in Latin America.[64]

The growing importance of trade during the nineteenth century may also be tracked in terms of the rising values of exports per capita. According to Bairoch (1991: 23), Europe's (*minus* Russia) per capita exports in current dollars rose from $3.3 in 1830 to 25.3 in 1912; the corresponding figures for Russia were $0.8 and $5.0; for North America, $5.3 and $20.6; for Africa, $0.2 and $3.2; for Latin America, $5.1 and $18.2; for Middle East, $1.0 and $3.7; for Sri Lanka, $0.8 and $16.1; for Indonesia, $0.8 and $5.2; for Thailand, $0.6 and $4.1; and for Philippines, $0.4 and $5.8. Although, India's per capita exports increased 12-fold between 1830 and 1912, it was still relatively small at $2.4 in 1912. China's per capita exports rose six-fold from a still lower base to reach a level of $0.6 in 1912. These figures are corroborated by alternative estimates of per capita exports between 1820 and 1900.[65]

Judging from their export ratios, most lagging countries had attained high levels of international integration by 1950. The export ratios for the two largest Asian countries, India and China, were 7.4 and 10.3 percent respectively. These ratios were higher for countries of middling size: 19.3 percent for Myanmar, 21.8 percent for Thailand, 30.2 percent for Nigeria, 46.3 percent for Zaire, 14.9 percent for Iran (in 1955), 19.4 percent for Egypt (in 1960), 8.2 percent for Turkey, 9.3 percent for Argentina, 9.6 percent for Brazil, and 14.1 percent for Mexico. The relatively lower ratios for Turkey, Argentina, Brazil and Mexico are due to several decades of import substitution. Smaller countries had achieved even higher export ratios: 38.8 percent for Sri Lanka, 30.4 percent for Algeria, 16.9 percent for Sudan (1960), 27.8 percent for Kenya, and 34.0 percent for Ivory Coast (1960). The comparable ratios for advanced countries were as follows: 23.2 percent in Britain, 15.6 percent in France, 9.7 percent in Germany (West), 11.2 percent in Spain, 22.2 percent in Canada, and 4.3 percent in United States. These numbers are not directly comparable since the share of non-tradable services increases at higher levels of per capita income, and this tends to reduce the export ratio for advanced countries.[66] Nevertheless, on a rough comparison, it would appear that in 1950 commodity markets in most lagging countries were at least as well integrated as in the advanced countries.

This is corroborated by the more rapid integration of markets for primary goods over the period 1876-80 to 1953. This may be inferred from an analysis of the commodity composition of world trade over this period. The division of world trade between primary goods and manufactures displays an extraordinary constancy over a period of some seven decades from 1876-80 to 1953. Primary products constituted 63.5 percent of world exports in 1876-80, 63.0 percent in 1913 and 63.3 percent in 1937; the share has been declining since the second world war.[67] Since world output of manufactures was increasing much more rapidly than that of primary goods over this period, a constant share of primary goods in world trade could only be achieved if the share of primary exports to primary production was rising and, conversely, the share of manufactured exports in world manufacturing output was declining.[68] One reason for the declining ratio of trade in manufactures was the import-substituting character of industrial growth. In addition, industrial growth may have spurred trade in primary goods as deficiencies in domestic availability of raw materials were met through expanded imports.

The division of the world into primary producing and industrial countries was firmly established by the 1870s. In 1876-80, 97.6 percent of the total exports of lagging countries in Asia, the Americas and Africa consisted of primary goods; at 21.9 percent of total exports, this ratio was much lower for lagging countries in Europe. At the opposite end, manufactures accounted for 88.1 percent of the exports of Britain and Ireland and 56.2 percent of the exports of North West Europe. United States and Canada, both resource-rich countries, occupied an intermediate position, with 85.7 percent of their exports consisting of primary goods and 14.3 percent of manufactures. The concentration of Africa, the Americas and Asia (excluding Japan) on primary production changed very little over the next seven decades: the share of manufactures in their total exports was 4.1 percent in 1883, 5.6 percent in 1955, and 8.5 percent in 1965.[69] On the other hand, the advanced countries increased their specialization in manufactures over the same period. The share of manufactures in total exports in 1899 was 64.3 percent in Britain, 54.7 percent in France, 69.6 percent in Germany, 42.5 percent in Japan, and 30.1 percent in USA; in 1957, these shares had risen to 82.8 percent in Britain, 67.8 percent in France, 87.1 percent in Germany, 88.8 percent in Japan, and 59.6 percent in USA.[70]

This geographic division of labor is confirmed by statistics on the regional distribution of world manufactured exports. In 1876-80, 89.3 percent of world manufactured exports originated in the advanced countries: 4.4 percent in North America, 37.8 percent in Britain and Ireland,

and 47.1 percent in North-West Europe. The lagging countries in Europe accounted for 9.2 percent, and all the lagging countries in Asia, the Americas and Africa contributed a minuscule 1.5 percent. These shares had changed very little some 60 years later. The share of the advanced countries in 1937 had declined marginally to 81.4 percent, while the share of the lagging countries stood at 18.6 percent. Latin America and Africa still accounted for 0.5 percent each, the lagging countries in Europe for 5.8 percent, and Asia accounted for 11.8 percent.[71] The increase in Asia was due in large part to the rise of Japan as an industrialized country.

Summary

A review of the literature on historical comparisons of levels of development suggests that disparities between now advanced and lagging countries around 1760 were most likely quite small and, once extreme observations at both ends are excluded, probably nonexistent.

The historical comparisons of per capita income use the method of backward projections of per capita income, with appropriate corrections for different price structures in the benchmark comparisons. Nearly always, the disparities around 1760 between the first cohort of now advanced countries (Britain, United States and France) and all other lagging countries (excluding those in Sub-Saharan Africa) were less than two to one. The disparities decline if Britain is excluded from the comparisons, and when corrections are made for declining per capita incomes in the Asian economies between 1760 and 1900. Finally, the disparities within the now advanced countries in 1760 were as large as the disparities between the first cohort of advanced countries and the lagging countries (excluding Sub-Saharan Africa).

The results from alternative comparisons fully support the results based on historical comparisons of per capita income. Once Britain is excluded, productivity levels in agriculture were comparable across most countries in early nineteenth century. In manufacturing, the productivity advantage may have belonged to some Asian countries. Comparisons of real wages yield similar results. This is corroborated by data on levels of urbanization which reveal no large differences across countries (regions) with comparable populations. Finally, anthropometric data show that populations in now advanced countries did not acquire their greater height until after, and perhaps well after, the eighteenth century.

While the disparities between now advanced and lagging countries were quite small around 1760, or even 1800, they expanded very rapidly over the nineteenth century. According to one estimate, the ratio of per capita income between advanced and lagging countries rose from unity in 1800 to three in 1900 and 7.7 in 1977. The disparities in manufacturing grew much more rapidly than in agriculture.

The global economy was largely a creation of the nineteenth century. The export ratio for the world economy rose from 1.04 percent in 1820 to 8.67 percent in 1913 and, after declining over the next three decades, climbed to 10.47 percent in 1970 and 13.5 percent in 1992. This expansion in world trade between 1820 and 1950 was based on a division of labor which assigned the production of primary goods to lagging countries in Asia, Africa and Americas and concentrated manufactures in the advanced countries. Most lagging countries contributed more than proportionately to this trade expansion, so that their export ratios rose more rapidly than in advanced countries, especially between 1870 to 1950. Over the same period, primary production became more integrated into the world economy while the opposite trend was recorded for manufacturing activities.

Although they started with low trade ratios in 1800, the economies of Asia and Africa were rapidly integrated into the global economy, so that by 1950 their trade ratios were comparable to or higher than those for lagging countries in Europe or Latin America. This creates some problems for theories which argue that economic growth is likely to be most rapid in countries which make the fullest use of all the opportunities for international exchanges. As colonies, the Asian and African economies followed this prescription but experienced very little growth in their per capita incomes.

Notes

1 A comparative review of economic policies during industrial epoch *I*, in chapter five, shows that lagging countries in Asia and Africa followed liberal economic policies towards manufactures, trade and foreign investments; while lagging countries in Latin America and Europe structured their relations with the global economy.

2 This Eurocentric thesis was not yet common in the late eighteenth century. Adam Smith (1776: 189, 206, 72) could write that China is 'much richer' than any part of Europe; further, that in manufacturing, China and India seem 'not to be much inferior' to any part of Europe.

3 Kuznets (1954: 145).

4 India had a per capita income of £25 in 1960.

5 These estimates include an early one by Clark (1957) and later more sophisticated ones by Bairoch (1981), Crafts (1984) and Maddison (1983, 1995).

6 Clark (1967: 18) reasoned that these comparisons are most useful when the 'levels of real income compared, or the commodities on which they are spent,

do not differ in too extreme a manner'. The first edition of this work appeared in 1940.

7   Growth rates for backward projections are from Maddison (1995: 23).

8   Growth rates for backward projections are from Maddison (1995: 23-24).

9   Bayly (1988: 33).

10 Moosvi (1977: 398) has shown that real wages in 1595 for Western Uttar Pradesh (India) were 1.52 times their levels in 1886-95 when both are converted into rice, and 1.56 times higher when measured in terms of wheat.

11 The 'developed' category includes United States, Canada, Australia, New Zealand, South Africa and Europe; the Third World includes all other countries.

12 The 'most developed' category includes Britain, France, Netherlands and United States.

13 We focus on Maddison (1983) rather than his later contributions (Maddison 1989, 1995), because it makes benchmark comparisons that are based on output indicators, unlike Bairoch (1981) and Maddison (1995) who use expenditure categories. The International Comparison Project (ICP) also employs expenditure categories. The first ICP estimates are available in Kravis, Kenessey, Heston and Summers (1975). Several revised versions of the ICP estimates have appeared since then.

14 We are assuming that per capita incomes in the latter countries remained unchanged between 1760 and 1820. Maddison (1983) does not provide data for 1760 for the lagging countries.

15 In 1820, Brazil and Mexico contained 55 percent of the population in Latin America.

16 The correction coefficient is the ratio of a country's purchasing power parity to its exchange rate.

17 Bairoch's (1981) correction coefficients are close to the Kravis-Heston-Summers estimates: see Kravis, Heston and Summers (1982).

18 Maddison (1983) and Bairoch (1981) employ different methods in their benchmark comparisons. Maddison's (1983: 29-30) benchmark estimates are based on levels of net output derived from 150 quantitative indicators of output in agriculture and industry, while estimates of services are based upon employment data and specific assumptions about productivity in the services sectors of advanced and lagging countries. On the other hand, the benchmark comparisons in Bairoch (1981), the International Comparison Project (ICP), and Maddison (1995) are based on expenditure categories. For a description of the ICP see Kravis (1986). Data for countries not included in ICP's benchmark comparisons are derived using various short-cut methods.

19 It is hard to imagine that a doctor in India or Thailand is less than a third as productive as a doctor in United States.

20 Samuelson (1964) established this on the basis of Heckscher-Ohlin theory. Since services are labor-intensive, lower wages will result in lower prices for services. While free trade will equalize prices of tradable goods across countries, differentials in prices of services are likely to persist. It follows that the

average price level–weighted sum of prices for services and tradable goods–across countries will vary inversely with wages. Kravis (1986) has shown that the correction coefficients that emerge from the ICP are inversely correlated with per capita income.

21 Consider the case of Ghana. The average relative price of goods *vis-à-vis* services was 2.76 for countries in the income class that included Ghana, assuming a relative price of 1.0 for countries in the highest income class (Kravis 1986: 17). An overvalued currency in Ghana will lower the gap in the price of services between Ghana and United States; import tariffs will raise the absolute prices of importables above US prices; while the prices of exportables should be the same as in United States. Given Ghana's small manufacturing sector (10 percent of GDP in 1965), it would take a very high overvaluation *and* very high import tariffs to push the overall price level in Ghana to the level of United States (World Bank 1986: 184). Judging from the evidence on black market exchange rates, the cedi was slightly *undervalued* in 1965; the official exchange rate in 1965 was 0.71 cedi to the dollar, compared to an exchange rate of 0.65 cedi to the dollar on the black market (Stryker 1990: 279).

22 Maddison (1995) was preceded by Maddison (1989). We chose to focus on the former because it covers a larger number of countries and the estimates often go back to 1820.

23 Maddison's (1995) comparisons start from 1820. The per capita incomes for 1760 are derived under the following assumptions: the backward projections for Britain and France used growth rates from Maddison (1983); a 25 percent decline in the per capita income of India and Bangladesh between 1760 and 1820; no change in per capita incomes for the other lagging countries between 1760 and 1820.

24 The annual growth rates between 1820 and 1980 for India, China and Brazil in Maddison (1983) were 0.40, 0.76, and 1.53 percent. The corresponding figures in Maddison (1995) are 0.36, 0.64 and 1.29 percent.

25 Bairoch (1988a: 399-400) has documented a decline of eight percent in the population of 73 large cities (more than 30,000) in India between 1800 and 1850.

26 Data on six districts in Gangetic Bihar for 1809-13 suggest that on average 18.6 percent of the total population in these districts was dependent on manufacturing (Bagchi 1976).

27 Maddison (1995: 38).

28 *The New Encyclopaedia Britannica* (Chicago: University of Chicago Press, 1993): 124-126.

29 Crafts (1984: 440).

30 If a correction of one third is warranted for India, a larger correction would be appropriate for Bengal (which included Bangladesh) which came under British rule in 1757 and suffered the worst excesses of a system of dual extortion practiced by the British East India Company and its employees in their private capacity.

31 Crafts (1984: 440) assigns a per capita income of $343 to France in 1830. Using growth rates from Toutain (1987: 76), this yields a per capita income of $294 for France in 1781-90. Cited in Bairoch (1991: 26).

32 It is unfortunate that comparative historical studies on real wages remain so rare despite the limited demands they make on data. At low levels of income, with food constituting the bulk of a worker's budget, real wages could be computed with data on nominal wages and prices of foodgrains.

33 Washbrook (1993) arrives at similar conclusions.

34 Agriculture includes foods, fibers, tobacco, hides and skins, and industrial fats and oils. The IUs for Egypt, India and Pakistan were converted from OUs using the conversion ratio (1 IU = 6.24 OUs) for Sri Lanka for which data was available in both units. Using Brazil's conversion ratio (1 IU = 7.15 OUs) would not have changed these results dramatically. At least for India and Pakistan, Sri Lanka's ratio seemed more appropriate.

35 These measures are in millions of direct calorie equivalents of subsistence output.

36 Rising per capita income augments the share of manufacturing and services in the economy, promoting urbanization since these activities are often concentrated in urban areas. Further, an economy's ability to support an urban population depends on labor productivity in food, a correlation that was likely to be stronger before 1800 when trade in bulky foodstuffs was limited. See Kuznets (1965) and Chenery and Syrquin (1975) for studies on patterns of development.

37 Bairoch (1988: 356).

38 Bairoch (1988: 215, 360).

39 Bairoch (1988: 400, 216). Using a higher cut-off point (at 10,000 people) for urbanization, Wrigley (1985) places the rate of urbanization in Europe (minus England) at 9.2 percent in 1700. Lieberman (1995: 797) claims that Southeast Asia had reached an urbanization rate of 5 percent (counting populations in cities of 30,000 or larger) in 1650; this was higher than in Western Europe.

40 Bairoch (1988a: 459).

41 Bairoch (1988a: 407).

42 Floud (1984) and Mandemakers and Van Zanden (1993).

43 Brennan, McDonald and Shlomowitz (1994a: 232; 1994b: 280).

44 Brennan et al. (1994a: 231).

45 Floud (1994: 16-19)

46 Advanced countries comprise all of Europe, United States, Canada, Australia, New Zealand, Japan and South Africa. All others constitute developing countries (Bairoch 1981: 7).

47 Bairoch (1981: 281, 7).

48 Bairoch (1991: 12).

49 The two estimates are from Maddison (1995: 227, 239) and Kuznets (1967: 7).

50 Kuznets (1967: 11). At least in part, the lower share of the rest of the world in global trade is due to the presence of several very large countries in this group, *viz.* China, India and the Ottoman Empire.
51 Batchelor, Major and Morgan (1980: 168).
52 Batou (1991: 21, 23).
53 The data for 1699-1701 and 1772-74 are from Rostow (1975: 120-21), the data for 1830-39 are from Kuznets (1967: 46-47).
54 Hughes (1990: 380-81). It is worth noting that India was still a manufacturing country: 83 percent of her exports to Britain in 1772-74 consisted of manufactures (Davis 1969: 119-20).
55 Rostow (1978: 669).
56 Maddison (1995: 239).
57 Maddison (1995: 227, 239).
58 Maddison (1995: 227, 239) and World Bank (1996: 212-213).
59 Lagging countries includes all countries in Asia, Africa and Latin America.
60 According to Mulhall's estimates, the export share of lagging countries increased modestly from 18 to 20 percent between 1800 and 1889 (Kuznets 1967: 11). Hanson II (1980: 20) provides similar figures: the lagging countries' share declined from around 22 percent in 1840 to 18 percent in 1900. According to Bairoch (1975: 93), the lagging countries in Asia, the Americas and Africa nearly doubled their shares in world exports from 16.0 percent in 1900 to 31 percent in 1950. According to an alternative estimate, excluding communist countries, the share of lagging countries in world exports went up from 20 to 26.3 percent between 1913 to 1953 (Kuznets 1967: 11).
61 Bairoch (1981: 7).
62 Between 1860 and 1911 Britain's export ratio declined from 16 to 13 percent, France's ratio increased from 16 to 24 percent, United States' ratio increased from 6.2 to 6.7 percent, and India's ratio increased from 1.0 to 4.6 percent (Hanson II 1980: 23).
63 Hanson II (1980: 20).
64 Bairoch (1975: 97). Since gross national product in Latin America was increasing more rapidly than in Asia, this implied a faster rate of integration for Asian economies.
65 Hanson II (1980: 26-27).
66 To increase comparability, we might look at ratios of exports to output in the tradable sectors (agriculture, mining and manufacturing). These ratios were very high for several lagging countries in 1960: 37.1 percent for Thailand, 64.2 percent for Sri Lanka, 55.1 percent for Myanmar, 41.8 percent for Egypt, 110.6 percent for Algeria, 109.2 percent for Zaire, 70.5 percent for Kenya, 66.9 percent for Ivory Coast, 54.5 percent for Nigeria, and 43.8 percent for Mexico. Britain had a comparable ratio of 52.8 percent, France of 31.2 percent, Germany of 39.2 percent, and Spain 22.9 percent (World Bank 1976). These ratios are biased against lagging countries since they include nonfactor service exports which are most likely a higher component of the exports of advanced countries.

67 Yates (1959: 37).
68 World industrial output increased by a factor of 9.4 over 1870 to 1938, while the volume of world trade increased by a factor of 4.33 over the same period (Rostow 1978: 662-669).
69 Lewis (1978: 226).
70 Kuznets (1967: 53).
71 Yates (1959: 50).

3

Theories: Orthodoxy and Dissent

'Any nation which by means of protective duties and restrictions on navigation has raised her manufacturing power and her navigation to such a degree of development that no other nation can sustain free competition with her, can do nothing wiser than to throw away these ladders of her greatness, to preach to other nations the benefits of free trade, and to declare in penitential tones that she has hitherto wandered in paths of error, and has now for the first time succeeded in discovering the truth.'

List (1841 : 308)

When economists turned their attention in the 1940s to economic growth, or more accurately, its paucity, in Africa and Asia, they were at once confronted by a curious inversion between orthodox theory and some hard facts about trade and growth.

For nearly two hundred years, orthodox trade theory had insisted that freeing international trade and foreign investments would improve efficiency and growth in all economies; it did not matter whether they were big or small, advanced or lagging, or whether they exported primary goods or manufactures. Yet these expectations were almost entirely belied by the facts in the lagging countries. Once the lagging countries had been converted into colonies or quasi-colonies, they maintained virtually open economies, with free or nearly free trade, free movement of capital and enterprises and, in the case of colonies, free movement of labor. But after nearly a century or more of virtual *laissez faire*, these dependent countries had made little economic progress. In several cases, their integration into the global economy had only produced immiseration.

How is it that orthodox economics had for nearly two centuries espoused theories of international trade that were increasingly at odds with the facts? Strangely, it might appear, the economists' devotion to the invisible hand was strongest in the field of international economics. They claimed that barriers to international exchanges not only deflected resources from their most productive uses, thus reducing incomes everywhere, but worse, they hindered growth by restraining competition, technology flows and that variety in consumption which sharpens men's acquisitive instincts. All this was welcome news too. It meant that growth could be had on the cheap, merely by bringing down the all-too-pervasive barriers to trade and investments. Just shut down the customs houses, and markets would do the rest.

From its inception, this *Ricardian* doctrine had an important political corollary.[1] It was considered perverse that any lagging country–rejecting its own best interests–should decide against free integration into the world economy. As a result, the classical economists gently prodded their governments to play the altruist, using force where necessary, to open up the lagging countries to commerce with civilized nations. As if this were not enough, the advanced countries were encouraged to take on a heavier burden–to intervene in the domestic affairs of lagging countries and set them on a more rational, progressive course. Integration into the global economy demanded good governance; and this only the West could provide.

As it turned out, the first half of this civilizing mission came close to being fulfilled. Over the nineteenth century, many lagging countries were laid open to the assault of global markets, creating primary-producing economies that nicely complemented those of advanced countries. This nearly complete submission to the invisible hand, however, failed to produce anything resembling sustained growth. After more than a century of insertion into world markets, the colonies and quasi-colonies were at the bottom of the economic pile, and often much worse than before. On the other hand, lagging countries which structured their incorporation into world markets had done visibly better: their *Listian* gamble had paid off rather handsomely. History had refused to oblige the orthodox economists.

When this dissonance between theory and facts was finally noticed, starting in the 1940s, it provoked a spurt of new thinking on labor markets, international trade, economic growth and the dynamics of global capitalism: innovations which mainstream economists would begin to assimilate some three decades later.[2] After being neglected for more than a hundred years, economic growth was now the central concern of a new branch of economics–development economics–which worried about why most lagging countries had gained so little from their integration into the world economy. Two broad responses to this question soon emerged. Some concluded that the problem with orthodox economics lay in its neglect of market failures; once these were incorporated, it would become clear why international integration turns out to be disequalizing. They came to be identified as the structuralists.[3] Others sought inspiration from Karl Marx, but turned his analysis of world capitalism on its head. They argued that global capitalism had never been a progressive force in lagging countries, or had ceased to be progressive somewhere along the way. Those who developed this radical critique of capitalism have been variously described as neo-Marxists, dependency theorists or world-systems theorists.

The review of theories undertaken here has two objectives. It is hard to believe that orthodox economists were naïfs: they could not *see* that international integration gave some very real advantages to advanced countries at the cost of lagging countries. We need to understand why and how they expunged the asymmetric effects of international integration from their theories–a journey that takes us from Adam Smith to David Ricardo. We review the heterodox theories, both old and new, in order to set the stage for our own eclectic account of the evolution of global inequalities that follows in chapter four.

The Classical and Neoclassical Economists

The orthodox defense of free trade went through a sea-change between Adam Smith and David Ricardo, switching from a concern with dynamic gains associated with a *growing* volume of trade to the purely allocative gains that flow from the *opening* of trade.

The analysis of dynamic gains from trade holds center stage in Adam Smith's *The Wealth of Nations*.[4] Almost at the outset, in chapter two, trade emerges as a fundamental principle of growth. The opening of trade, by extending markets, induces greater specialization in each country's production; in turn, this augments workers' skills, saves time, and encourages the invention and application of machinery.[5] These changes are cumulative, since productivity improvements lead to more specialization and additional rounds of increases in productivity, thus setting in motion an upward spiral of growth. Trade is truly an engine of growth in Smith's analysis.

Trade stimulates growth in other ways. By adding variety to the staples of consumption, as well as furnishing exotic luxuries, trade intensifies our cupidity, driving us to work harder and to save and invest. The classical economists waxed eloquent when describing the energy which a growing taste for variety might inject into a hitherto isolated economy, one whose resources had remained unutilized because of the want of goods upon which additional income could be spent.[6] Adam Smith elevated this consumption stimulus into a fundamental principle of social change in feudal Europe. Feudalism, he argued, had been brought down by itinerant traders peddling exotic 'baubles'. Unable to resist the lure of these baubles, as well as their convenience as stores of value, the great landlords were persuaded to pay for them, at first, by dismissing the great multitude of their retainers and 'unnecessary part of their tenants'. In time, as the feudals' appetite for 'baubles' grew so did their need for revenues and, at one remove, the pressure on their tenants to pay ever increasing rents. The peasants were willing to oblige, but at a price: they demanded greater security of tenure in exchange for higher rents.[7] Eventually, these demands produced an independent peasantry–and the end of feudalism.

Adam Smith identified several dynamic effects of trade that operated through deeper channels. The division of labor calls forth some professions, such as that of a porter, which may produce a stunting of the intellect, but it also creates others, such as that of a philosopher, which affoid opportunities for an indefinite growth of the higher faculties.[8] Similarly, the growth of trading classes, which closely follows the growth of trade, exerts some strong pressures towards greater probity in business as well as personal dealings. 'A dealer [trader] is afraid of losing his character, and is scrupulous in observing every engagement.' It is not surprising, concludes Adam Smith, that of all the nations in Europe, 'the Dutch, the most commercial, are the most faithful to their word'.[9] Not least, trade and the rise of manufactures produce conditions that improve governance, personal freedom and security of property.[10]

Adam Smith was keenly aware, however, that the cumulative growth initiated by trade did not operate with the same force in all economic activities. He knew that the division of labor went further in manufactures than in agriculture, and further still in manufactures that worked with metals.[11] This created some powerful asymmetries. A country with an initial competitive advantage in manufactures, upon entering trade, would be able to outsell all its rivals: an advantage that was almost certain to deepen with every new round of expansion in trade. Where would this cumulative process lead to? Wouldn't it end in the concentration of all the world's manufactures in a single country? This question generated some rather prescient exchanges during the eighteenth century, now described as the 'rich country-poor country' debate.[12]

This debate began with David Hume's prediction that the poor country would catch up with the rich. The rich country could not accumulate manufactures and grow indefinitely, since this would raise wages and the cost of 'provisions' (food and raw materials), and thereby induce manufacturers to move to the poor country to take advantage of its lower wages and cheaper 'provisions'. The rich country has the advantage of 'superior industry and skill (...) and the greater stocks of capital, of which its merchants are possessed, and which enable them to trade on so much smaller profits. But these advantages are compensated, in some measure, by the low price of labor in every nation which has not an extensive commerce, and does not much abound in silver and gold.'[13] Later, Hume conceded, in correspondence, that the 'rich country would acquire and retain all the manufactures that require great stock and great skill; but the poor country would gain from it all the simpler and more laborious'.[14]

Adam Smith was more categorical in his rejection of convergence. The rising wages in a growing economy would be more than offset by rising productivity in its manufacturing sector. Thus, in a discussion on productivity gains in manufacturing and its effect on price, he writes that although, 'in consequence of the flourishing circumstances of the society, the real price of labour should rise very considerably, yet the great diminution of the quantity will generally much more than compensate the greatest rise which can happen in the price'.[15] Wealth, in the Smithian economy, is 'self-reinforcing rather than self-destructive'.[16] In consequence, a rich country can never lose any branch of its manufactures or commerce to a poor country on account of its affluence alone. 'Some other cause, we may be assured, must have concurred. The rich country must have been guilty of some great error in its police.'[17]

Notwithstanding his analysis of the dynamic gains from trade, Adam Smith never wavered in his commitment to free trade. How did he accomplish this feat? Not surprisingly, his arguments against protection of manufactures were couched entirely in static terms–a sign of things to come. He concedes that 'regulations' can help to establish a manufacture sooner than it would have been acquired on its own, but 'it will by no means follow that the sum total, either of its industry, or of its revenue, can ever be augmented by such regulation. The industry of a society can augment only in proportion as its capital augments, and its capital can augment only in proportion to what can be gradually saved out of its revenue. But the *immediate effect of every such regulation is to diminish its revenue*, and what diminishes its revenue is certainly not very likely to augment its capital faster than it would have augmented of its own accord, had both capital and industry been left to find out their natural employments (italics added).'[18] Not a word about the direct and cumulative productivity gains that would follow from the early creation of a manufacturing sector. In another place, Adam Smith opposes the fostering of manufactures because this will divert capital from agriculture where it generates a surplus.[19] Once again, the argument is framed in terms of static efficiency losses, so familiar to later economists.

Adam Smith's analysis of the secular impact of mercantilist policies in Europe reveals the same inconsistency. He acknowledges that since 'the beginning of the reign of Elizabeth (...) the English legislature has been peculiarly attentive to the interests of commerce and manufactures, and in reality there is no country in Europe, Holland itself not excepted, of which the law is, upon the whole, more favorable to this sort of industry. Commerce and manufactures have *accordingly* been continually advancing during all this period (italics added).'[20] It is clear that Adam Smith attributes the progress of commerce and manufactures in England over the previous two hundred years to her mercantilist policies. On another occasion, he maintains that 'manufactures and foreign commerce together, have given birth to the principal improvements in agriculture'.[21] If mercantilism in Britain advanced manufactures and commerce, and both were responsible for the 'principal' improvements in her agriculture, making Britain one of the world's richest countries, why was free trade to be preferred to mercantilism?

Could it be that what Adam Smith really meant was that mercantilism was *now* bad for England, and bad *for* England also if other countries persisted in it? At least, one commentator, Low (1952: 324), in an essay on the 'rich country-poor country' debate, thinks that this was 'the central point of the *Wealth of Nations*'. 'Smith and [Josiah] Tucker,' he writes, 'were agreed that Britain was already a rich country and hence that there really was no need for the government to intervene to safeguard advantages which we were not in danger of losing.' Josiah Tucker, a contemporary of Adam Smith, agreed that the advanced country would retain its lead in manufacturing, but he showed greater candor in recognizing that 'the policy which was right for Britain would not necessarily be right for a poor and undeveloped country', and proposed measures for protecting infant industries in poor countries from foreign competition.[22]

The theory of comparative advantage, developed only a generation later by David Ricardo (1817), presented a very different account of international trade. It was defined by its narrow focus on the static effects of trade under constant production costs. Within this narrow framework, trade was always welfare improving, regardless of what goods were traded; the only asymmetry in the distribution of gains from trade arose from the size of the trading countries, and this favored the smaller country. This was a theoretical *coup d'etat* which, by grounding the analysis of trade in a purely static framework, universalized Britain's interest in free trade. Britain could now call upon a powerful theoretical tool to persuade lagging countries that free trade was in *their* best interest too. And should gentle persuasion fail, an occasional show of force against offending countries would not give anyone a bad conscience. The end would justify the means.

Ricardo's theory of comparative advantage set the standard for all orthodox theorizing in international trade. When the neoclassical economists rejected Ricardo's labor theory of value, they made sure to carry over his assumptions of fixed resources and fixed technology. Only a static framework would ensure that free trade is the best policy for all countries. It did not matter that in so restricting the theoretical framework, orthodox theory would have nothing to say about the impact of trade on employment, savings, capital accumulation, labor supply, human capital formation, technical change, consumer preferences, balance of power between trading nations, or national security. As the neoclassical economists refined their theory, it became necessary to make additional assumptions to rule out monopoly power, production and consumption externalities, learning by doing, increasing returns to scale, and irrational preferences for goods. With so many defenses, one has to concede that the theory of comparative advantage remains unassailable in its logic. It has fulfilled for nearly two centuries its primary task of disguising the interests of advanced countries as scientific theory.

The static assumptions of orthodox trade theory were not just a pedagogic convenience. Such a rationale would make sense only if the texts on international trade, after discussing comparative advantage, quickly moved on to more interesting questions regarding the long-term impact of trade on countries at different levels of development. But when the entire text is devoted to the static analysis of trade and trade policies, it is hard to see that their objective is pedagogic. The result of such a steady and unremitting diet of static analyses is unmistakable. It produces reification: mistaking the idea for the real thing. Comparative advantage becomes sacrosanct, the efficient and immutable outcome of natural forces–that can only be altered by market forces. Attempts to alter comparative advantage by means of tariffs not only reduce welfare but produce immiserizing growth.[23]

Until recently, orthodox trade theory protected itself from examination by eschewing all empirical analysis. For a long time, it was described as the 'pure' theory of trade–purified, one supposes, of any empirical concerns. Ricardo's (1817) theory of comparative advantage originated in 1817, but it would not be tested until 1951, only after it had been superseded by Heckscher-Ohlin theory.[24] It is still common for undergraduate texts in international trade to devote only one chapter to the facts of international trade, and none to its history. This theory is sufficient unto itself. Its elegance is taken as proof of its validity, and requires no attestation from facts. As a result, Haberler (1959: 498), eminent for his contributions to the theory of trade, could inform an audience of bankers in Egypt (still very poor after one hundred and twenty years of full incorporation into world markets) that it was his 'overall conclusion ... that international trade has made a *tremendous* contribution to the development of less developed countries in the nineteenth and twentieth centuries and can be expected to make an equally big contribution in the future, *if it is allowed to proceed freely* (italics added)'.

Karl Marx and the Classical Marxists

Marx believed that the forced incorporation of pre-capitalist societies into the world economy was necessary, inevitable, and fraught with revolutionary consequences.

The demise of pre-capitalist societies was inevitable because they could not resist the superior power–and firepower–of capitalism. Unlike previous social formations, capitalism did not merely reproduce itself. In the words of *The Communist Manifesto*, capitalism was driven by competition, and the resulting quest for markets, raw materials and investment outlet, to 'nestle everywhere, settle everywhere, establish connections everywhere'.[25] In short, its mission was to incorporate, by force of arms if they did not bend to market forces, all pre-capitalist societies into a single global economy.

The destruction of pre-capitalist societies in Asia was not only inevitable: it was also necessary. When examined from the vantage point of Western Europe, where the pace of historical change had quickened visibly since the sixteenth century, the rest of the world seemed to be marking time. The Asian societies were static; they showed no forward momentum because they lacked the principle of dialectical change.[26] Unable to fit these static societies into his four-fold schema of historical evolution, Marx invented a separate historical category–the Asiatic mode of production–to explain the absence of dialectical change in these societies. What set the Asiatic societies apart from European feudalism was the absence of private property in land; all land was owned by the state.[27] This was the foundation of Oriental despotism. Since there existed no landed magnates challenging its power, the state was under no compulsion to protect the merchants or peasants as a counterpoise to the power of landlords. Instead, the state was free to pauperize them. Marx has also spoken of the self-sufficient village communities in India, with their combination of agriculture and manufacturing, as the 'solid foundation of Oriental despotism'. But he provides no hint as to how these village communities were related to the absence of private property.[28]

Since Asiatic societies could not change on their own, the impetus for change would have to come from outside. Western capitalism was the *deus ex machina* that was already accomplishing this revolutionary task of integrating changeless Asiatic societies into the stream of world history. In the words of Marx, the British had a dual mission in India, 'one destructive, the other regenerating–the annihilation of old Asiatic society, and the laying of the material foundations of Western society in Asia'.[29] Colonialism had been elevated into an instrument of revolutionary change in Asiatic societies.[30]

This is a thesis of extraordinary power; it is Eurocentrism at its best. European bourgeoisie had a world historic mission: they would reconstruct all non-European societies in their own image, as a necessary prelude to the final transition to socialism. But how were these momentous changes going to be accomplished? Marx's ideas about an Asiatic mode of production, and its transformation under attack from European bourgeoisie, are worked out tentatively in his journalistic dispatches to the *New York Daily Tribune*; he does not elaborate upon these ideas in any of his major works. Nevertheless, Marx's brilliance does not fail even in his journalistic writings. Taken together, they provide an incomplete but suggestive account of how this transformation was being effected in India and China.

In part, the destructive half of the bourgeois mission was being effected through free trade. The free import of yarn was already destroying the self-sufficiency of India's unchanging village communities, turning them into 'mere farms, producing opium, cotton, indigo, hemp, and other raw materials, in exchange for British stuffs'.[31] Marx greets their destruction as the 'greatest' and the 'only *social* revolution ever heard of in Asia'.[32] China's village communities had somewhat greater staying power against European manufactures, since they combined agriculture with spinning *and* weaving.[33] Still, the forced opening of China had some profoundly unsettling effects: 'the oldest and most unshattered Empire on this earth has been pushed, in eight years, by the cotton ball of the English bourgeoisie toward the brink of a social upheaval that must have profound consequences for civilization'.[34] All this was, however, only the 'first impact of capitalist world commerce on such nations as the Chinese, Indians, Arabs, etc.' This would be followed by a more vital transformation. 'Capitalist production first makes the production of commodities general and, then, by degrees, transforms all commodity production into capitalist commodity production.'[35]

Although Marx did not elaborate on how this transformation to 'capitalist commodity production' would be effected, his perfunctory remarks suggest that the creation of private property in land was an integral part of this process. The British had already effected 'agrarian revolutions' in Bengal, Madras and Bombay by legislating into existence 'two distinct forms of private property in land–the great desideratum of Asiatic society'.[36] Nevertheless, Marx is severely critical of the two systems of land-tenure introduced into India, *Zamindari* in Bengal and *Ryotwari* in Madras; they are 'pernicious, both combining the most contradictory character–both made not for the people, who cultivate the soil, nor for the holder, who owns it, but for the Government that taxes it'.[37] Writing in 1853, some three quarters of a century after these new systems of land tenure were introduced, Marx was aware that the creation of large landholdings had not led to the creation of capitalist landholders. Instead, the *Zamindar* in Bengal had farmed his rights of revenue collection to others, who in turn had done the same, creating a many-layered class of intermediaries, none of whom had any direct involvement in farming.[38]

However, none of this would shake Marx's conviction that the British were laying, and would lay, the material foundations of a capitalist society in India. For nearly a century, the 'millocracy' (industrial capital) had made common cause with the 'moneyocracy' (merchant capital) and 'aristocracy' (the landed elite) in keeping India backward; their primary interest was in conquest, plunder and capturing her markets.[39] However, a backward and stagnant India could not continue to provide markets for Britain's expanding manufactures. The 'millocracy' was now convinced that India would have to be developed if her capacity to pay for British manufactures must continue to expand. As a result, conscious of their growing power in Britain, the 'millocracy' had begun to demand reforms in India's government, investments in her irrigation and the laying out of railways to develop her agriculture and link her economy to world markets.[40] Marx could scarcely contain his excitement at these developments.

In fact, Marx believed that Britain had already begun its task of 'regenerating' India. The unity of India, achieved and maintained by the dint of British arms, was even then being strengthened by the spread of railways and telegraphs and the slow emergence of a modern Indian middle class. Railways would at last end the isolation of India's villages and, in combination with steam ships, would bring India closer to the rest of the world, thus ending the isolation 'which was the prime law of its stagnation'.[41] More importantly, Marx believed, railways would bring industrialization to India. In a vast country possessed of coal and iron ores, railways would call forth, through backward linkages, industries producing iron, steel, machinery, as well as 'the application of machinery to those branches of industry not immediately connected with railways'.[42] In short, the British bourgeois would establish a united, capitalist and industrialized India just as surely as it had brought about the ruin of her ancient and archaic economy.

There was not much that Marx's immediate followers–the classical

Marxists–added to the master's grand vision of the transforming power of capitalism in pre-capitalist societies. Instead, they wanted to understand how the concentration of capitalist production, especially in manufacturing and finance, during the closing decades of the nineteenth century had altered the laws of motion of capitalism and, therefore, the prospects of a socialist revolution. First Hilferding (1910), then Bukharin (1917) and Lenin (1917), seized upon this concentration of capital, arguing that capitalism had now entered into a new phase, dubbed monopoly capitalism, characterized by the dominance of monopolies over world markets, control of banks over manufacturing, and a more direct control by these monopolies over state policies. Since monopoly capitalism led to a greater surfeit of capital, there was now a greater urgency to find investment outlets for the capital that could not be absorbed in the home countries.[43] This would intensify the rivalry amongst the leading capitalist powers for control of markets and resources in the rest of the world. This was the explanation for the imperialist grab of real estate in Africa and Southeast Asia in the fourth quarter of the nineteenth century.

Their recognition that imperialist rivalry had become more intense, however, did not persuade the classical Marxists to worry about its impact on the colonies. There is a general sense in their writings, of Hilferding (1910) and Lenin (1917) especially, that since monopoly capitalism encouraged direct control over pre-capitalist societies and increased exports of capital, this would hasten their incorporation into the world economy and eventual transformation into capitalist economies.[44] Another classical Marxist, Luxemburg (1913), arrives at the same conclusion, although she locates the impetus for imperialism not in the growth of monopolies but in the perennial failure of capitalism to realize surplus value within the bounds of its own economy. Capitalist economies can realize their surplus value only through exchange with pre-capitalist societies, an exchange that is always effected by violent means, thereby turning imperialism into a necessary outgrowth of capitalism from its very inception.[45]

Early Dissenters

Although free trade very quickly became a central doctrine of economic orthodoxy, it did not go unchallenged. Not surprisingly, the dissenting voices were loudest in lagging countries with their own industrial ambitions. Not only did these late industrializing countries do whatever it would take to develop their own manufactures, they also worked out several theories to support their interventionist policies.

Ironically, nearly all the central themes in these heterodox theories could be found in *The Wealth of Nations*. That the division of labor could be carried further in manufacturing than in agriculture; that manufacturing creates important economic, social and political spillovers; that manufacturing stimulates innovations in commerce and agriculture; that initially high manufacturing costs could be reduced through learning-by-doing; that substituting local manufactures for imports would save on the cost of transportation; that manufactures are indispensable for successfully executing wars; all these propositions enter into Adam Smith's analysis of the dynamic gains from trade. They were also summarily rejected in Ricardo's theory of comparative advantage. The dissenters in lagging countries lost no time in seizing upon these powerful themes in constructing their own defense of interventionist policies in support of late industrialization. The stone rejected by the builders become the cornerstone in the edifice of their heterodox theories.

One of the earliest works in defense of manufactures, Alexander Hamilton's (1791) *Report on Manufactures*, was also one of the most cogent, setting the tone for what was to follow. This defense of manufactures had a special irony, since the great abundance of land in United States in relation to its small population made it extremely unlikely, *a la* Adam Smith, that its capital could any time soon be employed productively in manufacturing. Hamilton was not deterred by the relative abundance of land in United States; he argued that an economy which combines manufactures with agriculture would be more productive than one which specializes in agriculture alone.

One finds in the *Report on Manufactures* as complete a statement on the advantages of manufacturing as may be found anywhere. The greater division of labor in manufacturing than in agriculture ensures, as Adam Smith had emphasized earlier, a more rapid growth of productivity in manufacturing. This creates a more diverse range of activities in manufacturing which increases productivity by facilitating a better fit between workers and jobs. Manufacturing augments factor supplies, employment and capacity utilization; it attracts immigrants and stimulates capital inflows, employs workers faced with temporary slack in their regular work, creates work that is better suited than agricultural tasks to the capacities of children, and allows work to occur round the year and into the night. It benefits agriculture too by creating a more steady demand for its products as well as creating demand for new agricultural products. Not least, the 'spirit of enterprise' finds a 'more ample and various field' for its activity in manufacturing; and this cannot fail to stimulate economic growth. Had the development economists of the 1950s read Hamilton's *Report*, their case for industrialization may well have been more persuasive.

With so many advantages, the development of manufacturing could not be left to market forces. Individuals might be discouraged by the fear of failure in 'untried enterprises' and the difficulty of competing against long-established manufactures which may also enjoy subsidies from their governments.[46] As a result, Hamilton (1791: 234-76) proposed a long list of interventions to stimulate manufactures, including duties or prohibitions on competing imports, prohibition on export of raw materials used in manufactures, subsidies on exports, drawback of duties on imported raw materials used in manufactures, encouragement of inventions and immigration of skilled workers, inspection of manufactured exports for quality, developing new financial instruments, and constructing roads and canals. It would appear that Hamilton was willing to give domestic manufactures all the help they could get to stand up to competition from British imports.

Over the next half century, the leading economists in United States continued to espouse protectionism. Two of them, John Rae (1834) and Friederich List (1841), are noteworthy because they sought to ground their arguments in an explicit theoretical framework. Rae (1834: ch. 1) developed a theory of growth which gave primacy to 'invention' as a source of growth. 'Invention is the only power on earth that can be said to create wealth.' He was at great pains to demonstrate how the centrality of innovation in his theory differed from Adam Smith's emphasis on capital accumulation as the leading source of economic growth. Adam Smith's opposition to protection makes sense once we understand his emphasis on capital accumulation; since protection diminishes output, it must also reduce capital accumulation and growth. On the other hand, if wealth is created by 'inventions', economic growth will be stimulated by 'rousing this [inventive] principle to activity'.[47]

Rae (1834: 53-55) presented an early case for protecting manufactures that was based on the recognition of externalities. A firm which cannot cover its initial losses may not be established even if it expects to become competitive with imports. Yet the innovations it has mastered may become available at no cost to other firms which, therefore, can break even or earn profits at the point of entry. These externalities may not be limited only to other firms in the same manufactures. 'Every useful art is so connected with many, or with all others, that whatever renders its products more easily attainable, facilitates the operations of a whole circle of arts, and introduces changes–the great agent in producing improvements–under the most favorable form.'[48] Protection is justified whenever the initial losses of a pioneering firm are exceeded by the sum of externalities it confers on all other firms in the economy. The concept of 'mental capital' or, alternatively, 'productive powers' is central to Friedrich List's theory of late industrialization. This is a comprehensive category that subsumes all the knowledge, values, social and political institutions of a country that are supportive of productive activities.[49] 'Mental capital' does not develop in isolation from a society's productive activities; 'the more goods that the material producers produce, the more will *mental production be capable of being promoted* (italics added)'.[50] In turn, a country's 'mental capital' has a profound impact on productive activities. The classical economists took the presence of 'mental capital' for granted, pursuing their analysis of economic development only in terms of 'exchange values', labor, capital and division of labor.[51] This has led to serious errors, since the task of economic analysis is to examine how 'the productive powers are awakened and developed, and how they become repressed and destroyed'.[52]

Agriculture and manufactures differ fundamentally in their capacity to create 'mental capital'. List provides an exhaustive analysis of the mechanisms by which manufactures advance the 'productive powers' of a country. 'Manufactories and manufactures are the mothers and children of municipal liberty, of intelligence, of the arts and sciences, of internal and external commerce, of navigation and improvements in transport, of civilization and political power. They are the chief means of liberating agriculture from its chains, and of elevating it to a commercial character and to a degree of art and science, by which the rents, farming profits, and wages are increased and greater value is given to landed property.'[53] On the contrary, agriculture is subjected to derision. In a condition of 'merely agricultural industry, caprice and slavery, superstition and ignorance, want of means of culture, of trade, and of transport, poverty and political weakness exist'.[54]

An agricultural country can never develop manufactures 'in the natural course of things'. It could never compete against older manufacturing nations, such as Britain, because their manufactures enjoyed 'a thousand advantages' conferred upon it by its more developed infrastructure, financial markets, access to larger markets both at home and abroad, greater accumulation of technical and marketing skills, and superior social and political institutions.[55] The agricultural nation must protect its manufactures until it has acquired a similar set of complementary factors which can enable it to compete on equal terms with established manufactures. If this entails a temporary loss of output, this will be 'made good a hundred-fold in powers, in the ability to acquire values of exchange, and are consequently merely reproductive outlay by the nation'.[56]

Explaining Polarization

Although global disparities widened dramatically over the two centuries following the Industrial Revolution, they received very little attention from economists until the 1950s.

In a way this was not surprising. Africa and Asia had performed quite well the tasks assigned to them in the global division of labor. They had produced a steadily growing supply of cheap raw materials; they had provided captive markets for manufactured exports from advanced countries; they had been open to foreign investments in their primary and commercial sectors; and many of them were hospitable sites for white settlements. Besides, the whole system had been quite easy to manage. All that it needed was open economies and small governments: results that had been reasonably well assured by appropriate displays of imperial power. Why worry about fixing something that had worked so well and for so long? Besides, had the economists chosen to worry, there would be trouble for their theories. Better not to worry!

The worrying started only after the second great war, when the colonial order began to cave in. France and Britain, not to mention lesser colonial luminaries, could not hold on to their empires much longer. They had been superseded by United States and Soviet Union, both of whom contested the ground held by the colonial empires. By a fateful turn of history, the two greatest powers now competed to capture the hearts and minds of the world's poorest nations. It was now time to worry about giving the lagging countries what *they* wanted; and what they wanted was economic growth, industrialization, education, technology and loans. Suddenly, there was a market for experts on the economies of lagging countries: in Washington, London, Paris and Moscow. Demand creates supply. And so, almost overnight, the new subdiscipline of development economics was born.

Once the field had been opened up, the hard questions could not be swept under the rug any longer. Why had disparities between advanced and lagging countries grown so wide, contrary to mainstream theory which predicted convergence? Why had the colonies stagnated when they were so well governed, some by the *creme de la creme* of Western nations? The first question led to two kinds of explanations. Several economists drew attention to market failures which tilted the balance of market forces in favor of the advanced countries. They came to be known as 'structuralists' since they drew attention to market failures and other structural characteristics of markets. Several others sought inspiration from Marx, but departed from his vision of capitalist development. They argued that global capitalism had created development in a small number of advanced countries and underdevelopment everywhere else. These revisionists described themselves as 'neo-Marxians', dependency theorists or world system theorists.

The seminal contribution to the structuralist critique of markets came from Raul Prebisch (1950a, 1950b). The problems of Latin America have their origins not in its internal conditions, but in the 'peripheral' position it occupies in the global economy, producing and exporting primary goods to countries at the 'center' in exchange for their manufactures. Since the income elasticity of demand for primary goods was smaller than that for manufactures, growth in the world economy unavoidably pushed down the terms of trade for primary goods.[57] This meant that gains from productivity increases in the 'periphery' were passed to the 'center' as lower prices. In addition, both labor and commodity markets in the 'center' enjoyed monopoly power while such restraints were lacking in the 'periphery'. These asymmetries exacerbated the tendency towards falling terms of trade in the 'periphery'.[58]

Gunnar Myrdal (1957) offered a more radical critique of markets since he rejected the central neoclassical concept of 'stable equilibrium' for analyzing social processes. Social systems are not in stable equilibrium. Instead, when change occurs in a social system, this generally calls forth other changes which tend to push the system further in the direction of the first change. In other words, social changes tend to be cumulative, both when the system is pushed upward and downward. The application of this principle to the global economy meant that when two economies, at different levels of development, are brought together, the natural operation of market forces tends to widen their initial inequalities. There are at least two 'backwash effects' producing this result. Trade between advanced and lagging countries expands the markets for manufactures and, given economies of scale in manufactures, reduces manufacturing costs and returns to capital in the advanced country. This leads to successive rounds of investments and export expansion in the manufactures of the advanced country. The polarization created by trade is deepened by factor movements. Attracted by higher returns, the lagging country also loses its capital and skilled labor to the advanced country.[59]

The early literature on development economics identified several more market asymmetries operating against lagging countries. Thus, since world markets set the prices for primary exports to equate wages in the primary export sector to subsistence wages, Lewis (1954, 1978a, 1978b) argued that the lower subsistence wages in the tropical countries–vis-à-vis subsistence wages in temperate primary exporting countries–implied that the terms of trade for tropical primary exports would be less favorable. Levin (1960) explained how global markets ensured that the primary producing sectors in many tropical countries would remain export enclaves. Since domestic wage labor and capital were scarce in these countries, and could not be mobilized quickly, they could develop their primary exports only by importing foreign capital and labor. This meant that the expansion of primary exports would bring few benefits to the exporting countries. Myint (1954) pointed out that peasants in lagging countries faced monopoly power at both ends of the market: as producers they faced the monopoly power of large trading companies; they also faced the same trading monopolies as buyers of imported consumer goods. These asymmetries depressed wages in lagging countries while also raising the prices of consumer imports.

The divergent growth experiences of United States and Latin America could also be explained by market asymmetries; this early example of hysteresis was developed by Baldwin (1956). Once market forces (aided by accidents of nature) had 'chosen' Latin America for the production of plantation crops, their fate was sealed. These plantation crops, characterized by increasing returns to scale, would produce large concentrations of landholdings and poor and mostly unfree peasants; the resulting unequal income distribution meant that simple manufactures would be slow to develop, thus perpetuating their dependence on a few primary exports. On the other hand, United States was 'chosen' for wheat production which, because of its limited economies of scale, supported small holdings and a free peasantry. This produced a more equal distribution of income and, therefore, more favorable demand conditions for the early emergence of a manufacturing sector. As a result, Latin American economies remained stuck with coffee, tobacco, sugar and bananas, while Americans produced wheat, textiles, steel, machinery, cars, ships and railways.

The neo-Marxists reversed Marx's thesis that capitalism could only be introduced into pre-capitalist societies from outside. Capitalism had *failed* to develop these societies, Baran (1952, 1957) argued, because it was introduced by foreign capital. Since foreign capitalists entered these societies in order to sell manufactures and extract raw materials, they formed political alliances with the largest landowners, stymied indigenous tendencies towards the growth of capitalist manufactures, and spawned a subordinate class of indigenous merchant capital (*compradors*) to handle the retail end of their activities. This alliance was bound to be detrimental to economic development wherever it took hold. The surplus appropriated by landlords was diverted to conspicuous consumption, while foreign capital dispatched its profits abroad. Income distribution too remained unequal, limiting the size of markets for mass produced consumption goods. When manufactures were eventually established, often again by foreign capital, it was to earn monopoly profits made possible by high tariffs. The result of all this has been 'a political and social coalition of wealthy compradors, powerful monopolists, and large landowners dedicated to the defense of the existing feudal-mercantile order'.[60]

This neo-Marxist critique was elaborated by a long line of contributors, the most notable amongst whom are Frank (1967), Amin (1970) and Wallerstein (1974). They have somewhat similar stories to tell. The progressive incorporation of regional and national economies, starting in the fifteenth century, into a single global economy by European mercantile capital, created a bipolar global economy, with a growing concentration of mercantile capital and, later, manufacturing and financial capital in Western Europe and the United States (the Center), and the conversion of the rest of the world (the Periphery) to primary production. The economic relations between the Center and the Periphery, dominated by capital from the Center, drained the latter of much of its economic surplus, a transfer that was effected at first through plunder, but later through capitalist (often, also monopolistic) production and exchange. These transfers 'underdeveloped' the Periphery, while they augmented capitalist accumulation at the Center. Wallerstein introduces an intermediate tier of countries (the Semi-Periphery) to which some countries from the Periphery might advance occasionally, or to which countries at the Center might sink under pressure from more powerful rivals.

Concluding Remarks

There exist some strong connections between a country's place in the global economy and the theories of trade that it espouses. The orthodox theories of trade were proposed, refined and upheld by economists from advanced countries, while their Listian opposites emanated mostly from lagging countries.

The orthodox theory of comparative advantage found its strongest proponents in Britain during the nineteenth century and, when the mantle of economic leadership passed to the United States, the theory moved its base across the Atlantic from one Cambridge to another. When the United States lagged behind Britain, her economists traded in heterodox theories of trade, but slowly, once she had caught up with Britain, the heterodox economists were displaced by others with a taste for orthodoxy. Occasionally, we do find economists from advanced countries who have taken a Listian view of integration, but this is because they identify with the interests of the lagging countries.

These connections lead to some sobering reflections on the uses of economics. For nearly two hundred years, economists from advanced countries have taught us that what was good for them, *a la* trade policy, was good for everyone else. They scarcely took notice of the growing polarization between advanced and lagging countries; neither did they recognize that this was a problem for the theory of comparative advantage. Was this social science or ideology? The passage from the contradictions in Adam Smith to David Ricardo's 'rigorous' statement of the law of comparative advantage, marks a descent into ideology from which the theory of trade has yet to recover: a recovery that is not likely to occur so long as free trade serves the interests of advanced countries–and advanced countries remain the arbiters of economic theory.

Notes

1 The opposite strategy which seeks to alter the terms under which this incorporation takes place will be described as *Listian*, after the mid-nineteenth century German economist, List (1841). Schwartz (1994: 60-63) describes this strategy as Kaldorian.

2 For an assessment of this later (mostly unacknowledged) impact of development economics on innovations in mainstream economics, see Bardhan (1993).

3 Hirschman (1981) has provided the best synoptic view of the emergence of structuralist thinking.

4 References to dynamic gains from trade may be found in other classical economists–including John S. Mill, John R. McCulloch, Robert Torrens and David Buchanan–but these gains are not central to their argument (Bloomfield 1981: 97). Mill (1848: 581) states that the 'indirect benefits' from trade 'must be counted as benefits of a high order'.

5 Minor improvements upon existing technology can be made by workers. However, the birth of major new technologies is owing to 'philosophers'; and men can be supported in this activity only by a very great division of labor (Elmslie 1994: 655).

6 Hume (1742: 296) has written that this 'perhaps is the chief advantage which arises from commerce with strangers. It rouses men from their indolence; and presenting the gayer and more opulent part of the nation with objects of luxury, which they never before dreamed of, raises in them a desire of a more splendid way of life than what their ancestors enjoyed.' In the same vein, Mill (1848: 581) writes that 'The opening of trade ... sometimes works a sort of industrial revolution in a country whose resources were previously undeveloped for want of energy and ambition in the people: inducing those who were satisfied with scanty comforts and little work, to work harder for the gratifi-

cation of their new tastes, and even to save, and accumulate capital, for the still more complete satisfaction of those tastes at a future time.' Also see McCulloch (1864: 92).

7 Smith (1776: 388-92).
8 Smith (1776: 15-16).
9 Smith (1762-63, 1766]: 538). See also Rosenberg (1964).
10 Adam Smith's (1776: 385) views on this subject are worth quoting in full:
'...commerce and manufactures gradually introduced order and good govern-ment, and with them, the liberty and security of individuals, among the in-habitants of the country, who had before lived in a continual state of war with their neighbours, and of servile dependency upon their superiors'.
11 'The nature of agriculture, indeed, does not admit of so many subdivisions of labour, nor of so complete a separation of one business from another, as manufactures.' This 'is perhaps the reason why the improvement of the pro-ductive powers of labour in this art [agriculture] does not always keep pace with their improvement in manufactures (Smith 1776: 5-6)'.
12 Low (1952) and Hont (1983).
13 Hume (1742: 310-311).
14 Quoted in Hont (1983: 276).
15 Adam Smith (1776: 243). 'The same cause, however, which raises the wages of labour, the increase of stock, tends to increase its productive powers, and to make a smaller quantity of labour produce a greater quantity of work. (...) There are many commodities, therefore, which, in consequence of these im-provements, come to be produced by so much less labour than before, that the increase of its price is more than compensated by the diminution of its quan-tity (Smith 1776: 86).'
16 Hont (1983: 300).
17 Smith (1762-63, 1766: 567).
18 Smith (1776: 425).
19 'By raising up too hastily a species of industry which only replaces the stock which employs it, together with the ordinary profit, it would depress a species of industry which, over and above replacing that stock with its profit, affords likewise a neat produce, a free rent to the landlord (Smith 1776: 637).'
20 Smith (1776: 392).
21 Smith (1776: 360).
22 Cited in Low (1952: 325).
23 Johnson (1967) and Brecher and Diaz-Alejandro (1977).
24 MacDougall (1951).
25 Avineri (1968: 32).
26 'Indian society has no history at all, at least no known history.' *New York Daily Tribune*, August 8, 1953, reprinted in: Avineri (1968: 125).
27 In a letter to Engels, Marx wrote, 'Berneir correctly discovers the basic form of all phenomena in the East–he refers to Turkey, Persia, Hindostan–to be the *absence of private property* in land. This is the real key even to the Ori-ental heaven (Avineri 1968: 6).'

28 Avineri (1968: 88).
29 Marx, *New York Daily Tribune*, August 8, 1853, reprinted in: Avineri (1968: 125).
30 *The Communist Manifesto* acknowledges that pre-capitalist societies could change from within. 'It compels all nations, on pain of extinction, to adopt the bourgeois mode of production; it compels them to introduce civilization into their midst, *i.e.* to become bourgeois themselves (Avineri 1968: 32-33).'
31 Marx, *New York Daily Tribune* (June 25, 1853), reprinted in Avineri (1968: 88).
32 Marx, *New York Daily Tribune*(June 25, 1853), reprinted in Avineri (1968: 88).
33 Marx, *New York Daily Tribune* (December 3, 1859), reprinted in Avineri (1968: 374).
34 *Neue Rheinische Zeitung*, February 1850, reprinted in Avineri (1968: 45).
35 Marx, *Capital*, vol. ii, ch. 1, sec. 2, reprinted in: Avineri (1968: 36-37).
36 Marx, *New York Daily Tribune*, August 5 & 8, 1853, reprinted in Avineri (1968: 130,126).
37 Marx, *New York Daily Tribune*, August 5, 1853, reprinted in Avineri (1968: 122).
38 Marx, *New York Daily Tribune*, August 5, 1853, reprinted in Avineri (1968: 122).
39 Marx, *New York Daily Tribune*, July 11 & August 8, 1853, reprinted in Avineri (1968: 100, 126-27). The interest of British rulers in India's development may be gauged from a single statistic quoted by Marx: 'the outlay during three Presidencies, with a population of seventy millions, up to 1851, for public works was only £93,000! Incredible as it may seem, the little State of Rhode Island has expended, until very recently, if not up to this moment, as much in Internal Improvements as the East India Company for the whole Empire!' *New York Daily Tribune*, June 25, 1853, reprinted in Avineri (1968: 79).
40 Marx, *New York Daily Tribune*, July 11 & August 8, reprinted in: Avineri (1968: 101, 127).
41 Marx, *New York Daily Tribune*, August 8, reprinted in: Avineri (1968: 126).
42 Marx, *New York Daily Tribune*, August 8, reprinted in: Avineri (1968: 128-29).
43 Lenin (1917: 63) writes: 'The necessity for exporting capital arises from the fact that in a few countries capitalism has become 'over-ripe' and (owing to the backward state of agriculture and the impoverished state of the masses) capital cannot find 'profitable' investment.'
44 Hilferding (1910: 322) wrote: 'The export of capital, especially since it has assumed the form of industrial and finance capital, has enormously accelerated the overthrow of all the old social relations, and the involvement of the world in capitalism.' Similarly, Lenin (1917: 65) wrote: 'The export of capital affects and greatly accelerates the development of capitalism in those countries to which it is exported. While, therefore, the export of capital may tend to a certain extent to arrest development in the capital exporting coun-

tries, it can do so only by expanding and deepening the further development of capitalism throughout the world.'

45 Luxemburg (1913: 371) writes: 'Force is the only solution open to capital; the accumulation of capital, seen as an historical process, employs force as a permanent weapon, not only at its genesis, but further on down to the present day.'

46 Hamilton (1791: 203).

47 Rae (1834: 29).

48 Rae (1834: 365).

49 List (1841: 158) takes a very broad view of 'mental capital'. 'The more the mental producers succeed in promoting morality, religion, enlightenment, increase of knowledge, extension of liberty and of perfection of political institutions–security of persons and property within the State, and the independence and power of the nation externally–so much greater will be the production of material wealth.'

50 List (1841: 159).

51 List (1841: 226) writes: 'He [Adam Smith] wrongly maintains that the revenues of the nation are dependent only on the sum of its material capital.'

52 List (1841: 138).

53 List (1841: 141-42).

54 List (1841: 141).

55 List (1841: 299-300).

56 List (1841: 226.

57 A proportionate increase in output in the 'periphery' and 'center' could restore equilibria in the markets for primary goods and manufactures only through a downward adjustment in the primary terms of trade.

58 Prebisch (1984).

59 The integration between advanced and lagging countries may also create 'spread effects' in lagging countries–expansion in markets for primary exports and transfer of technology from the advanced countries–but these 'spread effects' historically have been weak relative to the disequalizing 'backwash effects'.

60 Baran (1957: 195).

4

Sovereignty Matters

' ... a subject people resembles not only a convict but an invalid; it
suffers from debility as a result of its confinement. Under foreign rule
political and military traditions degenerate, cultural life decays and
economic activities, losing their national significance, are distorted to
meet the requirements of the colonial power. '

J. S. Furnivall (1948: 468)

A theoretical analysis of the global economy during industrial epoch *I* reveals that the potential for sustained economic growth in lagging countries was fundamentally linked to their sovereign ability to structure their economic relations with advanced countries.

The reasons for this may be stated succinctly. When advanced and lagging countries—with the former possessing comparative advantage in manufactures—were integrated, this concentrated manufactures, technology and capital in the former while the latter specialized in a diminishing range of primary goods.[1] This division of labor placed the advanced countries on a trajectory of growth while the lagging countries were likely to be caught in stagnation or worse. Only sovereign lagging countries, endowed with the power to *structure* their integration—to decide when, how fast and how far to integrate, what markets to integrate, and with whom to integrate—could resist the dynamics of disequalization created by international integration. There was double jeopardy in the loss of sovereignty. Their sovereignty eroded, lagging countries underwent unobstructed integration and, in addition, their markets and resources were appropriated to create rent for the advanced countries. Once lagging countries had lost their sovereignty, they did not have a prayer.

One gets a rather different account of these matters in Marx and the orthodox economists. Their writings suggest that sovereignty was often a hindrance to economic growth in lagging countries. This conclusion emerges from two deeply held assumptions of the nineteenth century, one partial and the other deeply flawed. Adam Smith first argued that international integration is a powerful engine of growth—a thesis that has since entered into the mainstream of economic thought. Most lagging countries, however, were too backward to manage their own integration into world markets; nor did they possess any internal dynamic which could in time propel them towards integration. The conclusion was inescapable. Only

70

colonization could transform these backward societies and prepare them for integration and growth. Not surprisingly, Marx and Engels were ecstatic when endorsing the conquests of African and Asian countries by Britain and France. This was their only chance of receiving the inestimable benefits of Western bourgeois civilization.

Stripped of pretensions, these arguments were mostly self-serving. Integration of the strong with the weak is nearly always good for the strong; a truism that could not have eluded the economists in advanced countries. The conscience of the strong, however, must be assuaged; the 'hanging' of the weak had to be made to look good. Starting in the nineteenth century, therefore, the lagging countries in Asia and Africa were given a bad name: they were variously represented by statesmen and scholars alike as stagnant, barbaric, primitive, semi-civilized, xenophobic, despotic, and lacking any real history. The last one was Hegel's favorite, in which Marx followed him blindly. It was unlikely that societies so deeply flawed would, or could, reform themselves. They had to be improved against their will. This is what made colonization a 'civilizing' force, even if it was often destructive and, occasionally, even brutal.[2]

What comes at first as a surprise, however, is the failure of neo-Marxists to recognize that sovereignty affected the prospects of capitalist development in lagging countries. Lagging countries, they argued, could not possess any real sovereignty. Paul Baran, a founding father of the neo-Marxist critique, was quite clear on this. The great wave of decolonization that began in the late 1940s, he argued, would not change the economic prospects of the newly independent countries; this 'precipitates merely a change in their Western masters'. He goes further, arguing that decolonization might even intensify exploitation since the new imperialism 'contains and preserves all its earlier modalities, but raises them to a new level' through the powerful medium of 'well-organized, rationally conducted' multinational corporations.[3] Following Baran's lead, most neo-Marxists paid little attention to sovereignty in their accounts of the evolution of international disparities.[4]

All this, however, is understandable. For all their revisions of Marx, the neo-Marxists never wavered in their commitment to the proletarian revolution. Instead, since capitalism could not deliver economic development to lagging countries, they emphasized the need to abolish it in a hurry. They could not have acknowledged that sovereignty improved the chances of capitalist development in lagging countries. At the least, this would mean that nationalist liberation was an alternative to socialist revolution. Wary of this competition, the neo-Marxists sought to devalue the significance of the decolonization movements that swept the world at the end of the second great war. Decolonization does not sever the ties of imperialist control. When an 'independent' country seeks to break away from foreign dominance, Baran (1957: 12) warned us, it is quickly cut down to size by 'diplomatic intrigue, economic pressure, and political subversion'. And should these efforts fail, the resistance hardens into a 'counter-revolutionary alliance of all imperialist countries'.

Asymmetric Market Forces

During industrial epoch *I*, market forces alone had the capacity to deepen global inequalities. This outcome is traceable to two factors: the presence of countries at unequal levels of capitalist development *and* asymmetries in the technologies of manufacturing and primary sectors.

Mainstream economists have always been at pains to show that international integration–resulting from the operation of free markets–works to the advantage of *all* participating countries. It did not matter whether these countries are advanced or lagging, large or small, or whether they export manufactures or primary goods.[5] The asymmetries–if any–in the distribution of gains from international integration, are biased in favor of countries that are small, lagging or primary producing. At their finest, these theories argue that free trade alone would ensure the convergence of all countries to identical levels of income.

The standard theories of trade are a 'set up', amongst the finest examples of tendentious theorizing in economics. They are set up to guarantee the 'right' results. The price paid for these results can be seen in the quaint models that occupy center stage in neoclassical theories of international trade, models in which there are no economies of scale or scope, no externalities, no learning by doing, no multiplier effects, no forward or backward linkages, and where nothing of consequence changes as a result of trade: *not* factors of production, technology, institutions, tastes, the relative power of domestic classes, or the relative power of the trading countries. If the durability of these constructs surprises us, it is because they disguise so deftly the powerful interests they are intended to serve.

Once we free the analysis of international integration from the restraints imposed upon it by standard theories, it is quite easy to show that the integration of markets for commodities, savings and skilled labor produce economic and demographic effects which are fundamentally asymmetric between advanced and lagging countries. These asymmetric effects produce a spiral of growth in the advanced countries and economic stagnation or decline in most lagging countries. This section is devoted to an examination of these asymmetric effects. A tabular summary of these effects is also presented in table 4.1.

Before we examine these effects, a few words of explanation about the terms 'advanced' and 'lagging' countries. Whether a country is advanced or lagging depends on the relative position it occupies on the scale of capitalist development. As a simplifying device, however, this distinction will generally be treated as dichotomous, so that all but a handful of the most advanced countries will be classified as lagging.[6] Capitalist development is synonymous with the development of markets for goods, capital, labor and land. Although these markets are interlinked, there is some disagreement about which of them played a pivotal role in the development of capitalism. Both Adam Smith and Karl Marx believed that the main stimulus to capitalist development came from the expansion of international trade in the seventeenth and eighteenth centuries; all other markets developed in response to this stimulus. Some recent Marxists, however, insist that capitalist development cannot occur unless conditions for the free operation of labor markets are first created.[7]

Since evaluations of capitalist development in each of the lagging countries could be time-consuming, we will equate capitalist development with a country's per capita income. A high correlation can normally be assumed to exist between the two, although exceptions will occur when rents on natural resources make up a large part of the national income. It follows from this that capitalist development during industrial epoch *I*– but not later–may also be measured as the share of labor employed in modern manufacturing, since this rises with per capita income. Significantly, this also means that advanced countries possess comparative advantage in most manufactures relative to lagging countries.

In order to analyze the disequalizing effects of international integration, we must begin with a clear recognition of the asymmetries in the production technology of manufacturing and agriculture during industrial epoch *I*. In general, manufacturing is characterized by increasing returns to scale, strong production and consumption externalities, and strong backward and forward linkages. On the other hand, agriculture is generally characterized by constant returns to scale, weak production and consumption externalities, and weak backward and forward linkages. In addition, technology transfers between countries encountered fewer obstacles in manufacturing than in agriculture. Although this list of differences is not exhaustive, a theory of international integration built upon these assumptions will arrive at results quite different from those of mainstream economics.

Table 4.1

Integration: Effects on Advanced and Lagging Countries

Locus of Integration	AC/ LC	Direct Effects: Economic	Indirect Effects: Economic	Indirect Effects: Other
Product Markets	AC	↑ MFG,	↓ Costs in MFG, COM,	↑ Power of K,
	LC	↑ PRI, ↓ MFG	↓ Comparative advantage in PRI	↑ Power of N, ↓ Power of K, ↓ Sovereignty, ↓ CDR, Unchanged CBR
Direct Foreign Investment	LC	Influx of AC firms into COM, MIN & plantations	Displacement of LC firms in COM, MIN & plantations; Displacement of skills in LC	↑ Power of K in AC, ↓ Sovereignty of LC
Financial Markets	AC	Savings inflow from LC	↑Capital formation	↑ Power of K
	LC	Savings outflow to AC	↓ Capital formation	↓ Power of K
Labor Markets	AC	Immigration from LC	↓ Wages, ↑ Human capital	↓ Costs in MFG
	LC	Emigration to LC	↑ Wages, ↓ Human capital	↑ Cost in MFG

AC=advanced country, LC=lagging country, MFG=manufacturing sector; MIN=mining; COM=commerce; PRI=primary sector; K= capitalists, N= landowners, CBR=crude birth rates, CDR=crude death rates

Free Trade. Free trade between countries at unequal levels of development initiates a cumulative process which concentrates manufactures, commerce, capital and technology in the advanced countries; at the same time, the lagging countries specialize in a shrinking range of primary goods. The result is growth in the advanced countries and economic stagnation or worse in the lagging countries.[8]

At the beginning of industrial epoch *I* the advanced countries had a modest comparative advantage in the key manufactures, including textiles, iron and steel, and machinery.[9] At first, this superiority derived from innovations in steam, textiles, and iron and steel, but it may also have depended to varying degrees on more efficient capital and labor markets, greater abundance of capital, superior management skills, a more disciplined labor force, and more effective political and social institutions. Over time, the cumulative actions of free trade both deepened and widened the advanced countries' superiority in manufactures, forcing the lagging countries to specialize in the production of primary goods. This cumulative development, however, lacks symmetry. We do not observe a similar deepening or widening of the lagging countries' superiority in primary goods. On the contrary, their comparative advantage in primary goods is likely to decline as productivity gains in advanced countries are extended to primary goods.

Free trade operates through several channels to deepen, as well as extend, the advanced country's comparative advantage in manufactures. The opening of trade expands the markets for manufactured exports; since it facilitates greater division of labor, this expansion reduces the unit costs of exports and, therefore, stimulates a new round of export expansion. The process is cumulative, since it deepens in every round the advanced country's original comparative advantage. At the same time, innovations in the original export industries become available to other manufactures, starting a process that extends the advanced country's comparative advantage to new lines of manufactures. Some of these manufactures no doubt enter as inputs into the original manufactures, adding to their growing comparative advantage and penetration of foreign markets.

This growth spiral also works its way through wider networks that include markets and political institutions. The growth in manufactures creates a growing demand for wage labor, technical and managerial skills, specialized financial services, scientific knowledge (including knowledge of markets and organizations), transportation, physical infrastructure, better property rights–most importantly, patents–and the removal of restrictions on competition and movement of labor. Gradually, these demand pressures are translated in a hundred ways, *via* market forces and political pressures, into more efficient labor and capital markets, better transportation networks, improved technical education and research, and a legal system that better safeguards property rights. In its early phase, when feudal restraints on production, property rights and markets were widespread, the energies of capitalists and workers were directed mostly at removing *existing* restraints instead of creating new ones.

The growth impulses emanating from manufactures also transform the primary sector. In part, this is due to the new, improved and cheaper inputs that manufactures can now supply to primary producers. The manufacturing sector also competes with the primary sector for labor, forcing the latter to adopt, more assiduously than before, these cost-saving inputs. In turn, as primary producers demand more and better inputs, this creates, *via* the dual action of markets and politics, a greater capacity in the manufacturing sector (and public research institutes) to meet this growing demand. After a period of import substitution, the declining costs in the primary sector eventually extend the advanced country's comparative advantage to a growing array of primary products.[10] It is not too long before the advanced country starts adding primary goods to its growing exports of manufactures.

The impact of manufacturing on the primary sector is also mediated by politics. In the early stages of capitalist development, agriculture provides by far the largest markets for manufactures. Thus, as soon as manufacturing capital can flex some political muscle, it begins to use this power to move agriculture off dead center. It pushes to free agriculture from its feudal restrictions, rationalize the systems of land tenure, increase labor mobility, improve rural transportation, bring schooling to the children of peasants, and put more money into agricultural research; these pressures increase in intensity with the importance of domestic markets for manufactures. Manufacturing capital is well compensated for its lobbying: a growing primary sector provides growing markets for their output, cheaper food and raw materials, and a more plentiful supply of workers.

The primary exports of lagging countries face competition from another source. Increasingly, with the growing applications of science to production in advanced countries, their manufacturing sector begins to produce a growing variety of cheaper substitutes for many of the primary exports of lagging countries. By the middle of the twentieth century, the list of these substitutes was long, and included such important products as plastics, aluminum, artificial fibers, chemical fertilizers, synthetic rubber, dyes and drugs; the list keeps growing, threatening the survival of primary exports that are vital to the economies of many lagging countries. In the long run, the continuing decline in the cost of these substitutes forces even the lowest-cost primary producers to bow out of production.[11]

The spiral of growth set off by integration in the advanced country is almost completely missing in the lagging countries. Since agriculture furnished few opportunities for division of labor, a point Adam Smith understood quite well, agricultural expansion in lagging countries occurred mostly on the basis of existing technology.[12] Technological externalities in agriculture too were more limited than in manufacturing. Improvements in seeds, insecticides, harvesting machinery, storage techniques and soil conservation techniques developed for one branch of agriculture were much less likely to find uses in others. The great number of production units, their dispersion over large areas, and regional variations in ecology, also did not help in the diffusion of these externalities. Finally, there was no lobbying from a dynamic manufacturing sector for improvements in agriculture. In the absence of cumulative technical changes, export growth in the primary sector of lagging countries could last only as long as surplus land was available. This placed narrow limits on export growth in all the land-scarce lagging countries.

The failure of export growth in lagging countries to stimulate cumulative technical progress would not have been a problem, if they could borrow technology from advanced countries. However, these transfers were discouraged by another asymmetry between manufacturing and agriculture. Technology transfers between advanced and lagging countries in manufacturing are impeded primarily by economic factors, such as different factor prices and size of markets. In agriculture, such transfers are complicated by the need to match soil type, precipitation, temperature characteristics, pests, plant diseases, pollinating agents, etc. As a result, most agricultural technologies developed in temperate countries could not be transferred to tropical countries with different ecologies and plant varieties.[13] Some of these technologies could have been adapted to tropical conditions; and such adaptations did occur but they were limited to export crops, whose prices declined as a result, transferring the benefits of higher productivity to the importing countries.[14]

The expansion of agriculture in lagging countries created few growth impulses *via* backward linkages either. Since the use of modern inputs in agriculture would become common much later–not till the first decades of the twentieth century–the growth of agriculture in lagging countries made few demands for inputs on the manufacturing sector. Even when these linkages were important, the technologically sophisticated nature of the inputs demanded, including agricultural machinery, fertilizers and pesticides, ensured that this demand could not be met by domestic manufactures and, hence, leaked out of the lagging countries.

The expansion of agricultural exports also lacked the capacity to call into existence efficient capital and labor markets or an integrated transportation network. This failure is easy to understand in lagging countries whose agriculture was dominated by peasant farms. The rising demand for labor on peasant farms was met mostly by mobilizing family labor. Their growing need for capital too was met through self-financing or borrowing on informal markets; the high transaction costs of lending to small and spatially dispersed farmers slowed down the entry of large-scale and more efficient financial institutions into agriculture. Even when agricultural production occurred in large farms–as in much of Latin America–this was based, more often, on a captive labor force, tied to the land by feudal restrictions. Similarly, growth based on primary exports was unlikely to create integrated domestic markets. The transportation needs of a primary export economy were well-served by a system of railways that radiated from the ports to the hinterland. It was unnecessary to create a reticulated network of roads, railways and communications that would

ticulated network of roads, railways and communications that would con-
nect the different regions, and thus create integrated domestic markets for
commodities, capital and labor.

Although the primary sector had the potential for creating stronger
forward linkages, most of them leaked to the advanced countries. The
cost savings to processing industries from local availability of raw materials were more than offset by higher capital costs and the paucity of
skills due to the absence of a modern manufacturing sector. Moreover, in
most cases, including the processing of mineral ores, the technology was
far too capital-intensive to be competitive in lagging countries. As a result, lagging countries could only process raw materials which were
costly to transport, or the processed product was bulky and had a large
domestic market. This explains why lagging countries could establish saw
mills, sugar refineries and cement factories; but cotton growing countries
had much greater difficulty competing with British textiles.

Classical economists often worried that rapid productivity growth in
manufactures would turn the terms of trade against the advanced countries. These fears were mostly unfounded. The tendency towards an adverse movement in the terms of trade for manufactures was opposed by
several countervailing forces, including a higher income elasticity of demand for manufactures, immobility of labor between countries, monopoly
power in manufactures, rapid population growth in the lagging countries,
and a growing supply of land.[15] In addition, the classical economists did
not allow for productivity growth in the primary sector of advanced
countries. Since this increased the supply of primary goods, it worked
against a decline in the terms of trade for manufactures. It also increased
the advanced countries' share in the production of several primary goods,
such as wheat, sugar, cotton, rice and tobacco; this would reduce any
redistribution of productivity gains from advanced to lagging countries, if
indeed such redistribution ever occurred. This relocation of primary production, of course, spelled trouble for lagging countries. It meant that
they would not only be forced out of manufactures (and commerce), but
they would also be crowded out of many lines of primary production. The
lagging countries occupied a progressively shrinking economic space in
the global economy during industrial epoch *I*.

Lagging countries with no surplus land had the worst deal in this set
up. In the absence of significant productivity gains, rapid expansion of
primary exports could only occur in the presence of substantial amounts
of surplus land. This meant that several of today's most populous countries (or regions) without surplus land, including India, China, Bangladesh, Egypt and Java–which today contain nearly half of the world's

population–had very limited prospects for growth based on primary specialization. Unable to compete with land-rich lagging countries, even a country as large as India would be boxed into exporting a narrow range of primary products, *viz.* jute, cotton, tea and wheat. The global markets had set a perfect trap for the land-scarce tropical lagging countries; they could neither industrialize nor could they develop through growth of primary exports. This trap only deepened with time as population growth depressed labor productivity in food and, therefore, wages, increasing the chances that gains from technical change in their export sectors would simply be transferred *via* declining prices to advanced countries.

We would be remiss if we did not clear up here a misconception concerning the sources of growth in United States, Canada, Australia, South Africa and New Zealand, countries which are said to owe their success to the growth of primary exports. Apart from the fact that these countries had switched to vigorous programs of industrialization at various points during the nineteenth century, the dynamics of these economies were not comparable to those of most lagging countries for another reason. At least till the end of the nineteenth century, free immigration integrated their labor markets with those of Britain, Germany, Holland and France, turning them virtually into extensions in space of the most advanced economies of the time. The human capital which these immigrants brought from their home countries, when combined with the natural resources of the temperate countries of settlement, quickly produced agrarian economies with strong comparative advantage in wheat, wool and dairy products–all of which enjoyed large and rapidly growing markets in the advanced countries. In addition, when these countries launched their own industrialization, the same flow of immigrants provided them with simultaneous access to the industrial skills of the advanced countries. It is about time that economic historians emerged out of the shadow of geographers and recognized the regions of temperate settlement for what they were, *viz.* spatial extensions of the world's most advanced economies.

Transfers of Savings. Orthodox analysis predicts that international integration of financial markets will transfer savings from capital-abundant (advanced) countries to capital-scarce (lagging) countries, thus helping to reduce international disparities.[16] This prediction is reversed in the global economy that we have constructed.

The reasons for this reversal should be transparent. International trade sets into motion cumulative forces which deepen and extend the advanced countries' initial comparative advantage in manufactures to other manufactures, commercial activities and primary production. The obverse of this is a progressive narrowing of the production base in lagging countries, which are not only pushed out of manufactures and commerce, but their comparative advantage in primary production too is eroded, so that they are forced to specialize on a shrinking range of primary goods. In other words, the global economy during industrial epoch I concentrated technological changes in the manufacturing, commercial and primary sectors of advanced countries, thus creating the paradoxical situation where savings flow from the capital-scarce lagging countries to the capital-abundant advanced countries. Of course, some savings were attracted into primary activities characterized by strong economies of scale. But once the higher early returns were exhausted, the profits from these initial investments return to the advanced countries.

Movements of Firms. The elimination of barriers to the international mobility of firms encourages entry of foreign firms (from advanced countries) into lagging countries, mostly into commerce, transportation, mining and plantations; and this has the effect of displacing capital and skills in the lagging countries.[17]

Foreign firms (from advanced countries) were likely to possess three advantages over indigenous firms in lagging countries. They could draw upon cheaper funds from the more efficient capital markets in their home country; they had better management and accounting practices; they had greater access to global markets. On the other hand, indigenous firms had the advantage of superior knowledge about local markets, including markets for products, labor and raw materials. Frequently, this meant that foreign firms had a competitive edge in large-scale export-oriented activities (including mining, plantation crops and large-scale manufactures directed towards exports), shipping, railways, international trade and the financial sector of lagging countries. In the long run, this would lead to the substitution of indigenous firms by foreign firms in all these activities.

Did the lagging countries gain from the entry of foreign firms? Orthodox economists think that they did, but their logic is flawed since they ignore the displacement effects of the entry of foreign firms on capital and labor in lagging countries. Consider the case where the entry of foreign firms results in an 'equivalent' displacement of existing indigenous firms: an increase in output, ΔQ, attributable to the entry of foreign firms in industry X results in the loss of ΔQ from the exit of indigenous firms in industry X. On the assumption that ΔQ is small, there would be no gains or losses to the lagging country if all the labor and capital employed by the displaced indigenous firms could be reallocated instantaneously to other uses.[18] Under these assumptions, it would not matter if foreign firms hired locally or from outside.

A realistic analysis of the displacement effects of the entry of foreign firms must begin by discarding the assumption that *all* the displaced capital and labor are reallocated to alternative uses. The greater part of the capital (physical and human) employed by the indigenous firms (that are eventually displaced) will most likely be lost, either because they are too specialized and have no alternative uses, or because the decline in returns to capital (due to competition from foreign firms) makes it difficult to replace them from depreciation funds.[19] In addition, the displaced workers may suffer loss of wages to the degree that they face frictional unemployment. The wage losses will be smaller if the foreign firms employ indigenous labor. Once these displacement effects are recognized, income losses from the entry of foreign firms become unavoidable.

These results remain unchanged even if the entry of foreign firms did not result in displacement of existing indigenous firms. By preempting valuable economic space now, the foreign firms ensure the continuing exclusion of indigenous firms which, with temporary support from the state, could become competitive and thus hold their ground against foreign firms. The current wage gains (if any) from the entry of foreign firms must then be offset against the failure of indigenous capital formation due to the unobstructed entry of foreign firms. These long-run potential losses could easily exceed the initial gains (if any) to indigenous labor.[20]

The displacement of indigenous firms (actual and potential) also reduces the diffusion of technology in the manufacturing and commercial sectors of lagging countries. Since foreign firms are better informed about markets in their home country, this will bias their hiring, sourcing and subcontracting activities towards their home country.[21] These biases redirect the flow of externalities away from lagging countries to the advanced country. A similar bias operates in the transmission of technology through more informal means; this is because of the limited social contacts that foreign firms are likely to maintain with indigenous populations, especially where cultural and racial differences intervene between the advanced and lagging countries.

Labor Migrations. Integration of the markets for unskilled labor has the potential for producing a strong equalizing effect on wages in the global economy.[22] However, for the most part, this potential was never allowed to come into play.

The advanced countries in Europe enforced strong restrictions on immigration through most of our period. Those outside Europe were more open, but they restricted immigration only to whites, many of whom came from the advanced countries in Europe. Non-whites did enter into United States but only as slaves. It is unclear if the removal of slaves from Africa improved wages of those left behind, since their capture was often accompanied by much destruction and brutality. On the other hand, the introduction of cheap slave labor into United States, a country with abundant land resources, gave it a strong comparative advantage in three major tropical crops (tobacco, cotton, and rice), thus robbing the tropical lagging countries of markets which might have been theirs.

There were significant labor outflows from India and China, two of the largest lagging countries, between 1870 and 1914, but this was directed to other lagging countries in Southeast Asia, East Africa and the Caribbean. While these outflows were large enough to depress wages in the receiving countries to the levels of India and China, they were still too small proportionally to increase wages in the two source countries.

Demographic Changes. The disequalizing effects of integration between advanced and lagging countries were reinforced by the different paths they followed in their demographic transition.

Integration increased the speed, and lowered the cost, of food deliveries to deficit areas, thus reducing the frequency and duration of famines everywhere. In addition, once cheap medical technologies for fighting diseases had been developed in the advanced countries, they quickly became available even to the poorest lagging countries. There was little political resistance to the transfer and spread of these technologies either. The largest landowners as well as the foreign-owned mines and plantations in the lagging countries would gain from the lower wages assured by a rapidly growing population.

Integration was not so even handed in its effects on birth rates. The disequalizing effects of integration made sure that birth rates in advanced countries would decline continually: the result of rising incomes, increasing participation of women in the labor force, rising urbanization, compulsory primary schooling, and a more equal distribution of income. Disequalization produced opposite effects in lagging countries, resulting from stagnation in per capita income, a more unequal distribution of income, destruction of home-based industries (which reduced the economic power of women in rural households), and an enduring political alliance between large landowners and foreign capital, both opposed to education and social reforms. As result, birth rates in lagging countries showed few signs of going down before the 1950s. When combined with falling death rates, the result was accelerating population growth, growing pressure on land, rising dependency ratios, and depressed wages in the subsistence sector: none of which helped the growth prospects of lagging countries.

Unequal Sovereignties

The global economy we have just examined remains a limited construct in the absence of states and classes. It is now time to inject politics into our analysis: to endow the advanced and lagging countries with classes and states, to give them unequal power, to examine their responses to integration, and analyze how all this affected the evolution of the global economy during industrial epoch *I*.

The political *dramatis personae* in this global economy consist of classes and states. In each country, there are three basic classes: capitalists, landowners and workers.[23] Capitalists derive their income from capital invested in manufacturing or commerce: they may be divided into two segments, depending on whether their dominant interests are in manufacturing or commerce. Landowners derive their income from land employed in primary production. Workers derive their income from labor, and may be divided into two segments, depending on whether they work in agriculture or manufacturing. These class distinctions become sharper with capitalist development.

The state consists primarily of all persons engaged directly in any one of its three-fold activities: defense, governance and production. Only the last needs some explanation. The state's production activities might include the construction and maintenance of infrastructure and, frequently, the management of public enterprises in manufacturing and the primary sector. In addition to the interests of its own personnel, the state embodies the interests of the dominant classes and the collective interests of the whole community. Which of these interests have the upper hand depends, among other things, on the level of capitalist development, the age of the state, the ethnic identity of state officials, the history of inter-state relations, and the ethnic composition of the population especially in relation to that of the state personnel.

Capitalist development encourages the ascendancy of capitalists over landowners for several reasons. It increases the share of manufacturing and commerce in the economy while concentrating these activities spatially; it augments the size of firms in manufacturing and commerce; it deepens the dependence of the military on manufactures, shipping and commerce; and improves both transportation and communication among the major urban centers. All these developments tend to increase the power of capitalists over the economy, their ability to articulate their collective interests, and their control over the state sector. This growth in the power of capitalists may follow different trajectories: it may be evolutionary as in Britain, or revolutionary as in France.

The advanced countries enjoyed military ascendancy over most lagging countries at the beginning of the nineteenth century, an advantage that grew with time. In large part, this was the result of capitalist development. Manufacturing, shipping and communications furnished the sinews of war: the advanced countries had a growing advantage in all three. The advanced countries also had a larger foreign trade, making it easier for them to raise revenues from import tariffs; and this enhanced their capacity to wage wars. The greater military capability of the advanced countries was also a historical product, a result of centuries of warfare made inevitable by the presence of a multitude of states in Europe, both large and small, whose shifting alliances succeeded in frustrating the imperial ambitions of any great power. These wars accelerated the pace of technological progress in weaponry, professionalized the army, and improved military strategy and discipline.

The stage is now set for an analysis of the global economy during industrial epoch *I*. We begin by examining the differential impact of integration on classes and states in the advanced and lagging countries; how this, together with a variety of exogenous factors, determined the manner in which the advanced and lagging countries responded to integration; how advanced countries were driven towards imperialism by the interests of their dominant classes; and, finally, what were the economic effects of imperialism on the lagging countries?

Integration Policies. The patterns of gains and losses created by integration ensure that the advanced countries will lean towards integration; although the response of lagging countries remains ambiguous.

These gains and losses are summarized in table 4.2. Integration creates gains for all segments of capital in the advanced countries by giving them access to markets and cheaper raw materials in lagging countries; these gains are shared with professionals and workers in manufacturing and commerce. The landowners in advanced countries lose since the primary sector faces competition from cheaper imports of food and raw materials. Wages in the primary sector of advanced countries may decline at first, but this is likely to be reversed as the slack in the labor force is taken up by the continuing expansion of manufactures. These gains and losses are reversed in the lagging countries. The capitalists and workers in their manufacturing sector lose, their landowners win, and their primary sector workers may win if they own land.[24] Commercial capital in the lagging countries may gain at first from the expansion of trade, but they are certain to lose out in the competition with superior foreign enterprises.

These asymmetric effects may also be observed in the state sectors of

Table 4.2
Winners and Losers Created by Integration

	Winners	Losers
Advanced Countries	Capitalists in manufacturing & commerce; urban labor; state	Landowners; tenants and peasants
Lagging Countries	Landowners; tenants and Peasants	Capitalists in manufacturing & commerce; urban labor; state

advanced and lagging countries. The state in advanced countries gains from integration, gains which are likely to increase with time. While revenues from import tariffs may decline, these losses can be made up by new taxes on the growing manufacturing and commercial sectors. The growth of manufactures, commerce and shipping enhances is likely to enhance the advanced country's military capability by creating better and cheaper weaponry, reducing dependence on imported military hardware, improving logistics, offering the mercantile fleet for military uses during wars, and providing intelligence about lagging countries that might have military uses. Once again, these gains are likely to be reversed in lagging countries. The loss of revenues from imports–due to the elimination of tariffs–and the dismantling of state monopolies will most likely force the state to retrench. The lagging countries are unlikely to recoup these losses by imposing new taxes on the declining manufacturing and commercial sectors; and it is doubtful if powerful landowners could be persuaded to make up for the lost revenues. The decline and eventual loss of manufacturing increases dependence on foreigners for military hardware. More seriously, the loss of commerce and shipping places the country's exports and imports in the hands of foreigners. The presence of foreign capital, whether in commerce, transportation, mining or plantations, threatens to convert the country into a dependency. In alliance with indigenous landlords, the foreign capitalists can undermine the autonomy of the state.

The transition towards integration is almost assured in the advanced countries since this is what their dominant capitalists want. But this transition may be slow. The landowners still wield considerable power, and they will seek to cut their losses by delaying the removal of tariffs on agricultural imports. Tariffs on manufactures too may persist, since landowners and capitalists may not yet be willing to tax their own incomes. In a bow to the working classes, immigration will be restricted or banned. The entry of foreign enterprises too will be discouraged, since capitalists generally find such competition too close for comfort; in some cases, this may also be seen as compromising national security. The most dynamic segments of capital will seek to bring down the remaining barriers to integration. However, success in this is likely to hinge on the contest between countries to gain reciprocal reductions from their largest trading partners.

The formulation of an appropriate response to integration is more problematic in the lagging countries. The landowners emerge as the only clear winners from integration, and they are likely to throw their full weight behind free trade. Opposing free trade are manufacturing and commercial capital, workers in manufactures and commerce, and various segments of the state sector. While the landowners have few allies in their battle for integration, they are powerful–the most powerful class in many lagging countries–ensuring that the opposing forces are more evenly matched than in the advanced countries.

The outcome of this close contest turns on several factors. The landowners' strength depends on land concentration, direct control over the reins of the state, and prior orientation towards primary exports. On the other hand, urban concentration, separation of handicrafts from farming, a tradition of craft guilds, and a strong state presence in manufacturing and mining give strength to capital and professional and urban workers; capital is weakened if it is dominated by ethnic or religious minorities. The efficacy of the state depends on its age, its ownership interests in manufacturing, national cohesion, the ethnic identity of the rulers, the balance of power between capitalists and landowners, and threats to its security from neighboring countries. Since these conditioning factors will vary from one lagging country to another, a variety of responses to integration will emerge in lagging countries.

This prognosis is fully supported by the economic policies of lagging countries in the first quarter of the nineteenth century–before most of them had forfeited their sovereignty. Some lagging countries at this time were moving towards a policy of integration; some were gearing up for industrialization; a few had withdrawn into hermetic isolation, wishing neither to integrate nor industrialize; and some had not yet faced the question since they were isolated by barriers of distance and geography. In addition, there were countries which had lost their sovereignty in an earlier wave of colonization and their economies were integrated into the advanced countries.

A collision between advanced and lagging countries was inevitable when the latter opposed integration. Conflicts were unavoidable even when the lagging countries favored integration because they might not move fast enough for the taste of advanced countries. More likely than not, their shift towards integration would be restrained by compromises with influential capitalists, powerful segments in the state sector, and concentrations of urban workers–resulting in varying levels of protection for manufactures, and restrictions on entry of foreign firms and on immigration. The landowners too might resist entry of foreign firms into primary production. In addition, import tariffs could not be given up altogether, since landowners would not tax themselves for the sake of a dogmatic adherence to free trade. None of these barriers to entry would be well received by the advanced countries.

In addition, the advanced countries were setting their sights on more ambitious goals. They did not merely want to level the playing field in the lagging countries, but to tilt it in their favor. They sought to control the markets in lagging countries so that they could earn monopoly rents and, if these were not enough, to take what else they could by force–without the intermediation of markets. Did there exist a parallel imperialism of lagging countries aimed at advanced countries? Certainly, the landowners in lagging countries would have wanted to end protection in the primary sector of advanced countries, and to monopolize their markets for primary goods. That this never happened is not surprising. The lagging countries lacked the power to enforce *their* imperialism.

In the event, it was the imperialism of advanced countries which prevailed; and willy nilly, most lagging countries adapted to its demands. Over the course of the nineteenth century, large swathes of the world had been converted into colonies of Britain, France, Germany, Belgium, Portugal and Netherlands. Many countries not directly colonized were forced to accede to 'open door' treaties: these quasi-colonies included the Ottoman Empire, Saudi Arabia, Yemen, Iran, Thailand and China. While South America and the lagging countries in Europe preserved their independence, Central America was kept under a tight leash by United States. How did these dramatic changes come about? What were their consequences for economic development in the lagging countries? Answers to these questions demand a more careful analysis of imperialism.

Imperialism. The taproot of imperialism is grounded in the interests of capital and labor in the advanced countries, although, occasionally, these interests are modified or superseded by strategic concerns. We now examine these interests, the political mechanisms that were employed to enforce them, and their consequences for the polities and economies of lagging countries.

Capital in the advanced countries consisted of three segments: manufacturing capital, engaged in manufacturing and located in the advanced countries; commercial capital, engaged in commerce between advanced and lagging countries; overseas capital, invested in the primary sector and infrastructure of lagging countries. Labor is best viewed as consisting of two segments: the industrial proletariat and a growing professional class including managers, engineers, accountants, lawyers and scientists.[25] We will identify the 'collective' goals of each segment of capital and labor, where the qualifier 'collective', as before, defines goals which any segment of capital or labor pursues *as* a class. Moreover, we assume, that these goals were pursued, at least during the first half of industrial epoch *I*, under conditions of competitive markets.[26]

All segments of capital in advanced countries shared one *encompassing* goal, *viz.* to restructure the economies of lagging countries to make them complementary with their own. For this, the economies of lagging countries would have to be opened up to capital, skills and enterprises from advanced countries. This was a simple demand–but it would reach into every nook and cranny of the lagging countries. It was a demand to reform taxes, trade policies, ownership laws, immigration statutes, official procurement laws, government contracts, state monopolies, and state-owned enterprises–until all entities, indigenous and foreign, were equalized in the lagging countries.

The different segments of capital and labor in advanced countries also had *specific* interests in lagging countries, which might conflict with each other. Manufacturing capital sought exclusive access to the markets and raw materials of lagging countries; it also wanted growth of these markets and in the supply of raw materials.[27] Commercial capital also demanded exclusive access to the markets and raw materials of lagging countries, but preferred to be free to sell their raw materials wherever they could get the best prices. Overseas capital sought exclusive access to investment opportunities in lagging countries; since this restricted investments in the primary sector, it was in conflict with the interests of manufacturing capital. On the other hand, overseas capital would oppose 'enforced bilateralism' in trade.[28]

The professionals and workers in advanced countries also had an *encompassing* interest in opening up the lagging countries; this would create employment for them, at home and in the lagging countries. For the same reason, they would support capital's bid to gain exclusive access to markets, raw materials and investment outlets in lagging countries; the last directly increased their chances of gaining overseas employment. However, the specific interests of professionals and workers clashed with those of capital. While capital favored open labor markets in advanced and lagging countries, labor was opposed to immigration and demanded exclusive access to skilled jobs in lagging countries.

Once we understand the interests of capital and labor in advanced countries *vis-à-vis* the lagging countries, the imperialist project becomes both transparent and inevitable. Capital and labor from *all* advanced countries have the same encompassing interest in opening up *all* lagging countries. This meant that advanced countries had a collective interest in opening up *any* lagging country that refused to integrate freely, or did not integrate fast enough. It was difficult to resolve this 'collective action' problem in a decentralized system of nation states. It could have been solved if there existed an advanced country that had a competitive edge *and* also possessed the military power to force open-door policies on lagging countries. Britain could have played this role; and, some have argued, that it did so during the first half of the nineteenth century. But such a role was difficult to sustain in the face of growing rivalries amongst advanced countries: that is, growing rivalries between the specific interests of their capital and labor. The encompassing interests were defeated by the specific interests of capital and labor.

The failure to enforce the encompassing goals freed the advanced countries' capital and labor to pursue their specific interests in lagging countries. This inevitably led to a grab for real estate. An advanced country could pursue its specific interests in a lagging country only by persuading the latter to discriminate against, or exclude, its own capital, enterprises, and skilled labor, and exclude competition from *other* advanced countries.[29] No indigenous government could have done all this–and survived. The lagging countries would have to be converted into colonies. Their governance would have to be taken over by the advanced countries.

The imperialist goals that we have defined thus far derive from the specific interests of capital and labor in advanced countries. This does not give a rounded picture of imperialism. Occasionally, the advanced countries may take actions to modify or even supersede the specific interests of capital and labor in its capacity as an umpire, arbitrating conflicts between different segments of capital and labor, or as a guardian of their collective interests. As a result, the advanced countries may pursue colonial policies that are in conflict with the short run interests of its own capital and labor. In seeking to eliminate its dependence on food imports from potentially hostile countries, an advanced country may be persuaded to promote productivity growth in food in its colonies, even though this threatens to raise wages and hurt its own capitalists. Alternatively, it may disperse some of its industries, including heavy industries, to the colonies in order to reduce risk of losses in the event of a war. Most likely, each of these motives was at work in Japan's policies towards its colonies.

In most cases, the states in advanced countries were eager to establish colonies because this served their own interests *qua* state. We have already drawn attention to the strong symbiosis between the state, on the one hand, and manufactures, commerce and shipping. The state's ability to raise revenues increases directly with growth of manufactures and commerce; industrialization also creates opportunities for state action in a growing variety of new areas, including infrastructure, education, labor markets, transportation and banking. This symbiosis alone might suffice to move the state to do the bidding of its capital and labor.

But of course capital and labor often had the ability to force the state to work for them. Under the conditions of competitive markets that prevailed during the early decades of industrial epoch *I*, the pursuit of these goals would require collective action. This was not too difficult for manufacturing, commercial and financial capital; they could do so through a variety of industry and business associations, through political parties, as well as their control of the press. Similarly, capitalist development enables industrial workers to voice their demands through trade unions, as voters, and through representation in political parties. As soon as their numbers permit, the professional workers too organize into associations to protect their interests.

Once these instruments of collective action were in place, the colonizing adventures of advanced countries moved into high gear. This process began early in the nineteenth century, with the number of participants growing over time, and was nearly complete by the end of that century. However, the colonization project did not embrace all lagging countries. Nearly all of Africa and most of Asia had been converted into colonies. Several countries in Asia managed to retain indigenous governments, although they were forced to sign 'open-door' treaties which opened them up to advanced countries. The lagging countries in Europe and the Americas retained indigenous governments that were, for the most part, also sovereign. The reasons for these variations in sovereignty across the lagging countries, are examined in chapter five.

We employ a four-fold taxonomy of sovereignty to capture these variations in sovereignty: colony, quasi-colony, dependency and sovereign country. A colony is sharply differentiated from the other three categories: *all* branches of its government are directly controlled by expatriates appointed *by* and *from* an advanced country. A quasi-colony retains an indigenous government, but is forced by 'open door' treaties to surrender control over policies affecting trade, foreign investments, foreign residents and, often, revenue collection and expenditure. Dependencies have their own governments, but their policy autonomy is constrained by the dominance of foreign capital in their economies as well as the threat of foreign military intervention. Sovereign countries have indigenous governments and are generally free to pursue their policies without any externally imposed constraints. These variations in sovereignty were very significant. It meant that some of them–the sovereign countries and dependencies–were freer than others–colonies and quasi-colonies–to structure their relations with advanced countries and, therefore, resist the disequalizing effects of global markets *and* colonial policies which discriminated against, expropriated, and depressed returns on all indigenous factors. The colonies and quasi-colonies were doubly handicapped in the race for economic growth.

Summary

The dynamics of the global economy during industrial epoch *I* are quickly summarized.

The free play of market forces, during industrial epoch *I*, concentrated manufactures, commerce, technology and capital in the advanced countries: while lagging countries specialized in a shrinking range of primary goods. This placed the advanced countries on a rising escalator, while the lagging countries ran on a treadmill.

Integration produced different gains and losses in advanced and lagging countries. It helped the dominant class (capitalists) as well as the state in advanced countries; it helped the dominant class (landowners) but hurt all other interests in lagging countries. The advanced countries chose integration; while the lagging countries might choose autarky, industrialization or integration. Even when the lagging countries chose integration, their embrace of it was not likely to be complete. This placed the advanced and lagging countries on a collision course.

The conflict between advanced and lagging countries ran deeper. The advanced countries also had greater power, which they employed to enforce the specific interests of their capital and labor *vis-à-vis* lagging countries. Since this called for discriminatory policies against capital and labor from all other sources–including other advanced countries and the lagging country–it inevitably led to colonization of lagging countries. However, for reasons examined later, this colonization did not embrace all lagging countries. The lagging countries in Europe and the Americas were spared colonization.

The loss of sovereignty was fateful for lagging countries. It led to integration and policies which excluded, discriminated against, and suppressed returns to all indigenous factors. The result was atrophy of capital, skills and technology in these countries. Conversely, most sovereign lagging countries experienced sustained growth.

Notes

1   These consequences flow from important differences in the technologies of manufacturing and the primary sector.
2   These views have not gone out of fashion. Peter Bauer (1969: 56), an eminent British economist, maintained that Asians and Africans could not have 'established law and order, safeguarded private property and contractual relations, organized basic transport and health services, and introduced some modern financial and legal institutions'.
3   Baran (1957: 14, 197).
4   Frank (1967) and Emmanuel (1969). Only Wallerstein (1979: 61, 145) recognizes the importance of a strong state in altering the terms under which the economy is integrated into world markets. Thus, a strong state enabled Russia to enter the world market as a 'semi-periphery'. Similarly, though Japan entered the world economy at the periphery, a strong state quickly elevated it to the status of a semi-periphery.
5   Departures from free trade were grudgingly admitted under the rubric of 'infant industry argument'; but these departures were expected to be exceptional and temporary.
6   A list of the advanced countries at the beginning of the nineteenth century would include Britain, France, Belgium, Holland and United States. Over time, new entrants would be added to this list.
7   Brenner (1976) claims that these conditions were in place in Britain and France by the end of the fifteenth century.
8   The account developed here draws upon the contributions of Smith (1776), List (1841), Lewis, (1954), Myrdal (1957), Myint (1954, 1958) and Hirschman (1958).
9   This is an idealized picture. In reality, several lagging countries may have retained their comparative advantage in some manufactures into the first decades of the nineteenth century.
10 It may be noted that since manufactures use primary inputs, cost reductions in the latter deepened their comparative advantage.
11 Over time, many handicraft exports from lagging countries have been displaced by machine-made substitutes produced in advanced countries.
12 Smith (1776: 6).
13 Power tools for use in agriculture and chemical fertilizers became available only in the twentieth century and were not widely used until much later.
14 Most lagging countries did not possess the scientific skills necessary for such adaptation. More importantly, the colonial governments in lagging countries had little incentive to improve productivity in their subsistence sectors.
15 Prebisch (1950a, 1950b) drew attention to the first three factors.
16 Mundell (1957).

17 We have substituted 'foreign firms' for 'foreign direct investment' since this helps to broaden our discussion. Foreign firms in lagging countries introduced not only foreign capital, but also foreign entrepreneurs, skills and labor. This opens up the discussion of the *displacement* effects of the entry of foreign firms on indigenous capital, entrepreneurs, skills and labor.

18 We assume perfect competition.

19 The same effects may be created when domestic firms are displaced by imports (Alam 1980).

20 This will depend on the time lag between the entry of foreign firms and the entry of indigenous firms. The smaller this lag the greater the likelihood that a net loss in indigenous incomes will result.

21 These biases are reinforced by at least three other factors *viz.* cultural differences between foreign firms and indigenous populations, conspiracies to minimize technology transfers to indigenous rivals and, not least, the racism of foreign firms.

22 The migration of unskilled labor too can have adverse effects if it drains a country of its younger workers with higher-than-average propensity to save.

23 Classes are defined with respect to their common interests; this does not mean that they are always capable of acting in concert on those common interests.

24 Wages in the export-oriented primary sector may not rise even in the long run if labor productivity in the subsistence sector does not rise.

25 Clearly, capital and labor may be disaggregated in other ways: we use a disaggregation that is relevant for the analysis of imperialism.

26 This assumption becomes less realistic over time; our objective in making this assumption is to show that a full-fledged imperialism can emerge even in the absence of monopolies.

27 The former gives rise to 'enforced bilateralism'–Myrdal's (1957) phrase– between advanced and lagging countries.

28 The prevalence of 'enforced bilateralism' in colonial trade suggests that manufacturing capital was the stronger party in this conflict (Kleiman 1976).

29 Policies which promoted the specific interests of capital and labor from advanced countries vis-à-vis lagging countries might include: excluding competition from indigenous firms, skills and manufactures; expropriating indigenous factors; using public investments for expanding arable land; creating an infrastructure for servicing primary exports; subsidizing immigration; reserving skilled jobs for expatriates; discouraging schooling; encouraging population growth; neglecting the subsistence sector; etc.

5

Mapping Sovereignty

*'... India was more and more ruled from London by men who had no
experience with the land they governed, by men who governed as
Englishmen and for Englishmen'.*

Mullet (1966: 20)

We will now construct a global map of sovereignty during industrial epoch *I*, describing the variations in sovereignty across different countries. A review of the historical evidence reveals a strong correlation across countries between sovereignty and economic policy regimes during this period.

The concept of sovereignty is rich in meanings and ambiguities; at different times it has meant different things to different people. While there are some who may prefer to retire the term from political discourse, we feel that it can still do useful service provided it is clearly defined.[1] It may even be possible to agree on two minimalist definitions of sovereignty. Most political scientists agree that sovereignty is an attribute of the state, and their discussions on sovereignty center around what are often described as its 'internal' and 'external' dimensions.[2] A state has internal sovereignty when it is the final authority over its territory and population—there being no rival to its authority inside or outside its territory.[3] On the other hand, external sovereignty depends on the actions of other states, on their *recognition* of a state's right to represent and act on behalf of a given territory and population. Under conditions that vary with time and place, external sovereignty confers a variety of protections under international laws and conventions.[4]

We start from the notion of internal sovereignty, but define it with reference to policies and classes. A country is sovereign to the extent that its policies, over some sustained period of time, are determined by, and in the interest of, indigenous classes, as opposed to foreign governments, foreign capital, or foreign labor.[5] Since policies are normally mediated—or formulated—and enforced by the state, sovereignty may also be defined as a characteristic of the state. A state, then, is sovereign when persons in authority—those who mediate, or formulate, and enforce policies—are indigenous *and* can determine the content of their policies free from con-

94

straints imposed by foreigners. On the other hand, the loss of sovereignty is complete, or nearly complete, when the persons in authority are foreigners who are appointed by, and are accountable to, foreign governments or foreign interests. Between these two poles lie countries which have indigenous governments but whose ability to formulate policies is curtailed by foreign powers or foreign capital.

Although sovereignty is nearly always an attribute of the state, it may sometimes be exercised outside the bounds of the state, or in opposition to it. A community that is not constituted as a state may choose, individually or by informal collective means, to sequester itself from world markets. A similar policy may be enforced in opposition to the policies of a state: thus, it was the aim of the *Swadeshi* movement in colonial India to negate the government's policy of free trade by refusing to buy British goods, especially textiles. A country's loss of sovereignty may also be truncated spatially, *e.g.*, when two or more foreign powers establish control over different regions of that country.

We also examine the connections between internal and external sovereignty. States do not exist in a political void. They are surrounded by other states, often with hostile aims, and if any state is to maintain its internal sovereignty, the hostility of other states must either be contained or neutralized. This is where 'external' sovereignty comes into play: it has been an important mechanism that states have employed to contain their hostility towards each other. The colonization of Asia and Africa during the nineteenth century is explained by the refusal of Western states to recognize their sovereignty and, thereby, admit them into the family of nations. This is what provided the moral and legal basis for their colonization. The states in Europe and the Americas avoided this fate because they were protected by membership in the family of nations.

A Taxonomy of Sovereignty

The construction of a taxonomy of sovereignty for industrial epoch *I* is facilitated by the presence of large and enduring sovereignty differentials during this period. We work with three correlates of sovereignty to develop a fourfold taxonomy of sovereignty.

The first correlate concerns the nationality of the leaders in the key branches of government, including the executive, legislature (if there is one), judiciary and the military. Are they nationals, normally resident in the countries they govern; or, are they foreigners appointed *by* and *from* another country, and to which they expect to return upon completion of their tenure in office? A country has an indigenous government when the chief persons in authority are indigenous; when they are 'foreigners', as the term has just been defined, it is a colony. A colony occupies the lowest rung on the ladder of sovereignty.

In the long run, indigenous governments are more likely to articulate the interests of indigenous classes than a government consisting of expatriates. Most importantly, this irreducible advantage derives from the greater density of their economic, political, ethnic, religious and historical ties to the indigenous population; this makes them more vulnerable to demands and pressures from different segments of society. Another factor might also be at work in most cases. When indigenous officials collide in their own wealth-creating activities with foreigners, they can employ their power in many subtle ways to frustrate the foreigners. Thirdly, the employment of locals in higher government offices has important backward linkages. It creates a demand for higher education, calling forth indigenous institutions of learning, a publishing industry and newspapers; in turn, these are likely to contribute to the creation of an indigenous middle class. Over time, these linkages may place indigenous governments under pressure to make the transition towards republican and democratic institutions and, in turn, this may lead to greater accommodation of indigenous interests.[6]

On the contrary, colonial governments are unlikely to accommodate indigenous interests; large landowners may be an exception. The colonies were run by foreigners, appointed by and from the metropole, who were responsive to the interests of the metropole. Not only did colonial officials enter office without any social ties to the societies they governed, but they were creative in minimizing social contacts with their subjects. Nearly everywhere, colonial governments created a system of apartheid, which carefully segregated whites from natives. At the same time, they were socially intimate with expatriates from the metropole–traders, shippers, bankers, and owners of plantations and mines–whose interests they promoted in a hundred ways, in opposition to the interests of indigenous competitors. In some colonies, the government relied on large indigenous landowners to repress the rural population and, in return, protected them from expropriation and high taxes.

Colonial rulers generally opposed the spread of education and skills among natives. Anxious to preserve their privileges, they felt threatened by natives who could read and write, or who had the capital and skills to compete with expatriates. Native education was weakest in the colonies which were expected to alleviate the unemployment problems of the metropole. In Africa and Southeast Asia, the colonial rulers introduced traders and workers from India, the Levant and China; as aliens, their loyalty was assured, and they would also deflect some of the native hostility away from the alien rulers. This policy relegated the indigenous population to the subsistence sector, or reduced them to unskilled hands on farms, mines and plantations owned by foreigners.

All indigenous governments, however, were not equal. They fall into three categories with varying levels of sovereignty. Several of them were forced by unequal treaties to open up their economies to the great powers; these are the quasi-colonies. They were obliged to limit their tariffs, to abolish state monopolies, to open up their economies to capital and enterprises from the treaty countries, and exempt the citizens of treaty countries from local taxes and courts. When these countries could not service their foreign debts, often contracted at very unfavorable terms, the great powers promptly stepped in to sequester their tax revenues; often, this led to direct control over their finances. Since the markets and resources in the quasi-colonies—unlike the colonies—were not monopolized by a single advanced country, this limited the ability of foreigners to extract rents from these countries.

The 'dependencies' rank above the quasi-colonies. They did not labor under treaties that explicitly constrained their freedom to act in their own interest. Instead, their sovereignty was compromised by the presence of large foreign corporations, often acting in collusion with local landed oligarchies. In times of crisis, whenever indigenous interests organized to challenge this alliance, the foreign corporations were quick to call upon their governments to redress the balance in their favor. Not surprisingly, the dependencies were continually shadowed by foreign gunboats: they suffered numerous invasions, leading to loss of control over their revenues, and even temporary foreign occupation.

Occupying the top rung in our taxonomy, sovereign countries are defined by exclusion. They have indigenous governments whose power to formulate policies is *not* constrained by 'open-door' treaties or the power of foreign corporations. Sovereign countries may be distinguished from dependencies on the basis of three indicators: the share of foreign enterprises in key sectors of the economy, the frequency of foreign military interventions, and the protectionist content of their economic policies. In addition, where ambiguity persists, we may examine the process of policy making for the presence of strong foreign influences.

A Map of Sovereignty: 1800 to 1960

We analyze the record of sovereignty by regions. A country-by-country examination would take up too much space; it is also unnecessary since regional patterns dominate the experience of sovereignty. The lagging countries are aggregated into seven regions: including Tropical Africa, Middle East and North Africa, South Asia, East and Southeast Asia, Latin America, Europe, and British settler 'colonies'.

Tropical Africa. The colonization of tropical Africa began in the 1880s, more than four centuries after the Portuguese first landed there. This delay was caused by the vulnerability of the European interlopers to Africa's pathogens; a reversal of the situation in the Americas. Since the Europeans could not make the Africans work for them *in* Africa, they transported them *out* of Africa, as slaves, for use on the farms, plantations and mines in the Americas. Moreover, since the Europeans could not yet venture into Africa's interior, they encouraged Africans to take over the capture of slaves by exchanging guns for their slaves. A happy exchange indeed, since the guns helped to make the slaves cheaper.

The first challenge to this regime came in 1807 when the British outlawed the slave trade. Anxious to replace lost opportunities, British capital now encouraged Africans to develop alternative exports. But the development of new exports gathered momentum only in the 1860s, after the ban on slavery in United States; this closed off the largest market for slaves. At about this time, demand for raw materials that could be produced in Africa also began to grow rapidly. More ominously, the Europeans were learning to survive in Africa's interior, with the help of new prophylactics and rapid-firing guns. A great throng of European prospectors now began to gather on Africa's shores; the long delay in colonization had helped to swell their numbers. The scramble for Africa began in the 1880s and by 1900 all of tropical Africa, barring Liberia and Ethiopia, had been colonized.[7]

Africa's decolonization occurred in a greater hurry. Sudan was the first African country to gain independence in 1956, followed by Ghana in 1957 and Guinea in 1958. Then the floodgates were opened, with 17 countries gaining independence in 1960 alone, and 13 more gained their independence during the 1960s. Portugal clung hardest to its African colonies, departing from Angola and Mozambique in 1975, only after years of bitter struggle.

North Africa and the Middle East. This region offered tempting targets for European colonization.[8] Most of it lay right across the Mediterranean, an easy distance from Europe; the coastal areas enjoyed a salubrious climate and contained fertile lands; and, not least, a thrust into Islamic lands would carry the satisfaction of humiliating an old and much feared adversary. But this region also presented some difficulties. Most of it was still united under Ottoman rule, an erstwhile great power whose break up, it was feared, might unleash costly rivalries amongst the European powers. The Europeans also feared–correctly, it turned out–that colonization would be met by strong popular resistance. These difficulties both delayed and limited direct colonization of this region.

Since direct colonization did not appear feasible, the advanced countries sought to open up the region to trade and investments. They did not have to start from a scratch. Britain and France already enjoyed, under the 'capitulations', extra-territorial rights over their subjects in the Ottoman empire; starting in the nineteenth century, other Europeans countries acquired similar rights for their citizens. More importantly, the original treaties were revised to expand the privileges granted to the Europeans. In time, the Europeans had obtained exemptions from local taxes, extended these privileges to local protégés, forced the dismantling of all state monopolies, and capped import duties in the Ottoman empire at three percent of the value of imports.

The British and the French had watched with apprehension the modernization of Egypt begun by Muhammad Ali in 1810. Their opportunity to strike came in 1838 when the Ottomans asked for their help in stopping Muhammad Ali's advance upon Istanbul. As a price for their support, the Ottomans signed in 1838 the Anglo-Turkish Commercial Convention which stipulated minimal tariffs, free access to domestic markets, and the dismantling of all private and state monopolies. Then, in 1840, with the support of France, the British mounted a military invasion of the Levant and Egypt. Muhammad Ali capitulated, giving up Syria, the Hejaz and Crete, agreed to reduce his military force to 18,000 men (which at one time numbered nearly a quarter million), and to comply with the terms of the Convention of 1838.[9] Finally, in 1882 just when nationalist forces were poised to assume control of Egypt, the British invaded Egypt and converted her into a *de facto* colony.

Meanwhile, Russia had extracted 'open-door' rights in Iran under two treaties signed in 1813 and 1828. The British demanded and received the same privileges in 1841; other European powers soon followed in their steps.[10] Morocco was next to capitulate, forced to sign an open-door treaty with Britain in 1856, though it resisted colonization till 1912.[11] Tunisia first ceded control over its finances to Britain and France in 1857, and colonization by the French followed in 1881.[12] Libya was returned to direct control of the Ottomans in 1835 and remained an Ottoman province until 1912 when it was occupied by Italy.[13] Finally, after their defeat in the first great war, the Ottoman empire itself was dismembered. Under the mandate of the League of Nations, Britain acquired Palestine, Transjordan and Iraq, while Syria (including Lebanon) passed under French control. Ironically, upon becoming mandates, these territories were freed from the burden of 'capitulations'.

Sovereignty returned to this region in stages, starting in the 1930s. Although Turkey raised its tariffs in small increments in 1907, 1915 and 1916, it had not acquired full tariff autonomy until 1929. Iran acquired tariff autonomy in the same year, and Egypt in 1930. The 'capitulations' were terminated in Turkey in 1923, in Iran in 1928, and in Egypt in 1937.[14] Although Egypt gained nominal independence in 1922, it was not until 1954 that the British agreed to end their military occupation over the next two years.[15] Iraq gained independence in 1932, although the British retained a strong influence over foreign affairs and military policy. The French ended their occupation of Syria and Lebanon in 1946.[16] Independence for the remaining colonies and mandates in the region came at various dates after the end of the second great war.

Latin America and the Caribbean. After breaking away from Spain and Portugal in the 1820s, this region preserved its independence through the second wave of colonization that swept the world in the nineteenth century. With one exception, none of the countries in this region was subjected to 'open-door' treaties by any of the great powers.[17]

Does this mean that these countries were sovereign through most of industrial epoch *I*? Gallagher and Robinson (1953) have argued that although Latin American countries escaped *re*-colonization, their economic policies came under the 'informal' control of Britain and later United States. This informal control was exercised by British and American corporations, sometimes acting on their own, but more often with support of their governments. They also maintain that 'the difference between formal and informal empire has not been one of fundamental nature but of degree'.[18] Essentially, this is the view that was later espoused by the Latin American writers of the dependency school.

We do not find any evidence of sustained foreign intervention in the economic policies of the South American countries. In his study of the Argentine economy, Ferns (1960:488) concluded that 'the British government has never had the power to oblige Argentina to pay a debt, pay a dividend, or to export or import any commodity whatever'. A study of the Peruvian economy between 1820 and 1870 led Mathew (1968) to the same conclusion. On the basis of extensive studies, Platt (1968, 1972a, 1972b, 1977) concludes that the British were unwilling to intervene militarily or diplomatically in support of their business interests in Latin America. Although the British landed their forces in Latin American on at least 40 occasions between 1820 and 1914, he argues that 'these coercions were designed to secure redress for damages that had already taken place, or to secure the security and fair treatment of existing trade. They were not intended to force British trade down Latin American throats, to promote the interests of British finance, or even to bring about any change in the form of government more favorable to British entrepreneurs.'[19] As to whether foreign businesses could act on their own to manipulate economic policies in Latin America, he thinks that this power was circumscribed in most cases by market forces.[20]

The claims of informal empire are even harder to sustain when we examine the content of economic policies in South America. A review of trade policies in the next section shows that most countries in this region began to impose punishing tariffs on imported manufactures soon after gaining independence. They also retained the right to tax foreigners and to set the conditions under which foreign investments entered the country. 'In the last decades of the nineteenth century,' according to Platt (1972a: 301), 'it became standard practice in most of the major state contracts to include a 'Calvo Clause', by which foreign contractors renounced any recourse to diplomatic intervention and agreed to abide by the decisions of the municipal law courts.' The presence of sovereignty is also demonstrated by the frequency with which these countries repudiated their foreign debts, without facing any sanctions. On the contrary, when the quasi-colonies in the Middle East failed to service their debts, their revenues were sequestered by the lending countries.

Central America and the Caribbean are more vulnerable to the charge of an informal empire. American hegemony over this region was conceded by Britain as early as the 1860s. This was clinched in 1904 when President Roosevelt declared that United States alone would police the region, maintain order and enforce their loan contracts with other nations.[21] It is clear that United States took these duties seriously. According to a Report of the House Committee on Foreign Affairs of the Congress, the United States intervened militarily in Central America, Cuba, Haiti and the Dominican Republic 34 times between 1885 and 1933.[22] The result, in the words of Schoonover (1991: 172), was that the Central American countries 'surrendered to metropole interests control of the major elements of their internal communications, public utilities, national debt, currency, state revenue, and other economic activities that produced the national wealth'. In time, this growing dependency is also reflected in the monopolization of this region's trade by United States. The data for

1948 show that United States enjoyed a virtual monopoly over the exports of this region.[23]

South Asia. The British colonization of this region began in 1757 and was substantially complete by the end of this century; the last major indigenous state–that of the Sikhs–was absorbed into the British empire in 1843. India's princely 'states' constituted a system of indirect rule within the British empire in India.[24] In the meanwhile, the British ousted the Dutch from Sri Lanka in 1796 and completed the annexation of the still independent central kingdom of Kandy in 1815. Only Nepal and Afghanistan managed to retain a large measure of autonomy over their internal affairs.[25]

The colonial presence in India ended in 1947, when it was also partitioned to create the new state of Pakistan consisting of two territorial units separated by India. In 1971, the eastern wing of Pakistan seceded, forming the independent state of Bangladesh. Sri Lanka gained its independence in 1948. Both India and Sri Lanka had acquired a measure of self-government before their independence, the former in 1935 and the latter in 1931.

Southeast and East Asia. Apart from Java and northern Philippines, which were colonized earlier on, the erosion of sovereignty in this region began in the early decades of the nineteenth century and was nearly complete by the end of the century. Only Japan recovered quickly from this erosion and then went on to acquire colonies of her own in Taiwan and Korea.

Colonization encountered its first major success in Myanmar. The Anglo-Myanmar war of 1824-26 led to the loss of Arakan and Tenasserim; a second war in 1852 led to the loss of lower Myanmar; the rest of Myanmar, now landlocked, was acquired by the British in 1886. The French entered the contest in 1862 when they began the colonization of Vietnam, and by 1908 all of present-day Vietnam, Cambodia and Laos had been brought under French rule. The sultanates of the Malay peninsula and Sarawak were brought under a complex system of direct and indirect British rule between 1874 and 1914. The Dutch began to extend their control beyond Java in the first decades of the nineteenth century, but this process would not be completed till the end of the nineteenth century. Similarly, the Spaniards extended their control to the southern islands of Philippines in the second half of the nineteenth century, but lost it all to United States in 1898.[26]Colonial rule in this region was terminated within a decade after the end of the second great war.

China's defeat in the first Opium War made the first dent in her isolationist policy. The treaty of Nanking, signed in 1842, forced China to open four ports to British trade, limit her tariffs, and confer extraterritorial rights on the British. Similar privileges were extended to United States and France in 1844. The treaty of Tientsin signed in 1858 opened the doors to China wider: Britain, United States, France and Russia gained access to eleven more ports; their ships could now sail down the Yangtze; tariffs were fixed at 5 percent; and trade in opium was legalized.[27] The penetration was deepened by the Mackay treaty of 1902 which opened up still more ports and abolished several internal taxes on trade.[28] China did not regain tariff autonomy until 1929 but this was followed by colonial incursions from Japan. Sovereignty came when the Chinese communists gained victory over the Nationalists in 1948.

Having read the writing on the wall, Thailand, on its own initiative, signed an 'open-door' treaty with Britain in 1855. This treaty fixed the import tariff at 3 percent, took away the state's right to engage in trade or own monopolies, conferred extraterritoriality on foreigners, but retained the right to impose internal transit duties. In a bid to balance British influence, Thailand extended these treaty privileges to eleven more Western powers. These diplomatic maneuvers succeeded because they coincided with the self-interest of Britain and France, who found an independent Thailand useful as a buffer between their territorial acquisitions in Southeast Asia. Under a revision of the treaties in 1926, Thailand was allowed to raise her tariffs while agreeing to remove all inland transit duties.[29]

Japan's isolationist policy was breached when Commodore Perry's infamous black ships steamed into Yedo Bay in 1854. In the treaties that followed, the Japanese agreed to open several ports to foreign trade, to grant extra-territoriality to foreign traders and, after revisions of 1866, accepted a tariff of 5 percent on all exports and imports. Two years later, in 1868, Japan began a process of forced modernization which misleadingly has been described as the Meiji Restoration, but was nothing short of revolutionary. Japan quickly modernized its military, and in 1895 inflicted a stinging defeat on the Russian navy. Japan's commercial treaties were revised in 1899, permitting her to raise tariffs from 5 to 15 percent. Eventually, in 1915, Japan acquired full tariff autonomy.[30]

Europe. Europe's lagging countries were not subjected to colonization during the nineteenth century. On the contrary, nearly all the European territories in the Ottoman empire gained their independence before the end of the century. Albania, the last of these possessions broke away from Ottoman control in 1907. Admittedly, there were peoples in European countries who felt excluded from their own governance, but nearly always they shared nearly equal rights with other citizens. Thus, although Ireland is sometimes described as a colony of Britain, this is a misnomer. The Irish enjoyed full representation in the British parliament since at least 1829.

British Colonial Settler States. The British colonies of white settlement, including Canada, Australia, New Zealand and South Africa, had acquired internal self-governance, including the right to be governed by elected representatives, long before they acquired complete sovereignty over their external political relations. Most importantly, their elected parliaments were empowered to formulate land, labor, trade and fiscal policies, without interference from Britain. Canada had acquired self-government in 1848, Australia in 1850, New Zealand in 1856 and South Africa in 1853. Some other British colonies with large numbers of white settlers, such as Rhodesia, also enjoyed considerable internal self-government.[31]

Explaining the Map of Sovereignty

It is now time to explain the map of sovereignty during industrial epoch *I*. Why were some countries colonized, while others retained varying levels of sovereignty? Did only the most backward countries lose their sovereignty, so that their colonial status was merely a proxy–and not a cause–of their poor growth record?

The claim that only the most backward countries were colonized is quickly rejected if backwardness is construed in economic terms. We know from the evidence presented in chapter two that once outliers are excluded, differences in per capita income across countries around 1800 were quite small. In fact, according to some estimates, the Asian countries were ahead of countries in Latin America and Southern and Eastern Europe. Comparisons based on several alternative indicators of development–including output structure, labor productivity, urbanization and anthropometric readings–yield similar conclusions. Yet, Latin America and Europe retained their sovereignty, while Asia and Africa were colonized or reduced to quasi-colonies.

There is another problem in equating backwardness with colonization. It is not clear why backwardness *per se* should attract colonization. An advanced country which sought the highest returns on its colonial 'investments' would prefer to colonize countries that were rich in resources and had large markets; this would make the most backward countries undesirable as colonies. Admittedly, there were other motives at work. Colonization could be aimed at potential economic rivals. Once again, it is not the most backward countries which would be targeted for preemptive colonization. In some cases, colonies were acquired for their strategic value, but any connection between a country's strategic value and backwardness would have to be accidental.

The skeptics will argue that what mattered for sovereignty was a country's *potential* for development, not its actual state of development. Conditions which favored the prospects of development in a country also favored the preservation of its sovereignty. What were these conditions? At various times, these have been equated with rational political institutions, security of property rights, religious values emphasizing material success, temperate climate, and racial characteristics which supported physical energy and intellectual vigor.

On a superficial review of the evidence, these arguments might appear plausible. Consider a color-coded global map of sovereignty in 1900, with colonies, quasi-colonies, dependencies and sovereign countries painted red, pink, off-white and white, respectively. On such a map, nearly all of Africa is painted red, with two patches colored pink or off-white.[32] Asia, with the exception of Japan, is painted red or pink; Japan would soon make the transition from pink to white. On the other hand, North and South America are painted white or off-white, and all of Europe, Australia and New Zealand are painted white. The contrast between Europe and its overseas offshoots, on the one hand, and the rest of the world, is clear. It is tempting to mistake these correlations for causation, and attribute the sovereignty of Western nations to their superior climate, civilization or race. But this claim will not stick unless we can identify causal mechanisms which translated the civilizational, cultural or racial 'superiority' of some countries into greater sovereignty.

The most celebrated account of such a causal mechanism may be found in Gallagher and Robinson (1953). They argued that 'British policy in the late, as in the mid-Victorian period, preferred informal means of extending imperial supremacy rather than direct rule.'[33] Colonies were established only when the informal structures of control established over a country were unable to 'provide a framework of security for British enterprise'. Why is it that such informal structures failed only in Africa and Asia? Gallagher and Robinson (1953: 13) provide a simple answer: they were lacking in governance. 'In satellite regions peopled by European stock, in Latin America or Canada, for instance, strong government structures grew up; in totally non-European areas, on the other hand, expansion unleashed such disruptive forces upon the indigenous structures that they tended to wear out and even collapse with use.'

This thesis is fleshed out by Robinson (1972), who argues that there were strong 'institutional barriers' to the integration of Africa and Asia into the world economy. Informal control worked only when there existed an indigenous class of 'exporters-importers' and institutions which permitted them to play a mediating role between the global and the domestic economy. In the white colonies 'the international economy worked through neo-European attitudes and institutions which enables their export-import sectors to convert British economic power into colonial political collaboration with empire.'[34] In Africa and Asia, where markets were less developed–their economies were not differentiated from their socio-political institutions–there did not exist a sufficiently strong class of traders to perform this mediating role. As a result, this collaborative role was forced upon 'non-commercial, ruling oligarchies and land-holding elites', who were inept, borrowed heavily, went bankrupt, thus inviting greater foreign interventions: all of which provoked 'xenophobic, neotraditional uprisings'. It was at this point that the Europeans stepped in to recreate the terms of an effective collaboration between the international and domestic economy.

This theory does not square with the facts. With the exception of Chile, instability was endemic in Latin America during the nineteenth century; most Latin American countries took decades to reestablish stable and unified governments after the overthrow of Spanish colonial rule, and even later, rebellions and military coups remained rife.[35] Landes (1997: 313) writes that independence in Latin America came as a 'surprise to [its] inchoate entities that had no aim but to change their masters' so that its history in the nineteenth century was 'a penny-dreadful of conspiracies, cabals, coups and countercoups–with all that these entailed in insecurity, bad government, corruption, and economic retardation'. Yet, not one of these countries was re-colonized. Equally important, the 'collaborating classes' in Latin America were not playing by the rules of the game. They frequently defaulted on international debts, set very high tariffs on imported manufactures, imposed restrictions on the entry of foreign investments, and organized state monopolies to raise export prices. These aberrations sometimes provoked responses from the great powers; but their imperialist actions had limited aims and never led to colonization. The lagging countries in Europe acted with greater pluck, doing whatever was needed to industrialize their economies. Yet this never threatened their sovereignty.

There is a second problem with Robinson's (1972) thesis. If colonization occurred because of a breakdown in the structures of informal control, and its objective was to recreate these structures–to 'reconstruct and uphold a collaborative system that was breaking down'–we might expect that once colonial rule had succeeded in these objectives, it would, having outlived its utility, abolish itself.[36] But this never happened. In many cases, colonial rule persisted for centuries; and it was abolished only when it was faced with worse alternatives. This casts serious doubt not only on the thesis that colonization was called forth by a breakdown in systems of collaboration in lagging countries. It calls into question the claim that advanced countries 'preferred' informal control to colonialism. The argument that countries in Latin America and Europe had greater ability to deter conquests, will not stand up to scrutiny either. The combined population of Latin America in 1820 was less than Britain's, and at the time only four countries in this region had a population exceeding one million.[37] It strains credulity to suppose that these countries returned their independence because they could oppose a determined invasion by the great powers. The British mounted armed assaults on these countries with impunity–at least forty between 1820 and 1914–several ending in the occupation of their port cities and customs houses. Central America and the Caribbean were even more vulnerable, and endured thirty-four military interventions between 1885 and 1933 from United States alone.[38]

On the other hand, the colonization of Asia and Africa was not always a cakewalk. The French took several decades, deployed large forces–at one time exceeding one hundred thousand troops–and tens of thousands dead, to conquer and pacify Algeria. They suffered a stinging defeat in 1870, three decades after first landing their troops in Algeria.[39] In India, the British enjoyed a crushing superiority in their early military encounters with native forces, often defeating forces ten times larger than their own; but this superiority diminished rapidly with time, and in the last wars–waged during the 1840s and 1850s–the opposing forces were equally matched in strength.[40] In the last decades of the nineteenth century, with an overwhelming superiority in military hardware, the Europeans took twenty-five years to occupy West Africa. In some of their later engagements in Africa, the French were forced to field troops comparable in strength to that of their adversaries.[41] Even as late as 1896, the Ethiopians almost completely mowed down a large force of invading Italians.

We still need to explain why virtually all of Africa and Asia were painted red or pink, whereas Europe and its overseas extensions were painted white or off-white. The argument that Western nations escaped colonization because of some superiority over Asian societies, will not hold water; at least, during the early decades of the nineteenth century, this superiority was mostly chimerical. Instead, we must search for some systemic biases in the global system which targeted some countries for colonization and spared others. In fact, such biases did exist, and they were rooted in a growing sense of superiority and exclusiveness that pervaded Europe during industrial epoch *I*, a superiority of race and religion, which reinforced Western unity when confronted with non-European societies. Race and religion united all Western peoples into a club, a 'family of nations', that separated and distanced them from all other societies that were defined as outsiders, adversaries and, in time, as backward races and civilizations. This is what restrained and reoriented the imperialist ambitions of the great Western powers. The complex ties that bound the great powers to this Western 'family of nations' restrained their imperialist ambitions against its weaker members; but their racism, religious bigotry and civilizational arrogance also sanctioned wars of subjection against all 'inferior' civilizations, because they possessed nothing that was worth preserving.

What we are saying is that European understanding of sovereignty, of what qualified a nation to claim sovereignty, was integrally linked to categories of race and civilization. The emergence of Europe as an autonomous cultural domain was deeply conditioned by the challenge of Islam. The dramatic rise of Arabs during the seventh century drove the Byzantines out of the Levant and Africa, established a threatening Arab presence in Spain, and converted the Mediterranean into an Arabian sea. Thus pushed back and confined to the European land mass, Christendom was forced to turn inward, economically and culturally, in order to forge the unity, the ideas and the emotions with which to hold back the Islamic challenge that would not go away for a thousand years. The Christian Europe that emerged from these conflicts harbored a deep antagonism towards Islam. This was a civilization born out of adversity, confined spatially like no other great civilization, and, therefore, animated by a deep urge to overcome and destroy its tormentors. Not surprisingly, this created an aggressive energy that was combined with a strong sense of exclusiveness.

This exclusiveness was deepened when the Europeans eventually broke through the Islamic *cordon sanitaire* in the fifteenth century to encounter other non-Western societies. These explorations led to the creation of export economies in the Americas based at first on the use of Indian labor and, when their ranks had been depleted by abuse and disease, they were replaced by black slaves from Africa. Similarly, in the Indian Ocean, the Portuguese and, later, the Dutch, French and British deployed their superior maritime power to monopolize a domain of trade that had hitherto been open to all nations. Slowly, these demonstrations of power bred a contempt for *all* non-European peoples and cultures. A color consciousness now entered into the distinction between Europe and the 'Others'. Europe was now both Christian and white, and the 'Others' were non-Christian and non-white. Soon the 'Others' were construed as less than human–as sinners, uncivilized, savages, children, brutes and animals. These denigrations had a powerful instrumental value. They were employed to justify the colonial enterprises in Asia and Africa as a necessary, if painful, prelude to civilizing the 'lesser breeds'.

The political correlates of this European exclusiveness have seldom been addressed by the social sciences. It restricted membership in the 'family of nations' to Europeans and their overseas cousins; all others were pariahs, not fit to associate with the twice-born nations. In a rare essay, Strang (1966) has developed the implications of this disjuncture; he maintains that this created two political universes, one European and another non-European. This segregation proved fateful. It ensured 'that non-Western polities could not call on Western actors or opinion for support. They were not members of the Western community of recognition, supported by generalized third parties on the basis of common ethnic and religious identities, shared conceptions of collective purposes, or the needs of an 'automatic' balance of power. Colonialism in Asia and Africa did not ramify back into Western national or international society to challenge the aims and nature of the imperialist.' On the other hand, the re-colonization of the former white colonies in the Americas was not acceptable because they 'shared in the moral, religious, and racial world of the Great Powers. (...) Policy in the Americas did reflect back into the social, cultural, and political worlds of Europe.' [42] The same logic applied *a fortiori* to the lagging countries of Europe. Not only were they exempt from colonization, but the European powers were under moral pressure to help Eastern Europe break away from the moribund Ottoman empire.

We need to dispose of another argument which credits sovereignty in some lagging countries to the rivalries amongst the great powers. It has been argued that the Latin Americans were saved by the resolve of United States, first proclaimed in the Monroe doctrine of 1820, to keep the European powers out of the Western hemisphere. This resolve, however, would not have any teeth for several more decades. The British, French and Germans launched numerous armed forays into Latin America throughout the nineteenth century, often leading to the capture of their port cities and customs houses, without military interference from United States. [43] Rival imperialist ambitions may have been a more serious deterrent to colonization in Europe itself. Not only did the rivals live in the same neighborhood, they were more equally matched, raising fears that colonial adventures so close to home might get out of hand. These balancing acts, however, did not apply to North Africa, demonstrating that other powerful forces were at work. Besides, the European powers could have acted jointly, or with tacit support from their rivals, as they so often did elsewhere, to force 'open-door' policies upon Eastern and Southern Europe. But this never happened: no European country was subjected to open-door treaties.

Sovereignty Differentials in Tariff Policies

Our theory of the global economy predicts that sovereign countries will use their control over economic policies to *structure* their economic relations with the advanced countries. Most importantly, this would involve the use of tariffs to promote industrialization.

A comparison of trade policies during industrial epoch *I* shows that tariffs varied systematically with sovereignty. A policy of free or nearly-free trade remained the norm in the colonies: to use Bairoch's (1993: 41) striking phrase, they were an 'ocean of liberalism'. When colonial rulers were forced by their fiscal needs to impose even modest tariffs, they were often fully offset by countervailing excise taxes on domestic production. Harnetty (1965) has documented how the Manchester textile lobby moved into action in 1859 when British India proposed modest increases in tariffs from three-and-a-half percent to five percent on yarn, and five to ten percent on cotton piece goods. Their opposition was decisive, leading to a retraction of the proposed increases a year later, and by 1882, all duties on textiles had been abolished. When a duty of five percent was imposed again in 1895, it was accompanied by an equivalent excise duty on all Indian textiles.[44] In Egypt, Lord Cromer believed that growth of a protected cotton industry in Egypt 'would be detrimental to both English and Egyptian interests', and he followed through by imposing an excise tax of eight percent on local textiles to offset an import duty of eight percent.[45] Indian textiles were granted modest protection in the 1920s, only because of growing competition from Japanese imports.

The situation in the quasi-colonies was only slightly better. The Ottoman Empire began the nineteenth century with a three percent limit on their import tariffs; this was raised to eight percent in 1861, and raised again to 11 percent in 1907 in order to pay off foreign debts. Upon entering the war, Turkey doubled its import duty to 22 percent, and in 1916 replaced this with differentiated tariffs ranging from eight percent for foodstuffs to 16 percent for wholly manufactured goods.[46] By the 1860s, Morocco, Tunisia, Algeria, Yemen, Thailand, Saudi Arabia, Japan and China had also been tied down by 'open-door' treaties which generally limited their import tariffs to five percent or less. Japan regained tariff autonomy in 1915; others had to wait till the late 1920s. Nearly everywhere, this was followed by an active use of tariffs in support of industrialization.

The dependencies of Central America and the Caribbean first implemented deliberately protectionist tariffs towards the end of the 1950s. This delay should not be attributed to external pressures alone. The small domestic markets in these countries made import substitution very costly: a difficulty that was compounded by opposition from their powerful landowning elites.[47] However, this did not prevent them from using tariffs for revenue purposes. The ratio of tariff-revenues to imports in Nicaragua was 34 percent in 1928 and rose to 50 percent in 1933.[48] The dependencies were also more independent in their responses to the depression of the 1930s. Instead of depreciating their currencies, most dependencies resorted to some form of exchange control; Costa Rica and El Salvador were the exceptions.[49] A system of differentiated tariffs that would support import-substituting industrialization was introduced in most of these countries in the 1950s.[50]

Tariffs were the main source of revenues in nearly all the sovereign countries; and eventually, all of them structured their tariffs to offer protection to existing and new industries. The larger Latin American countries introduced protectionist tariffs soon after they gained independence. One of the first acts of the Peruvian government, upon attaining independence in 1821, was to impose a duty of 20 percent on all imported goods; domestic manufactures threatened by imports were protected at twice this rate. By 1926, these rates had gone up to 30 percent for non-competing imports, while imports which competed with domestic manufactures faced duties of 90 to 100 percent. Mexico started out with low duties in 1821 but by 1827 she had placed 54 of her imports on a prohibited list; cotton goods that were not on this list paid very high duties. Argentina introduced protectionist tariffs in 1822 and raised the rates again in 1835; in turns these tariffs were reinforced by internal duties which discriminated against imports. In 1822, Chile also set tariffs with a protective intent, and many of these rates were clearly prohibitive. Similarly, in 1844 Brazil had tariffs of 30 percent on most manufactures including cotton; over the next few years, duties on machinery and raw materials were lifted, thus raising the protectionist impact of existing tariffs on consumer goods. It would be hard to reconcile any of this with commitment to liberal trade policies.[51]

During the third quarter of the nineteenth century, several countries, including Brazil, Mexico, Chile and Colombia, revised their tariffs downwards. This was not due to any external pressures or, conversely, weakness in internal protectionist demands. In part, the revisions became necessary because domestic handicrafts were unable to meet the growing demand for manufactures. More importantly, the growing volume of trade made it possible to cut the duties without affecting the total revenues earned from tariffs. Despite this trend towards liberalization, tariffs remained the most important source of revenue in nearly all of South America, and some key industries continued to receive protectionist treatment. In 1859, the average tariffs on textiles was 50 percent in Brazil, and in Colombia it was still higher at 88 percent.[52]

Protectionism in South America increased during the last decades of the nineteenth century. There was a growing demand for tariffs to counter declining import prices during this period, resulting from lower costs of oceanic transportation. Some countries met these demands by leaving the earlier specific duties unchanged, and since these were based on inflated values, the declining import prices raised the implicit *ad valorem* tariff rates. Several countries left the average tariffs unchanged but varied individual rates, giving higher effective protection to domestic industries. As a result of these measures, by 1913 the ratio of tariff revenues to total imports in Brazil, Uruguay and Venezuela were higher than in Australia, Canada and United States.[53]

At the opening of the nineteenth century, most European countries still carried the legacy of mercantilist policies, which included high tariffs, import prohibitions and navigation laws which discriminated against the use of foreign shipping in the country's carrying trade. As late as 1820, prohibitions on imports of manufactures were common in the Austro-Hungarian empire, France, Russia, Spain and Sweden (which then also included Norway). With the exception of France, these countries also imposed duties on internal movements of goods. Import prohibitions were rare in Britain, but its manufactures were still protected by an average tariff rate of 50 percent. Switzerland, the Netherlands and Portugal had relatively liberal trade regimes, with tariff rates on manufactured imports of ten, seven and 15 percent respectively. Manufactures in Denmark were protected by 30 percent tariffs. Amongst larger countries, Prussia alone had a liberal trade regime with no prohibitions and average tariffs on manufactures of ten percent.[54]

Protectionist barriers in the larger European countries rose after the Napoleonic wars to counter the rise of British manufactures.[55] In 1841 France still relied on prohibitions to exclude most manufactured imports; all other imports paid duties ranging from 40 to 60 percent.[56] The tariff law of 1838 in the Austro-Hungarian empire 'imposed *ad valorem* duties of 60 percent on most cotton, wool, iron and earthenware manufactured goods, and very high specific duties on everything else, not to mention many remaining prohibitions'. These policies remained in force till 1851. Russia's attempt to introduce liberal tariffs in 1819 met with fierce opposition and was followed in 1822 by a strongly protectionist regime which included high tariffs and 'prohibitions affecting nearly all locally produced manufactures'. Similarly, in 1825 Spain prohibited the import of about 650 mostly manufactured goods and imposed very high tariffs on all others. The list of prohibitions was reduced to 93 in 1841, but the remaining prohibitions covered most consumer manufactures, and all other imports paid duties ranging from 15 to 50 percent *ad valorem*. Not all the smaller countries in Europe moved towards liberal trade policies. Upon seceding from the Netherlands, Belgium opted for a protectionist regime that included prohibitions on imports and very high tariffs on nearly all manufactured goods. Trade policies in Sweden and Norway also remained heavily protectionist during this period.[57]

The Anglo-French trade treaty of 1860 inaugurated a period of trade liberalization that embraced virtually all of Europe over the next two decades. This liberalization made deeper inroads in the smaller countries; Germany and Britain were the only large countries that were on the list of the most liberal countries in 1875. However, even at the height of this trade liberalization, the manufacturing sector in several countries continued to receive a substantial degree of protection. In 1875, the average tariff on manufactures was 15-20 percent in the Austro-Hungarian empire, Russia, Spain, Portugal and Denmark, 12-15 percent in France, 8-10 percent in Italy and 9-10 percent in Belgium. It should be emphasized that these rates are averages across *all* manufactured imports; most likely, they concealed higher levels of protection for specific industries.[58]

This liberalization interlude did not last very long. Britain excepted, the protectionist tendencies were revived in 1879 and continued to gain momentum during the succeeding decades. According to calculations based on a standard list of commodities for all countries, the average import tariffs for manufactures in 1913 were 84 percent in Russia, 34 percent in Spain, 28 percent in Romania, 28 percent in Finland, 25 percent in Sweden, 22 percent in Bulgaria, and 20 percent in the Austro-Hungarian empire, Serbia and Italy. Whether one looks at these indices, or some others (such as the ratio of import duties to value of imports, or tariffs on the import of British manufactures) they point to the presence of strong protectionist policies in nearly all the countries of Europe.[59]

United States moved slowly towards protectionism. The turning point came after the war of 1812 when growing revenue demands led to a doubling in tariffs. Once in place, there was no turning back from these high tariffs, apart from a reversal during the 1840s and 1850s, until the end of the second great war. The ratio of duties to dutiable imports was 54.4 percent in 1829-31, reached a low of 20.6 percent in 1857-61, went up to 46.7 percent in 1867-71, reached a high of 55.3 percent in 1931-33, and was 28.3 percent in 1944-46. When the costs of freight from Europe are also added, United States must be counted amongst the most protectionist countries in the world during this period.[60]

Although their domestic markets were quite small, the former British colonies of settlement lost little time in introducing protectionist tariffs once they had attained self-government. Victoria introduced its first protectionist tariffs in 1867. The first Australian tariffs of 1902 were somewhat less protectionist, with import duties varying between 5 and 25 percent. On a rough calculation, their import tariffs on manufactures were 16 percent, not much lower than the average tariffs of 19 percent for continental Europe. Canada introduced its first protectionist tariffs in 1879, with *ad valorem* duties on manufactures ranging between 20 and 30 percent. In 1887, these tariffs varied between 25 and 35 percent, and in 1914 they stood at 26 percent. New Zealand introduced its first protectionist tariffs in 1888, and in 1914 the average tariffs on manufactures ranged between 15 and 20 percent, comparable to the average for continental Europe.[61]

Sovereignty Differentials in Other Policy Areas

Import tariffs formed only a part, albeit a central part, of the arsenal of policies employed by lagging countries to promote industrialization. In the interests of economy, only some general remarks are offered on the relationship of these industrial policies to sovereignty.

Gerschenkron's (1962) thesis on late industrialization in Europe is pertinent here, since he maintained that government interventions in support of late industrialization increased with economic backwardness. In backward Russia, government interventions were more pervasive than in France or Germany. The Russian government protected domestic manufactures, set up banks to offer loans to manufactures, and used official procurements to create markets for them. When none of this worked, it assumed entrepreneurial functions, setting up industries in the public sector.[62] The French and German policy was generally limited to offering protection against imports.

Sovereign lagging countries outside Europe followed the same pattern: they employed a variety of instruments to support their industrialization, starting as early as the first decades of the nineteenth century. The Mexican government started promoting industries shortly after its independence in 1821. They set up an industrial bank in 1830 to provide subsidized loans and machinery on credit to private entrepreneurs. During its twelve-year life span, the bank made a pivotal contribution to the development of Mexico's modern textile industry.[63] We encounter the most systematic early effort at state-led industrialization in Egypt between 1810 to 1838. By the end of this period, state monopolies had made investments worth $12 million in a broad range of industries including foundries, textiles, paper, chemicals, shipyards, glassware and arsenals. At their height, these industries employed some 30,000 workers. However, nearly all these industries failed when Egypt was forced, following her defeat in 1840, to abolish all state trading monopolies and drastically curtail its military establishment, thereby cutting off these nascent industries from state subsidies as well as their largest markets.[64]

Nearly all the former colonies and quasi-colonies adopted vigorous policies of industrialization upon gaining sovereignty. When they regained some measure of policy autonomy during the 1920s and early 1930s, Turkey, Iran, Egypt and Iraq introduced a variety of measures to support industrialization and economic development. They imposed differentiated tariffs and quantitative restrictions on imports; offered credit, tax relief, and reduced railway rates to domestic manufactures; domestic manufactures were given exclusive access to government procurements; manufactures were established (in Iran and Turkey) in the public sector; growing public investments were made in infrastructure, education and training. Because of their greater sovereignty, Turkey and Iran pursued these policies more vigorously than Egypt or Iraq.[65] A similar switch in industrial policies would be observed in nearly all the colonies when they gained their independence after the second great war.

On the contrary, not only did colonial governments refuse tariff protection to their industries, they rarely promoted industries by any other means. In the words of Fieldhouse (1981: 68), 'no colonial government had a department of industry before 1945. The state almost never actively encouraged indigenous entrepreneurs to invest in local import-substituting industrial production. The government did not provide medium or long-term loans to help would-be capitalists, though the banking system, owned by banks in the metropolis and geared to the needs of import/export trade, was seldom willing to provide these essential credit facilities to non-Europeans.'

Summary

It is the main thesis of this book that sovereignty–defined as the capacity of a state to articulate the interests of indigenous classes–is an important category in explaining variations in the development experience of lagging countries at least in the two hundred years from 1760 to 1960.

Our taxonomy of sovereignty is based on three criteria: the presence of an indigenous government, imposition of 'open-door' policies, and dominance of foreign capital. This leads to a fourfold taxonomy of sovereignty: in descending order, they include sovereign countries, dependencies, quasi-colonies and colonies. Under this taxonomy, Europe and South America were sovereign in 1900, while Africa and Asia consisted almost wholly of colonies and quasi-colonies.

The strong correlations we observe between sovereignty, on the one hand, and race and civilization are not accidental. In order to contain their conflicts, the European states had evolved into a 'family of nations', an arrangement based on recognition of the sovereign rights of each state: rights which were protected by a complex nexus of international laws and conventions, as well as a delicate balancing of power amongst the constituent states. The European experience had also developed racist doctrines, which excluded all non-Western states from membership in the 'family of nations'. This had fatal consequences. It delegitimized the non-Western states and excluded them from the nexus of protections available to Western nations. This explains why nearly all the Asians and Africans were herded into colonies and quasi-colonies during the nineteenth century; while Europe and the Americas retained greater sovereignty.

Our theory of the global economy predicts a positive correlation between sovereignty and protectionist policies. This was fully supported by a review of trade policies during industrial epoch *I*. Nearly all the sovereign countries were heavily protectionist, while the colonies practiced free trade.

Notes

1 Falk (1993: 854).
2 The state is defined with reference to a territory, a population inhabiting that territory, and a system of governance having authority over that population and territory (James 1986: 1-22). See Waltz (1979: 96), Hinsley (1986: 26) and Philpott (1995: 357) on the two dimensions of sovereignty.
3 Hinsley (1986: 26).
4 External sovereignty is the more ambiguous of the two dimensions of sovereignty. Thus, it may be conferred upon a 'state' that has no effective authority over the territory or population over which it claims jurisdiction. Further, this is not a one-state-one-vote system; votes cast by powerful states may count for a lot more.

5   A class is indigenous to a country when its members have permanent residence there, are born there and expect to die there.

6   Most lagging countries with indigenous governments, even the quasi-colonies–such as Iran, Thailand, China, Turkey–had made some progress towards representative institutions by 1935. The colonies had not yet established any elective institutions at the federal level. Their legislative councils consisted of appointed members, few of them indigenous (Easterlin 1996: 63).

7   Liberia was colonized by freed black slaves from United States, with the military and financial support of United States, which continued to protect her from encroachments by the British and French. As in other colonial settler states, the Americo-Iberians established themselves as a permanent ruling elite, the natives were dispossessed, excluded from government, forced to make illegal payments and perform corvee labor on private farms and public projects (Clower *et al.* 1966: 3-10). Although Ethiopia escaped colonization, she was brought firmly under the influence of Italy, with support from the British and French, an arrangement that was ratified by the Tripartite Agreement of 1906 signed by the three powers. These powers exercised extraterritorial privileges in Ethiopia (Zewde 1991: 85, 111, 150-51).

8   At the beginning of the nineteenth century, this region consisted of Iran, Morocco, the Ottoman empire, and the Ottoman regencies of Tunisia, Algiers, Tripoli and Egypt. The first three regencies enjoyed various degrees of autonomy from Istanbul, while Egypt acquired *de facto* autonomy under Muhammad Ali in 1805.

9   Mansfield (1991:59).

10   Issawi (1982: 19).

11   Laroui (1989: 487).

12   Fieldhouse (1967:182).

13   Laroui (1989: 499).

14   Issawi (1982: 21-22,159).

15   Although Egypt was declared 'an independent sovereign state' in 1922, it remained a British protectorate for the next twenty years, with British officials in command of the army, police and bureaucracy (Mansfield 1991:179).

16   Aroian and Mitchell (1984: 204).

17   The commercial treaties signed by governments in Latin America and Britain sought to guarantee most favored nation treatment for Britain's trade; they did not restrict the height of tariffs. The only exception was the Anglo-Brazilian Commercial Treaty which set an upper limit of 15 percent on British imports into Brazil (Platt 1968: 315).

18   Gallagher and Robinson (1953: 151).

19   Platt (1968: 330).

20   Platt (1972a: 297-300).

21   Platt (1968: 350).

22   Ronning (1970: 29-32).

23 In 1948, the share of United States in the exports of Guatemala, El Salvador, Honduras, Nicaragua and Costa Rica was 90, 76, 70, 74 and 78 percent respectively (LaFeber 1984: 91).

24 Panikkar (1932).

25 On Nepal's independence, see Hussain (1970).

26 Dixon (1991: 57-84).

27 Michael and Taylor (1964: 119-141).

28 Cain and Hopkins (1993: 436)

29 Ingram (1955: 33-35, 134).

30 Sugiyama (1988: 34-36).

31 *The New Encyclopaedia Britannica* (1993).

32 The three exceptions were South Africa (white), Liberia (pink) and Ethiopia (pink).

33 Gallagher and Robinson (1953: 12).

34 Robinson (1972: 129).

35 Strang (1996).

36 Robinson (1972: 139).

37 Maddison (1995: 112).

38 Platt (1968) and Ronning (1970: 29-32).

39 Cherif (1989: 464-67).

40 Ness and Stahl (1977).

41 Crowder (1971: 1, 7).

42 Strang (1966:33-34). Similarly, Philpott (1995) maintains that international relations in Europe were regulated by a 'constitution' consisting of 'norms of sovereignty'. These norms defined who were the legitimate polities, who could become one, what are the prerogatives of these polities. The norms of sovereignty defined by the Treaty of Westphalia limited membership to European and Christian nations (the Ottoman Empire was an exception). In 1885, at the Berlin Conference, the European powers divided the world into civilized (European) states and barbarian peoples who could not enjoy sovereign rights until ' they had learned the art of governing'.

43 When Mexico defaulted on her foreign loans in 1861, the French, with the support of Britain and Spain, invaded Mexico, right under the nose of United States, even setting up a puppet government in Mexico City. This government was soon overthrown, *but only after the French withdrew their troops*.

44 Chaudhuri (1983: 868).

45 Issawi (1982: 158).

46 Issawi (1982: 20-22)

47 The smallness of their markets may be seen from their populations even in 1950: Costa Rica (863,000), Panama (816,000), Nicaragua (1,052,000), Honduras (1,513,000), El Salvador (1,859,000), Dominican Republic (2,136,000) and Guatemala (2,876,000) (Maddison 1995: 218). At this time, less than 1 percent of all farm owners in this region controlled nearly 40 percent of farmland (Barry 1987:8).

48 Bulmer-Thomas (1987: 348).

49 Bulmer-Thomas (1987: 54).
50 Bulmer-Thomas (1987: 168).
51 Platt (1972: 75-79) and Potash (1983: 19, 21, 139).
52 Bulmer-Thomas (1994: 141) and Platt (1972: 78-80).
53 Bulmer-Thomas (1994: 141-42) and Stein (1957: 84).
54 Bairoch (1988b: 6).
55 Britain and some smaller countries (Switzerland, The Netherlands, Portugal and Denmark) moved towards freer trade during this period.
56 Bairoch (1988b: 15).
57 Bairoch (1988b: 17-23).
58 Bairoch (1988h: 42).
59 Bairoch (1988b: 76).
60 Bairoch (1988b: 141).
61 Bairoch (1988b: 139, 145-49).
62 Trebilcock (1981: 205-291).
63 Potash (1983: xi, 46-48, 125).
64 Issawi (1982: 154), Crouchley (1938: 69-71) and Batou (1991: 181-218).
65 Issawi (1982: 14, 22) and Jalal (1972: 6, 88-89 and 104-105).

6

Measuring Sovereignty Differentials

*'The PAST says to the people of England of the PRESENT: 'I have
sinned. I have beggared the people of India. ... I have driven them from
making cloth to raising opium. I have destroyed the power of concentration. I have produced famine and pestilence. I have converted people who
were free into slaves'.*

Henry Carey (1847: 408)

*'A manufacturing country Egypt never can become–or at least for ages; a
country giving perpetual cause of anxiety to the European Powers by the
restlessness of her Rulers, she cannot be allowed to continue–but by the
peaceful development of her agricultural aptitude she may interest and
benefit all'.*

John Bowring[1] (1837)

The stage is now set for exploring the economic consequences of variations in sovereignty across lagging countries during industrial epoch *I*.

Our objective is to measure the differential impact of higher levels of
sovereignty on a country's export orientation, growth rates, levels of
industrialization, and human capital. In order to quantify this differential
impact, or 'sovereignty differential', we estimate reduced-form equations
of the form: $Y = \alpha + \beta U + \delta V + \varepsilon$, where Y is a measure of economic
performance, U is a set of sovereignty dummies, V is a set of economic
and social factors affecting Y, and ε is the random error term. The sovereignty dummies are derived from a five-fold taxonomy of sovereignty:
consisting of sovereign countries, dependencies, quasi-colonies, newly
independent countries, and colonies.[2] This provides us with a basic set of
four sovereignty dummies: sovereign countries (*SOV*), dependencies
(*DEP*), quasi-colonies (*QC*) and newly independent countries (*NIC*), with
colonies (*COL*) as the base category. The sovereignty differentials in Y are
given by the estimated β coefficients of these sovereignty dummy variables. Thus, the *SOV*-coefficient measures the excess of Y in sovereign
countries over Y in the colonies, all other things remaining the same.

The sovereignty differentials are also estimated for several alternative
taxonomies of sovereignty. These alternative taxonomies are derived by
successively merging the intermediate categories (dependencies, quasi-
colonies and *NIC*) in the original five-fold taxonomy into the two polar
categories (sovereign countries and colonies). Thus, the category 'sovereign countries' is expanded successively to include dependencies, quasi-

Table 6.1
Complete Set of Binary Comparisons

Group I	Group II
SOV	COL
	COL-NIC
	COL-NIC-QC
	COL-NIC-QC-DEP
SOV-DEP	COL
	COL-NIC
	COL-NIC-QC
SOV-DEP-QC	COL
	COL, NIC
SOV-DEP-QC-NIC	COL

SOV=sovereign countries; DEP=dependencies; QC=quasi-colonies; NIC=newly independent countries; COL=colonies

colonies and *NIC*; and the category 'colonies' is expanded to include *NIC*, quasi-colonies and dependencies. Altogether, this gives rise to ten different taxonomies of sovereignty. However, instead of presenting results on all the sovereignty differentials for each taxonomy, we report estimates of sovereignty differentials only for comparisons between the polar categories in each of the ten taxonomies. A list of these polar categories is presented in table 6.1.[3] The sovereignty differentials are expected to decline progressively as comparisons between the primary categories are extended to more inclusive categories, since this reduces the sovereignty-gap between the two sets of countries in the comparisons. Thus, the sovereignty differentials are expected to decline when *NIC*, *QCC* and *DEP* are successively merged into *COL*; or alternatively, when *DEP*, *QCC* and *NIC* are merged into *SOV*. A pattern of declining sovereignty differentials in our results will confirm the correctness of our taxonomy of sovereignty.

The sovereignty differentials in the structural variables are estimated for 1960 (1965 in one case), the earliest year for which national accounts data become available for a large and representative sample of lagging countries. A test of our hypotheses at this late date, when colonialism was in full retreat, perhaps sets them up for failure. We have shown earlier that colonial governments, starting with the onset of the second great war, began to show greater accommodation towards indigenous interests, and this may have reduced the sovereignty differentials that we seek to measure.[4] At the same time, the structural parameters of interest to us–export orientation, industrialization levels, and stocks of human capital–could not have responded quickly to policy changes, so that if sovereignty differentials in these parameters were large to begin with, they could not have vanished in 1960. At least, this was our expectation, and it was fully supported by the results. Our estimation exercises yielded large sovereignty differentials in export orientation, industrialization levels, literacy rates, and average years of schooling in the labor force in 1960 (1965 in one case). Similarly, we observed large differentials in growth rates of per capita income between 1900 and 1950. Nearly always, the statistical tests showed that these differentials are robust.

Although we do not find any *a priori* reasons for suspecting that only backward countries were vulnerable to colonization, we chose to address these concerns empirically. First, we introduced a dummy variable in our regressions for countries whose 'superior' initial conditions may have set them apart from others. Similarly, we address concerns about institutional deficiencies in Sub-Saharan countries by (i) introducing a dummy variable for these countries and, alternatively, (ii) estimating the sovereignty differentials by dropping these countries from our sample. Finally, we develop a test to check if the sovereignty differentials are proxies for some missing institutional factors not incorporated in our regressions. This involved estimating sovereignty differentials in the structural parameters for 1960 and 1980 (circa) when large and systematic differences in sovereignty across lagging countries were a thing of the past; this was done for identical sets of countries. A similar exercise was undertaken for the sovereignty differentials in growth rates. The results were conclusive. In every case, the sovereignty differentials in the structural parameters declined significantly with the lapse of time; similarly, the differentials in growth rates between 1950 and 1992 were negative. These results would be difficult to explain if our basic taxonomy of sovereignty was merely a proxy for differences in hidden growth factors across the lagging countries. It is unlikely that the hidden institutional differences across countries suddenly vanished, or weakened, at about the same time as the colonies were dismantled.

Although empirical analyses of the economic impact of colonialism are quite thin, they generally support our results.[5] In an ambitious comparative historical study covering 23 countries from 1850 to 1914, Morris and Adelman (1988) employed factor-analytic techniques to show, amongst other things, that foreign economic dependence had an adverse impact on economic growth. The thesis that advanced countries monopolized the markets of their colonies was tested by Kleiman (1976) who found that in the early 1960s, the shares of Britain, France, Italy, Belgium and Portugal in the export and import trade of their colonies were larger, often much larger, than their shares in the trade of *all* lagging countries.[6]

In a similar study, Svedburg (1981) found that in 1967 the shares of advanced countries in the foreign direct investments of their colonies were higher than in non-colonies. Two studies investigating relative returns to British investments in the colonies and non-colonies produced mixed results. Svedburg's (1982) calculations show that returns on the capital stocks of British companies in the colonies were considerably higher than in other lagging countries between 1938 and 1957, and especially between 1950 and 1957. Similar estimates were made by Davis and Huttenback (1988) in a study using firm-level data from an earlier period. They found that British investments in the colonies yielded higher returns than home investments in the two decades before 1880, but this relationship was reversed in the three succeeding decades.'

Sovereignty Differentials in Export Orientation

Our empirical estimations show that erosion of sovereignty increased export orientation, measured as the ratio of exports to national output: a tendency that varied directly with the age of the colony.

The relationship between sovereignty and export orientation is likely to be complex, especially if we take into account the dynamic effects of sovereignty (or its erosion) on comparative advantage. On the one hand, export orientation is likely to rise with the loss of sovereignty. We have seen earlier in chapter five that since the early nineteenth century most sovereign countries protected their manufactures, while quasi-colonies and colonies maintained virtual free-trade regimes In addition, colonies biased their incentives towards primary production: their infrastructure served exports and imports; the remaining investments went into irrigation and land reclamation; they pushed down wages, redistributed indigenous land to expatriates, forced the commercialization of agriculture, and encouraged the entry of foreign capital into primary production. Many of these measures would take time to mature, creating a positive link between (primary) export orientation and the age of the colonies.

While they biased incentives towards primary production, colonial policies also produced an opposite effect. Most colonial governments used both discriminatory policies and informal pressures to gain monopoly control over the markets and resources of their colonies. Since this was likely to depress export prices in the colonies, we may expect that this would have discouraged primary production for exports. By the same token, these discriminatory policies discouraged investments in the colonies from sources other than the home country, and this too may have reduced primary production for exports.

The relationship between sovereignty and export orientation is complicated also by the cumulative effects of trade between advanced and lagging countries. Our theoretical model in chapter four suggests that once a country acquires comparative advantage in *some* manufactures, this is likely to be extended to other manufactures and in time to primary goods. The obverse of this is that a lagging country specializing in primary production faces a progressive erosion of its comparative advantage so that over time it is forced to concentrate production on a diminishing range of primary goods. Most likely, these cumulative effects increased export orientation in the sovereign countries while reducing it in the quasi-colonies and colonies. However, the positive effects of sovereignty on export orientation, *via* industrialization, are likely to materialize with a considerable lag–only at advanced levels of industrialization.

Given these contrary effects emanating from the erosion of sovereignty, we must turn to empirical analysis to determine the *net* impact of loss of sovereignty on export orientation. We estimated an export function of the form: $RX = \alpha + \beta U + \delta V + \varepsilon$, where RX is the ratio of exports of goods and non-factor services to gross domestic product, U is a vector of dummies relating to sovereignty, V is a vector of other independent variables affecting RX, and ε is a random error term. The V-variables include a country's population density (*DEN*), population divided by surface area as a rough proxy for land endowments; population (*POP*), as a measure of the size of the economy, and square of population; a dummy variable for oil-producing countries (*OIL=1* for major oil-producing countries); a dummy variable for Sub-Saharan Africa (*AFR=1* for all countries in Sub-Saharan Africa); and a dummy variable for Japan and countries in Western Europe (*LEAD=1*).[8] The U-variables include four dummy variables for sovereignty: *SOV=1* for all sovereign countries, *DEP=1* for all dependencies, *QC=1* for all quasi-colonies, *NIC=1* for newly independent countries, with colonies as the base category. In addition, we included a multiplicative dummy variable, *AGECOL*, to capture the age of the colonies; this is the product of a colonial dummy (*CL=1* for all countries that were colonies at any time between 1921 and 1960) and the age of the colony. A list of the independent variables used in our regressions may be found in table 6.2.

The export function was estimated for a sample of 86 lagging countries in 1960.[9] The regressions have fairly high explanatory power, with an adjusted R^2 equal to 0.60; the F-statistics are statistically significant at the one percent level. The coefficients for all the sovereignty dummies are

Table 6.2
Independent Variables in Regressions on Structural Variables

Variable	Definition
PCI	Per capita gross domestic product in 1960
POP	Population of country in 1960
$(PCI)^2$	PCI squared
$(POP)^2$	POP squared
DEN	A country's population in 1960 divided by its area
OIL	OIL=1 for oil-rich countries
LEAD	LEAD=1 for Japan and countries in W. Europe
MUSLIM	Percentage of population that is Muslim
CHRISTIAN	Percentage of population that is Christian
CL	CL=1 for countries that were colonies at any time between 1921 and 1960
AGECOL	A product of CL (CL=1 for all countries that were colonies at any time between 1921 and 1960) and years between colonization and independence or 1960, whichever comes first
CL-MUS	Product of CL and MUSLIM
CL-CHRIS	Product of CL and CHRISTIAN
AFR	AFR=1 for countries in Sub-Saharan Africa
COL	COL=1 for all countries that were colonies in 1950
NIC	NIC=1 for all colonies that gained independence during 1940-1950
QC	QC=1 for all countries that were quasi-colonies through most of the century leading up to the 1950s
DEP	DEP=1 for all countries that were dependencies
SOV	SOV=1 for all countries that were independent in, or before 1921, and had sovereign status thereafter

negative, as expected, but only *NIC* (with a coefficient of -10.52 percentage points) is statistically significant at the five percent level; the other sovereignty dummies are not significant at the ten percent level. *AGECOL* appears with an expected positive sign and is statistically significant at the one percent level; it has a value of 0.05, suggesting that a hundred years under colonial rule increased export orientation by 5 percentage points. When the regressions are estimated without *AGECOL*, the negative coefficients for *SOV* and *DEP* are statistically significant at the one percent level; the two remaining sovereignty dummies are not significant at the ten percent level.[10]

Sovereignty Differentials in Industrialization

We now present results which demonstrate that levels of industrialization across lagging countries in 1960 were positively correlated with their historical record of sovereignty.

The bias towards manufactures in sovereign countries emanated from several sources. Some protection for manufactures was unavoidable even when landlords dominated these countries. Since the landlords were unwilling to tax their own incomes or the imported luxuries they consumed, they raised revenues mostly from tariffs on ordinary consumer goods, and these were often quite steep. A few industries were protected for their security value, or because the ruling elites had a financial interest in them. State procurements were generally reserved for domestic suppliers, creating yet another instrument for promoting domestic industries. Further, whenever the balance of domestic forces became more favorable to industrialization, as it eventually did in most sovereign countries, they moved quickly towards an industrial policy that deliberately promoted import substituting industrialization.

This bias towards manufactures in sovereign countries was accentuated during global recessions. This connection was most visible during the depression of the 1930s when most sovereign lagging countries responded to the declining value of their exports by devaluing their currencies; and not a few imposed exchange controls, raised tariffs and engaged in deficit spending, thereby giving a boost to domestic manufactures. The colonies responded to the same crisis with deflationary fiscal and monetary policies, which depressed demand for all manufactures.

Most colonies created an opposite bias towards production of primary goods. In addition to their policy of free trade, they implemented measures to reduce wages and land costs in primary production. In Africa, peasants were evicted from the best lands; they paid poll taxes, and provided free labor on public projects and the farms of white settlers; formal schooling was discouraged; and, if labor was still not cheap enough, cheaper labor was imported from India and China. At the same time, the supply of land was augmented by draining swamps, clearing forests and investing in irrigation projects. The movement of goods into and out of the country was subsidized by investing in infrastructure that serviced international trade. In addition, white settlers were encouraged to engage in primary production with grants of agricultural lands and mining rights, and subsidies on loans and transportation.

Industrialization in the *QCC* was discouraged by weak consumer demand, the result of a distribution of income which favored foreigners. We have seen how free international integration displaces indigenous capital, enterprises and skills in the *QCC*, effects which were augmented by the discriminatory policies of colonial governments and expatriate enterprises.[11] This concentrated incomes in the hands of foreigners, who repatriated them or spent them on imported consumer goods, ensuring that the expansion of the export and commercial sectors in the *QCC* did little to create a mass market for consumption goods. Consumer demand in the colonies was also held in check by the neglect of the food sector, which depressed wages and the marketable surplus in agriculture.

The growth of manufactures in the *QCC* also suffered from a paucity of indigenous entrepreneurs, capital and skills resulting from the displacement effects of integration. Once a country has been eroded of an indigenous base of capital, enterprise and skills, it is not easy to establish modern manufactures even when domestic markets have been recreated by growth based on primary exports. Arguably, expatriate enterprises in commerce, mining and plantations could step into the breach, but it is not difficult to see why they would be reluctant to break rank by diversifying into manufactures. Since investments in manufactures threatened to undermine the economic order on which colonies were founded, they were certain to raise eyebrows and might provoke sanctions from the expatriate community as well as colonial governments. There was another problem. Since the hiring policies of expatriate enterprises generally excluded locals from managerial and skilled positions, this was certain to offset any cost advantage the colonies may have derived from lower wages and proximity to markets or raw materials.

Sovereignty differentials in industrialization are estimated within a framework developed by Clark (1957), Kuznets (1965), Chenery and Taylor (1968) and Chenery and Syrquin (1975) for studying patterns of development across countries and over time. We estimated reduced form equations of the form: $MFG = \alpha + \beta U + \delta V + \varepsilon$, where *MFG* is the percent share of manufacturing output in gross domestic product, *U* is a vector of dummies relating to sovereignty, *V* is a vector of other independent variables affecting *MFG*, and ε is a random error term. These regressions are estimated for 1960, the first year for which data on national income accounting become available for a large number of lagging countries.

The rationale for the control variables included in these regressions is quickly summarized; a list of these variables is presented in table 6.2.[12] Per capita income (*PCI*) affects output structure *via* demand and supply forces. Rising *PCI* increases the proportion of income spent on manufactures; it also increases investments in education and skills, thus producing a growing stock of human capital which is likely to shift the country's comparative advantage towards manufactures. Population *(POP)* serves as a proxy for the size of the domestic economy. For any given level of protection offered by natural and policy barriers, a larger domestic economy offers a larger number of product markets in which firms can operate at efficient scales of production. In addition, since the strength of externalities often depends on proximity of contacts, a larger manufacturing sector creates greater externalities, thus setting into motion cumulative reductions in all-round costs and growth in the size of the manufacturing sector. The square terms for *PCI* and *POP* allow for non-linearities in the relationship between these variables and *MFG*.

The Heckscher-Ohlin theory of factor endowments suggests that *MFG* may depend on a country's factor endowments. Thus, a country with a rich endowment of natural resources relative to its population is likely to persist longer on the path of primary-based growth before turning to industrialization. Given the difficulties of constructing a comprehensive index of a country's resource endowments, we employ instead a crude but simple proxy, *viz.* population density (*DEN*), defined as a country's total population in 1960 divided by its area. In addition, we introduce a dummy variable (*OIL*=1) for the oil-rich countries. Industrialization in these countries was likely to be depressed by the inflated wages resulting from their windfall gains.

The anti-industrial bias of colonial policies is likely to diminish with time. This bias is strongest in the early expansionist phase of colonialism when the indigenous presence in manufacturing, commerce and the government is swept aside by integration and discriminatory policies. However, once colonial rule is firmly established, the indigenous classes may begin to recover some of the ground they had lost before–as local intermediaries to metropolitan firms, recruits in colonial armies, workers in mines and plantations, or low and mid-level employees in the government. These gains may give rise to a national consciousness and, in time, political parties articulating the interests of indigenous traders and workers. In order to capture any dilution in the anti-industrial bias of colonial policies brought about by these changes, we introduce an interactive dummy variable (*AGECOL*): a colonial dummy (*CL*=1 for all countries that were colonies any time between 1921 and 1960) multiplied by the age of the colony in 1960. We expect *AGECOL* to have a positive effect on levels of industrialization in 1960.

We control for the effects of institutional factors on industrialization in several ways. Differences in the initial conditions across countries are minimized by restricting our empirical analysis to lagging countries in 1900. In addition, we vary the sample of lagging countries by making the definition of lagging countries more restrictive. Since it might be argued that Japan and countries in Western Europe had superior initial conditions, we include a dummy variable, *LEAD*=1 for these countries. A second dummy variable, *AFR*=1 for all countries in Sub-Saharan Africa, is also included to accommodate opposite concerns about their initial conditions. It should be noted, however, that this does not distinguish between adverse conditions created by the greater racism of colonial policies and adverse factors specific to Sub-Saharan Africa which operated independently of colonialism.

The sovereignty differentials in industrialization were first estimated for a sample of 95 lagging countries, consisting of all countries that had a per capita income in 1900 that was equal to or less than 50 percent of per capita income in United States.[13] In the interests of economy, we only report results on sovereignty differentials in industrialization and the relevant adjusted R^2s and *F*-statistics. The sovereignty differentials are defined as the excess of *MFG* in Group 1 countries, with higher levels of sovereignty, over *MFG* in Group II countries with lower levels of sovereignty, while controlling for all other factors affecting industrialization. A complete list of these binary comparisons was presented earlier in table 6.1.

The first set of ten sovereignty differentials, reported in the top panel of table 6.3, shows that sovereignty had a positive, large and statistically significant impact on industrialization in 1960.[14] As expected, we observe the largest differential between sovereign countries and the colonies, *viz.* 11.9 percentage points; this is larger than the average industrialization of 8.6 percent in the colonies. The differentials decline only modestly to 11.1, 10.7 and 9.5 percentage points as the base category is expanded successively to include *NIC*, quasi-colonies and dependencies. The first three coefficients are statistically significant at the one percent level, and the fourth at the five percent level. The differentials between *SOV-DEP* and the remaining polar categories are also quite large, ranging between 8.2 and 7.7 percentage points, and statistically significant at the one percent level. The sovereignty differentials between *SOV-DEP-QC* and the two remaining polar categories are smaller, at 5.1 and 4.8 percentage points, but they are still about half the average levels of industrialization in the relevant polar categories. The least favorable comparison, between *SOV-DEP-QC-NIC* and *COL*, yields a differential of 3.3 percentage points that is statistically significant at the ten percent level.[15]

These results validate our five-fold taxonomy of sovereignty. If the sovereignty rankings are correct, we would expect to observe declining values of the sovereignty differentials as group II countries are expanded to include countries with higher levels of sovereignty; or alternatively, as group I countries are expanded to include countries with lower levels of sovereignty. These expectations are fully sustained for both comparisons.

Table 6.3

Sovereignty Differentials (SD) in Industrialization: 1960

Group I	Group II	SD: I over II (% points)	MFG in II (% GDP)	$\bar{R}^2$	F
		All lagging countries (n=95)			
SOV	COL	11.9**	8.6	0.54	10.2**
	COL- NIC	11.1**	9.7	0.54	11.1**
	COL-NIC-QC	10.7**	9.9	0.55	12.4**
	COL-NIC-QC-DEP	9.5*	10.3	0.54	13.3**
SOV-DEP	COL	8.2**	8.6	0.52	10.3**
	COL- NIC	7.7**	9.7	0.52	11.3**
	COL-NIC-QC	7.7**	9.9	0.53	12.7**
SOV-DEP-QC	COL	5.1*	8.6	0.49	10.1**
	COL- NIC	4.8*	9.7	0.49	11.1**
SOV-DEP-QC-NIC	COL	3.3+	8.6	0.49	10.8**
		All lagging countries *minus* Sub-Saharan Africa (n= 63)			
SOV	COL	10.9*	12.5	0.37	4.0**
	COL- NIC	10.2**	13.1	0.38	4.5**
	COL-NIC-QC	10.1**	12.9	0.39	5.1**
	COL-NIC-QC-DEP	9.0**	13.1	0.40	5.5**
SOV-DEP	COL	7.1*	12.5	0.34	3.9**
	COL- NIC	6.6*	13.1	0.35	4.4**
	COL-NIC-QC	6.8*	12.9	0.36	5.0**
SOV-DEP-QC	COL	5.0+	12.5	0.32	3.9**
	COL- NIC	4.8+	13.1	0.33	4.4**
SOV-DEP-QC-NIC	COL	2.4	12.5	0.31	4.1**

(**),(*) and (+) denote statistical significance at 1, 5 and 10 percent levels.

The sovereignty differentials between group I and group II countries decline in all but one of the comparisons as the group II countries are expanded; it stays unchanged in one comparison. Similarly, the sovereignty differentials between group I and group II countries decline in every case as group I countries are expanded to include countries with inferior levels of sovereignty. It is unlikely that these strong patterns are the result of some happy coincidence.

These results did not change when the sovereignty differentials were estimated for four alternative country samples—two larger and two smaller than the original sample—obtained by varying the definition of lagging countries. The two larger samples were obtained by increasing the cutoff percentage for the definition of lagging countries from 50 to 60 and 75 percent of the per capita income of United States in 1900; the two smaller samples were derived by lowering the cutoff percentage to 40 and 30 percent.[16] A comparison of the results (not reported here) across all five country samples shows steadily declining absolute values for each of the sovereignty differentials as the sample size becomes more restrictive. Importantly, however, the sovereignty differentials for the smaller samples remain statistically significant. Thus, seven of the ten sovereignty differentials for the smallest sample of 88 countries are statistically significant at the one percent level, one at the five percent level, and only two are not significant at the ten percent level.

Although the regressions control for the impact of size of economy on output structure through two proxies, POP and POP[2], it is possible that these controls do not work well. Accordingly, two additional sets of sovereignty differentials were estimated for samples of large and small countries, with a small country defined as one with a population of 5 million or less in 1960.[17] The regressions for the large countries yield much larger sovereignty differentials than before, all significant at the five percent level.[18] The sovereignty differentials for the small countries are somewhat smaller than before with all but one of these differentials significant at the one percent level. This variance in the size of the differentials perhaps reflects the fact that domestic markets were a less binding constraint for industrialization in the larger sovereign countries.

We carefully investigated if the sovereignty differentials are affected by the large number of Sub-Saharan countries (*AFR*) in our sample countries.[19] In particular, since *AFR* lagged behind the other colonies in their levels of industrialization in 1960, this raised concerns that factors specific to these countries—and not their status as colonies—might account for the results on sovereignty differentials. The critical question here is whether this industrial lag was due to factors specific to *AFR* and *unrelated* to colonialism, or whether this was due to the specific character of colonialism in this region. Amongst others, Lenski and Nolan (1984) and Crenshaw (1995) have argued that *AFR* lagged behind the agrarian societies of Asia and Europe in their level of skills, both technical and social, because of their horticultural heritage; Asian and European farmers relied on the plow while most farmers in *AFR* still relied on the hoe at the end of the nineteenth century.[20] On the basis of some simple correlations and regressions, Lenski and Nolan (1968) claim that the values of several economic and demographic indicators do in fact depend on whether a country was horticultural or agrarian. These statistical results, however, lack credibility since they do not introduce any control variables other than a country's status in the global system.

The thesis that *AFR*'s industrial lag derives from deficiency in skills and organization rooted in their horticultural legacy does not always square with the facts. In West Africa, where they had not been displaced by European settlers, indigenous peasants created during the first half of the twentieth century a sizable commercial economy based on the cultivation of cocoa and coconut palm, accomplishments which demanded high levels of energy, thrift, skills and enterprise.[21] One supposes that with appropriate inducements, these same capacities could have been employed to develop a manufacturing sector producing at least the simpler non-durable consumer goods. We must also contend with the question that if Africans lacked the preparation to invest in manufactures, why was this slack not taken up by the large number of Europeans, Levantines and Indians in Africa. This suggests that the deficiency in *AFR* was not one of culture or skills but one of incentives; and this is what placed Africa behind other colonies.

Similarly, it is unlikely that *AFR* faced more serious problems with an industrial labor force than other countries. South Africa and to a lesser degree Rhodesia, the two Sub-Saharan countries which were free to pursue a program of industrialization before 1950, succeeded in developing a modern industrial sector primarily on the backs of an African labor force. Moreover, had the Africans been incapable of acquiring skills and threatening the jobs of white workers, why would the whites in South Africa go through all the unpleasantness of erecting a system of apartheid to exclude competition from black workers. In a survey of 63 manufacturing firms in Nigeria, Kilby (1961) found that the quality of the labor force depended upon wages and working conditions, and found no evidence of any cultural aversion to wage employment. Finally, African labor could not have been the obstacle to industrialization, since Africans could be replaced by cheap Indian and Chinese labor as they had been on the plantations, mines and ports. All this leaves the matter of a lag in *AFR*'s industrialization still begging for an explanation.

We may look for an explanation of this industrial lag in the greater severity of colonial policies in *AFR*. Colonial policies in Sub-Saharan Africa–leading to the expropriation of fertile lands, the neglect of education, the exclusion of indigenous peoples from government, the immigration of whites, the insertion of alien intermediaries from India and Lebanon, and employment of forced labor–were pushed farther here than in India, Egypt or Malaysia.[22] Africans entered into the modern sectors of their economies–the mines, plantations, railways and ports–as unskilled workers; nearly all skilled jobs were appropriated by expatriates. The stronger discrimination against Africans was motivated, and justified, by a racist ideology which assigned them the lowest rank in the hierarchy of races, and sometimes regarded them as less than human. Most likely, this was facilitated by Africa's tribal fragmentation, which weakened the threat of large-scale resistance to colonial excesses. Whatever the reasons for these excesses, they produced two consequences which alone might account for the industrial lag of these countries: a greater concentration of income in the hands of foreigners and the nearly complete exclusion of Africans from skilled jobs.[23]

Significantly, however, our estimates of sovereignty differentials in industrialization are not visibly affected when we control for *AFR*'s industrial lag. First, consider the values of the sovereignty differentials estimated without the Sub-Saharan countries. The new sovereignty differentials, reported in the second panel of table 6.3, are only modestly smaller than their previous values; three of these sovereignty differentials are significant at the one percent level, four at the five percent level, two at the ten percent level, and only one is not significant at the ten percent level.[24] There is a more noticeable decline in the values of these differentials relative to the average levels of industrialization in the base categories whose values are now higher because of the exclusion of *AFR*.[25] A third set of sovereignty differentials, not reported here, was estimated for the full sample of lagging countries but with the addition of a dummy variable (*AFR*=1) that controls for the presence *AFR*. The coefficients for *AFR* in these regressions are always negative with values ranging between -1.7 and -3.3 percentage *points*, but only three of them are statistically significant at the ten percent level. The values of these sovereignty differentials are nearly identical to those reported in the second panel of table 6.3. In addition, the first seven sovereignty differentials are statistically significant at the one or five percent levels; the ninth is significant at the ten percent level; and the eighth and tenth are not significant at the ten percent level.

It may still be argued, despite the exclusion of advanced countries from our sample and the incorporation of two dummies (*LEAD* and *AFR*) to control for differences in initial conditions, that our sovereignty dummies are merely proxies for differences in initial conditions amongst the lagging countries. This conjecture was tested by estimating sovereignty differentials for a common sample of 83 lagging countries in 1960 and 1980 but with an unchanged taxonomy of sovereignty. If the sovereignty differentials in 1960 are due to missing institutional factors, then the equalization of sovereignty after 1960 should not affect our results on sovereignty differentials.[26] However, a comparison of the two sets of estimates in table 6.4 reveals a systematic and significant decline in the absolute values of the sovereignty differentials between the two dates; there is a larger decline in the values of the sovereignty differentials rela-

Table 6.4

Sovereignty Differentials (SD) in Industrialization: 1960 and 1980

Group I	Group II	SD: I over II (% points)	MFG in II (% GDP)	$\overline{R}^2$	F
		1960			
SOV	COL	7.5**	9.3	0.65	13.7**
	COL- NIC	7.5**	9.7	0.66	15.3**
	COL-NIC-QC	6.5**	9.8	0.66	16.7**
	COL-NIC-QC-DEP	4.4**	10.3	0.63	16.5**
SOV-DEP	COL	6.1**	9.3	0.65	14.9**
	COL- NIC	6.1**	9.7	0.66	16.6**
	COL-NIC-QC	5.4**	9.8	0.66	18.4**
SOV-DEP-QC	COL	4.0**	9.3	0.63	14.9**
	COL- NIC	4.0**	9.7	0.64	16.8**
SOV-DEP-QC-NIC	COL	2.5+	9.3	0.62	15.8**
		1980			
SOV	COL	5.1*	12.3	0.53	8.7**
	COL- NIC	4.6*	13.2	0.53	9.3**
	COL-NIC-QC	4.6*	12.8	0.54	10.3**
	COL-NIC-QC-DEP	3.1+	13.4	0.53	10.8**
SOV-DEP	COL	4.4*	12.3	0.54	9.6**
	COL- NIC	4.1*	13.2	0.54	10.3**
	COL-NIC-QC	4.2*	12.8	0.54	11.6**
SOV-DEP-QC	COL	2.8	12.3	0.53	10.0**
	COL- NIC	2.3	13.2	0.52	10.8**
SOV-DEP-QC-NIC	COL	2.8	12.3	0.52	11.2**

(**),(*) and (+) denote statistical significance at 1, 5 and 10 percent levels.

tive to the average levels of industrialization in the base categories in 1980, which are substantially higher than in 1960. All but one of the sovereignty differentials in 1960 are significant at the one percent level; none are significant at the one percent level in 1980, six are significant at the five percent level, one at the ten percent level, and three are not significant at the ten percent level.

In tests employing Leamer's extreme bounds analysis, we find that most of the sovereignty differentials in the top panel of table 6.3 are robust.[27] The independent variables in the regressions were disaggregated into three subsets, as follows: $Y = \alpha + \beta_i\,I + \beta_m\,M + \beta_z\,Z + \varepsilon$, where I is a vector of always-included variables, M is a vector of sovereignty dummies, and Z is a subset of other explanatory variables. The I-variables were defined to include *PCI*, *PCI*^{2}, *POP* and *POP*^{2}, and the Z-variables included *DEN*, *OIL*, *LEAD*, and *AFR*. In order to check the sensitivity of the sovereignty differentials in the top panel of table 6.3 to changes in specifications, the earlier regressions were re-estimated with all linear combinations of the Z-variables. A comparison of the high and low estimates for each of the sovereignty differentials reveals that the first four sovereignty differentials, between *SOV* and the four polar categories, are robust at the five percent level of significance. The sovereignty differential between *SOV-DEP* and *COL* is robust at the ten percent level, and the differentials between *SOV-DEP*, on the one hand, and *COL-NIC* and *COL-NIC-QC* are significant at the five percent level. Only the last three sovereignty differentials failed the test of robustness at the ten percent level. These results are in keeping with our theory which predicts that sovereignty differentials will decline as the sovereignty gap between group I and group II countries becomes smaller.

Sovereignty Differentials in Human Capital

The sovereignty differentials in human capital–measured as adult literacy rates in 1960 and, alternatively, average years of schooling in the labor force in 1960 and 1965–provide strong support to the thesis that erosion of sovereignty depressed levels of human capital in lagging countries.

The causation from sovereignty to human capital operated through several channels. The erosion of sovereignty always led–via greater integration–to the displacement of manufactures and indigenous enterprises in the quasi-colonies and colonies. The indigenous skills lost through these displacement effects could not be replaced by the growth of primary export activities, since the latter employed fewer skills, and when they did, these skills were mostly supplied by expatriates. Many of the colonies in Africa and Southeast Asia encouraged the immigration of workers for employment in mines and plantations, thereby restricting the access of indigenous workers to the most rudimentary labor skills in the new export activities.

The displacement of skills resulting from greater integration was nearly always magnified by discriminatory policies. Under the 'open-door' treaties forced upon the quasi-colonies, the great powers secured exemption from local taxes and local courts for their own enterprises and citizens. In the colonies, foreign enterprises were granted preferential access to government procurements and contracts, bank loans and transportation; they often received land and mineral rights as outright gifts or at highly subsidized prices; and, in some cases, they were shielded by laws from indigenous competition.[28] Faced with these handicaps, indigenous enterprises in the quasi-colonies and colonies were almost completely pushed out of the most profitable operations in banking, international trade, transportation, and mining. This process was carried farthest in Sub-Saharan Africa and Southeast Asia, where indigenous enterprises nearly died out because of a colonial policy which encouraged petty traders from India, China and the Levant to take up positions which metropolitan capital did not find profitable.[29]

The exclusion of indigenous peoples was most visible in the public sector of the colonies. The highest positions in colonial public services were monopolized by expatriates; when settlers were available, or colonial governments were expected to relieve the burden of unemployment at home, the indigenes were also displaced from clerical jobs.[30] The exclusion of indigenous elites from all higher offices in the colonies led to the atrophy of indigenous institutions for the management of conflicts and, worse, prevented them from developing skills for handling the social stresses and conflicts created by their insertion into the international economy. The racist and centrist colonial regimes undermined the capacity of indigenous peoples to evolve political mechanisms for solving their local collective problems.

The official policy of discrimination was mirrored by colonial enterprises. At first, this appears irrational since, unlike governments, business enterprises are expected to worry about their bottom line, which could benefit greatly from the employment of cheaper indigenes in skilled and managerial positions.[31] This discrepancy was not due to racial prejudice *per se*. Since the colonies were often held by small expatriate forces, colonial rulers worked hard to cultivate a mystique of racial superiority. Most importantly, this demanded minimum social contact between the rulers and the subjects except in relations of subordination; this meant that all positions of authority in the government and colonial enterprises had to be held by whites, preferably white expatriates.[32] Colonial enterprises were in no position to object, if they ever felt so inclined, since their profits often depended upon privileges handed out by colonial governments. Moreover, once these racial distinctions were in place, they acquired a life of their own. Soon, the white expatriates would band together to ensure that no natives would ever threaten their privileges.

The hiring of expatriates in skilled jobs created another negative feedback. To the extent that expatriates monopolized skilled jobs, this reduced the demand for institutions of higher learning in the colonies, virtually ensuring their absence in the smaller colonies. Since this, in turn, greatly reduced the supply of indigenous skills, it ensured that when skilled positions became available they could only be filled by expatriates. This meant that colonial enterprises could now perpetuate the white monopoly over skilled jobs without 'discriminating' against the indigenes. The dominance of expatriates over skills also eliminated the diffusion of skills through social contacts. Not only did the expatriates live in their own enclaves, but they protected their monopoly over skilled jobs by discouraging the transfer of their skills to indigenous workers.

Colonial policies which concentrated incomes in the hands of expatriates affected indigenous education in other ways.[33] Most importantly, this reduced the ability of the indigenous population to *pay* for education. Indirectly, this income concentration also affected the supply of education. Nearly everywhere, philanthropy has been a major source of funding for education, but there is very little evidence that colonial enterprises or expatriates directed their philanthropy towards education in the colonies. Almost all the private institutions of higher learning–as well as hospitals– set up in India during British rule, resulted from the munificence of indigenous landlords and traders, even though their share in the national wealth had shrunk dramatically under colonial rule. Perhaps the expatriates understood that educating the natives would undermine the durability of the colonial empires upon which their own profits depended.[34]

The bias against education in the colonies was reinforced by fiscal and political constraints. Since they could not impose tariffs on imports–a major source of revenues for sovereign governments–colonial governors operated on a tight financial leash; this meant that after they had met demands for infrastructure, internal security and defense, there was very little left over for improving the education and health of their subjects.[35] This did not worry the colonial rulers overmuch, since they had concerns that educated natives did not make loyal subjects. These concerns were reflected in colonial education policies which often emphasized basic vocational skills over literacy, employed school curricula to disparage indigenous cultures, undermined indigenous systems of learning, displaced indigenous languages from schools, and used public schools to spread Christianity. The British East India Company made its first allocation to education in 1817, sixty years after they took over the collection of revenues in Bengal. In the meanwhile, countless village schools as well as institutions of higher learning closed down as the Company appropriated their properties and funds, or terminated the rent-free status of their land holdings.[36] Government expenditure on education in Egypt was cut back drastically in 1883 when she passed under British rule; scholarships were reduced, tuitions were increased and rote learning and discipline were emphasized over the quality of education. Colonial education in Africa was adapted to the 'mental capacities' of their subjects; simple vocational skills such as basket-weaving were emphasized over literacy; and higher education was not introduced until after the second great war. Not a single college had been set up in all of Sub-Saharan Africa before 1945, not counting those in South Africa. Ghana's first technical college opened in 1951. Notwithstanding their overwhelming dependence on agriculture, there were only 154 university graduates in agronomy in the British and French colonies in Africa at the time of their independence.[37]

The use of alien languages for schooling, as well as the mixing of schooling with proselytization, discouraged education in the colonies. The imposition of alien languages burdened the schools with a persistent problem of teacher shortages. Not only did this disbar the graduates of indigenous schools from teaching, but they could be replaced only slowly in the absence of higher institutions of learning that employed alien languages; as a result, teaching, for a long time, was limited to what could be done by expatriates. The alien languages also compounded the problems of learning for pupils who now had to first master the rudiments of a new language before acquiring knowledge even of the most elementary kind. In addition, the first generation of students in any family could not expect to advance their learning process outside the schools. The use of schools for missionary work made matters worse. Many parents chose illiteracy for their children rather than risk losing them to alien religions.

Colonialism has been credited with creating a class of wage workers in Africa, thereby helping to advance it on the road to capitalist development.[38] It has been argued that Africa would have no wage workers without the coercive policies of colonial rulers. Several objections to this thesis are quickly advanced. Wage labor is not created by coercion alone; incentives might have worked even better. Second, if coercion was necessary to extract profits from mines, why should we assume that only colonial rulers possessed the capacity for coercion? Third, are we to suppose that the interest of advanced countries in Africa's resources would have vanished in the absence of colonies, or that indigenous rulers would be incapable of developing their resources on their own, or that lacking indigenous technology they would have prevented foreign corporations from developing those resources? If the value of Africa's resources was not predicated on colonial rule, then it may be expected that instruments for their exploitation–including wage labor–could also be created without colonialism. Finally, we may be allowed to question the advantages of a wage-labor created by racist and often brutal policies which led to high turnover and high mortality rates in the labor force. Africans were quite able and almost certainly would have preferred to develop their lands into commercial farms, instead of working on them as wage labor. It is not obvious that an economy organized into plantations, with a labor force drawn forcibly from subsistence farms, is preferable to commercialized peasants who organize production for domestic and world markets.

To summarize the argument: we predict that the loss of sovereignty during industrial epoch *I* led to lower levels of literacy; lower average levels of schooling in the labor force; lower levels of technical, scientific and managerial skills; lower levels of entrepreneurship; and diminished aptitudes for conflict resolution and governance. This section explores only the first two connections, since data on specialized forms of capital are not available. Still we are fairly certain that sovereignty differentials for higher-order skills are likely to be much larger than those we estimated for adult literacy rates and average years of schooling.

Adult Literacy Rates: 1960. Our estimations reveal large sovereignty differentials in adult literacy rates across lagging countries in 1960; in addition, we did not find any evidence to support concerns that these results are proxies for missing institutional factors.

The methodology for these estimates is the same as before. We estimated reduced form equations of the form: $LITERACY = \alpha + \beta U + \delta V + \varepsilon$, where *LITERACY* is the adult literacy rate in 1960, *U* is a vector of dummies relating to sovereignty, *V* is a vector of other independent variables affecting adult literacy, and ε is a random error term. Although *LITERACY* is a narrow measure of human capital, it has the advantage of being a direct measure and, therefore, is likely to be more reliable than measures of average years of schooling in the labor force, which are derived under a variety of assumptions from less reliable data on enrollments and age-specific mortality rates. The use of adult literacy rates for cross-country comparisons also raises concerns about whether the definitions of literacy employed to collect data were comparable across our sample of countries.[39] While such concerns cannot be dismissed, it would appear that political pressures to overstate literacy rates would be strongest in countries with the lowest literacy rates, so that our estimates of sovereignty differentials are likely to be weighed down by these biases.

The control variables employed in estimating sovereignty differentials in adult literacy are quickly summarized. Whether literacy is regarded as a consumption or investment good, an increase in per capita income (*PCI*) will increase the demand for literacy; the higher demand for literacy as an investment good results from the growing skill-intensity of production at higher levels of per capita income. Adult literacy is likely to increase with rising population density (*DEN*), since this is likely to lower the costs of education, for users as well as suppliers. The inclusion of *LEAD* reflects concerns that the high levels of adult literacy in Japan and Western Europe are due to their head start in education. A dummy for Sub-

Table 6.5
Sovereignty Differentials (SD) in Adult Literacy: 1960

Group I	Group II	SD: I over II (% points)	LITERACY in II (%)	$\bar{R}^2$	F
		All Lagging Countries (n=86)			
SOV	COL	62.6**	24.7	0.79	23.2**
	COL- NIC	51.7**	29.8	0.75	20.1**
	COL-NIC-QC	43.6**	29.1	0.74	21.1**
	COL-NIC-QC-DEP	17.2**	30.7	0.73	21.8**
SOV-DEP	COL	60.9**	24.7	0.78	24.3**
	COL- NIC	50.2**	29.8	0.74	21.5**
	COL-NIC-QC	42.2**	29.1	0.74	22.7**
SOV-DEP-QC	COL	24.2**	24.7	0.76	23.4**
	COL- NIC	16.9*	29.8	0.73	21.5**
SOV-DEP-QC-NIC	COL	21.0**	24.7	0.76	25.8**
		All Lagging Countries *minus* Sub-Saharan Africa (n=56)			
SOV	COL	39.5**	51.5	0.75	12.7**
	COL- NIC	33.9**	49.8	0.75	13.5**
	COL-NIC-QC	35.4**	44.1	0.75	15.0**
	COL-NIC-QC-DEP	17.5*	44.5	0.75	15.9**
SOV-DEP	COL	37.7**	51.5	0.74	12.8**
	COL- NIC	31.9*	49.8	0.74	13.8**
	COL-NIC-QC	33.4**	44.1	0.74	15.4**
SOV-DEP-QC	COL	7.2	51.5	0.71	12.3**
	COL- NIC	2.3	49.8	0.71	13.5**
SOV-DEP-QC-NIC	COL	6.6+	52.5	0.72	13.8**

(**),(*) and (+) denote statistical significance at 1, 5 and 10 percent levels.

Saharan countries (*AFR*) is included for the opposite reason. Since Islam is often regarded as a barrier to modernization, we include *MUSLIM* to control for the percentage of Muslims in a country. On the contrary, it has been argued that Christianity was a positive force in modernization over the past two centuries; hence, the inclusion of *CHRISTIAN*, defined as the percentage of population that is Christian. Further, Muslim populations in the colonies may have resisted colonialism and conversion to Christianity by refusing to attend government or church-run schools, whereas Christians may have been attracted to the same schools because of their religious affinity with the colonial rulers. In order to test these hypotheses, we include two interactive dummies: *CL-MUS* and *CL-CHRIS*, where these are defined as the products of *CL* (a dummy variable for all countries that were colonies at any time between 1921 and 1960) and *MUSLIM* and *CHRISTIAN* respectively. A list of these variables may be found in table 6.2.

The sovereignty differentials in adult literacy rates were estimated for a sample of 86 lagging countries which had a per capita income in 1900 equal to or less than 50 percent of the per capita income in United States in 1900.[40] The results reported in the first panel of table 6.5 show that our explanatory variables account for a rather high proportion of the variation in adult literacy rates across countries; the values of adjusted R^2s vary between 0.73 and 0.79. All the sovereignty differentials appear with the expected positive signs, and all but one of them are statistically significant at the one percent level; the remaining differential is statistically significant at the five percent level. In addition, the sovereignty differentials are large, varying between 62.6 and 16.9 percentage points, compared to average adult literacy rates in the base categories which range between 24.7 and 30.7 percent. The largest sovereignty differential, at 62.6 percentage points, is more than two-and-a-half times as high as the average adult literacy rate in the corresponding base category. Even the smallest sovereignty differential of 16.9 percentage points is more than half the average adult literacy rate of 29.8 percent for the relevant base category.[41]

In results not reported, the adult literacy rates in the colonies increase with the age of the colony. *AGECOL* always appears with positive coefficients, ranging between 0.08 and 0.10, that are statistically significant at the one percent level. This calls for a downward adjustment in the sovereignty differentials. Thus, the sovereignty differential in adult literacy between sovereign countries and a colony with a hundred years under colonial rule, would have to be adjusted downward by eight to ten percentage points; this would still leave a sovereignty differential of 52.6 to 54.6 percentage points for these comparisons. Following a similar adjustment, the sovereignty differential in adult literacy between *SOV-DEP-QC-NIC* and a colony of the same age would lie between 11 and 13 percentage points. The sovereignty differential between sovereign countries and the oldest colonies–with three hundred years of colonial rule–would still be quite high at 34.5 percentage points.

The sovereignty differentials in adult literacy decline for every increase in the scope of group I and group II countries. The sovereignty differential of 62.6 percentage points between *SOV* and *COL* declines to 51.7, 43.6 and 17.2 percentage points for successive expansions in the scope of the group II countries to include *NIC*, *QC* and *DEP*. Similarly, an expansion in the scope of group I countries to include *DEP*, *QC* and *NIC* reduces the differentials from 62.6 percentage points to 60.9, 24.2 and 21.0 percentage points. The same pattern of declining sovereignty differentials is observed for all other expansions in the scope of sovereignty categories. These patterns support the thesis that a wider sovereignty gap between lagging countries will be accompanied by larger sovereignty differentials in the literacy rates. In addition, these results confirm, as they did before, the correctness of our sovereignty rankings.[42]

Once again, we investigate how our results are affected by the presence of a large number of Sub-Saharan countries in our sample, especially since these countries have lower literacy rates than other colonies.[43] The proper way of addressing this issue depends upon what we think are the causes of Sub-Saharan Africa's lower literacy rates. If the lag is due to factors specific to this region–and have not been caused by colonialism–then we need to control for them in one of two ways: by excluding all Sub-Saharan countries from our sample, or by adding a dummy variable (*AFR*=1 for all Sub-Saharan countries) to control for these countries. If however, the lower literacy rates in Sub-Saharan Africa are due to the greater severity of colonialism in this region, then we must introduce a different base category for our sovereignty dummies, *viz.* colonies in Sub-Saharan Africa. The latter procedure strikes us as the more plausible one.

It is tempting to argue that Sub-Saharan Africa's lag in literacy rates was due to its pre-literate past and horticultural legacy, and not the result of colonial policies. The contention that *all* countries in Sub-Saharan Africa were pre-literate needs to be corrected. According to Curtin (1964: 31), perhaps as 'many as a third of the people south of the Sahara lived in societies that were literate in the sense that Europe was literate during the middle-ages–that is, at least a class of scribes could read and write'. Several communities in West Africa, the Sahel region and the horn of Africa had strong traditions of literacy that long pre-dated the colonial period. There is evidence that some of these societies had very high rates of literacy; enrollment rates among boys belonging to the *Dyula*, a trading community spread over Ghana, Ivory Coast and Burkina Faso, was 90 percent in 1959.[44] It should also be noted that low literacy rates were not confined to pre-literate cultures. According to one source, literacy rates in the Middle East, a region with the oldest tradition of literacy, could not have been much above two percent in 1800.[45] Low literacy rates were also common in parts of Europe and Latin America during the nineteenth century.[46]

Attributing Sub-Saharan Africa's lower literacy rates to her pre-colonial past runs into other problems. First, it is puzzling that some six to eight decades of colonial rule and international integration should have failed to elevate literacy levels in this region to the modest levels for the other colonies. Is there any evidence that Africans were indifferent or averse to the advantages they could have derived from literacy? Ranger

(1965: 59) has shown that there were 'from the beginning some African societies which enthusiastically welcomed Western education'. In the absence of public schools to meet this rising demand for education, in several places this task was assumed by the private sector. Private 'bush' schools accounted for more than two-thirds of the primary enrollment in Southern Nigeria up until the 1940s and Northern Rhodesia in 1938, and more than five-sixths of the enrollment in Uganda in 1938.[47] It would appear that missing schools, not missing students, were responsible for Africa's lag in literacy.

Africa's literacy lag is more credibly attributed to the entrenched racism of her colonial rulers. Racism, always a powerful tool of domination in the colonies, struck deeper roots in Africa because of the continent's long association with the Atlantic slave trade. Davidson (1994: 320) has argued that it was the transatlantic trade in black Africans that provided the earliest and strongest impetus for European racism.[48] This long-lasting trade, accompanied as it was with savage brutality towards the slaves, was unacceptably odious. But there was great profit in it too; and the pecuniary motive prevailed over moral qualms. The solution was to garnish slavery with a healthy dose of racism. Thus began the degradation of Africans to a subhuman status, to the level of beasts, so that the brutality inflicted upon them might be excused as no more offensive than cruelty towards animals. This dehumanization was in an advanced stage when imperialism burst into Africa in the late nineteenth century. Africa had been mythologized as the dark continent, with no history, inhabited by a race of sub-humans no higher than children in their intelligence.

This degradation had some unpleasant consequences for Africans. They were excluded, to a greater extent than other subject peoples, from their own government; they were almost completely pushed out of primary exports (except in West Africa); they faced competition, even in their capacity as unskilled labor, from cheaper indentured workers from India; they received virtually no advanced schooling; their primary schools frequently emphasized manual skills and the saving of souls over literacy; and (in East, Central and Southern Africa) they were pushed out of their best agricultural lands to make room for white settlers. In part, Africa's misfortunes were also due to her late colonization. Africa's topography conspired to delay colonization till European military superiority became overwhelming, making it easier for her colonization to be effected with a thoroughness that would have been more difficult a hundred years ago.[49]

We also investigated if Sub-Saharan Africa's putative historical handicaps had any visible effects on the earlier reported estimates of sovereignty differentials. To this end we first re-estimated sovereignty differen-

Table 6.6
Sovereignty Differentials (SD) in Adult Literacy:
1960 and 1980

Group I	Group II	SD: I over II (% points)	Literacy in II (%)	$\bar{R}^2$	F
		1960			
SOV	COL	60.52**	24.9	0.78	18.9**
	COL- NIC	54.3**	29.4	0.73	15.9**
	COL-NIC-QC	44.1**	28.9	0.72	16.6**
	COL-NIC-QC-DEP	11.5	30.7	0.71	16.6**
SOV-DEP	COL	59.4**	24.9	0.78	20.7**
	COL- NIC	53.0**	29.4	0.74	17.5**
	COL-NIC-QC	43.0**	28.9	0.73	18.3**
SOV-DEP-QC	COL	26.0**	24.9	0.77	20.3**
	COL- NIC	18.9*	29.4	0.72	17.4**
SOV-DEP-QC-NIC	COL	22.5**	24.9	0.77	22.4**
		1980			
SOV	COL	23.1*	42.8	0.62	9.5**
	COL- NIC	14.7	46.6	0.60	9.1**
	COL-NIC-QC	9.4	46.7	0.60	9.9**
	COL-NIC-QC-DEP	4.3	47.8	0.61	11.0**
SOV-DEP	COL	13.0+	42.8	0.63	10.3**
	COL- NIC	13.1	46.6	0.60	10.0**
	COL-NIC-QC	8.1	46.7	0.61	11.0**
SOV-DEP-QC	COL	13.8	42.8	0.64	11.4**
	COL- NIC	7.9	46.6	0.61	11.1**
SOV-DEP-QC-NIC	COL	15.0**	42.8	0.64	12.6**

(**),(*) and (+) denote statistical significance at 1, 5 and 10 percent levels.

tials in adult literacy by dropping all Sub-Saharan countries from our sample. A review of the results, reported in the second panel of table 6.5, shows that although smaller than before, the sovereignty differentials are still quite large: the first seven sovereignty differentials range from 17.5 to 39.5 percentage points. Seven of the ten sovereignty differentials are statistically significant at the one or five percent levels, one at the ten percent level, and two are not significant at the ten percent level. Not surprisingly, the sovereignty differentials with the lowest values, or with *t*-values not significant at the ten percent level, relate to comparisons which greatly dilute the differences in sovereignty between group I and II countries.

The sovereignty differentials in adult literacy were re-estimated with a dummy variable (*AFR*=1) for all countries in Sub-Saharan Africa. The results (not reported here) are similar to those reported in the second panel of table 6.5. The first seven sovereignty differentials are statistically significant at the one percent level, with values ranging between 20.0 and 44.5 percentage points; the tenth differential is significant at the ten percent level; the remaining two, although positive, are not significant at the ten percent level. The largest sovereignty differential, at 44.5 percent between *SOV* and *COL*, is twice as large as the average adult literacy rate in the base category.[50]

Sovereignty differentials were also estimated with a modified taxonomy of sovereignty. Colonies were split into two categories, colonies in Sub-Saharan Africa and all others, with the former serving as the base category for our sovereignty dummies. Not surprisingly, these estimations yielded sovereignty differentials that were significantly larger than before, and nearly always statistically significant at the one percent level.

In order to test if the taxonomy of sovereignty is a proxy for missing institutional factors, we estimated sovereignty differentials for an identical set of countries in two different time periods, 1960 and 1980. If the sovereignty differentials in 1960 are due to missing growth factors which are correlated with our taxonomy of sovereignty, then these growth factors would not be affected by the decolonization that occurred since 1960 and, in consequence, the sovereignty differentials would survive unchanged for regressions in later periods. In short, we would expect the sovereignty differentials to remain substantially unchanged between 1960 and 1980. This is not confirmed by the results in table 6.6.[51] The sovereignty differentials in 1960 range from 11.5 to 60.5 percentage points; in 1980, they vary from 4.3 to 23.1 percentage points. More importantly, eight of the sovereignty differentials in 1960 are statistically significant at the one percent level, one at the five percent level, and only one is not statistically significant at the ten percent level. By contrast, seven of the ten sovereignty differentials in 1980 are not statistically significant at the ten percent level; the remaining three are statistically significant at the one, five and ten percent levels.

The basic results on sovereignty differentials in table 6.5 were not sensitive to changes in the definition of lagging countries. Three new samples of lagging countries were obtained by setting the cutoff points in our definition of lagging countries at 75, 40 and 30 percent of the per capita income in United States in 1900; this gave us samples with 93, 82 and 79 countries respectively. The results of the first two samples differed very little from those reported in table 6.5, although the sovereignty differentials for the smallest sample were considerably larger than those for the other samples.[52] This would suggest that differences in sovereignty had a greater impact on adult literacy in countries that were least developed in 1900.

The robustness of the results in table 6.5 was tested using Leamer's extreme bounds analysis.[53] The independent variables in the regressions were disaggregated into three subsets, as follows: $Y = \alpha + \beta_i \, \text{I} + \beta_m \, \text{M} + \beta_z \, \text{Z} + \varepsilon$, where I is a vector of always-included variables, M is a vector of sovereignty dummies, and Z is a subset of other explanatory variables. The I-variables in these exercises are *PCI, PCI², MUSLIM, CHRISTIAN, CL-MUSLIM, CL-CHRISTIAN* and *AGECOL;* and the Z-variables are *DEN, OIL, LEAD,* and *AFR.* In order to check the sensitivity of the estimated sovereignty differentials in the top panel of table 6.5 to changes in specifications, the regressions were re-estimated with all linear combinations of the Z-variables. A comparison of the high and low estimates for each of the sovereignty differentials reveals that the first three sovereignty differentials between *SOV* and the first three polar categories are robust at the one percent level of significance; only the sovereignty differential relative to the fourth polar category is not robust at the ten percent level. The sovereignty differentials between *SOV-DEP* and all three polar categories are robust at the one percent level. The remaining three sovereignty differentials are not robust at the ten percent level. Alternatively, the six sovereignty differentials with the highest values are robust at the one percent level, while the four differentials with the lowest values are fragile. These results show that sovereignty differentials are both large *and* robust for large differences in sovereignty between countries, but as the differences between sovereignty categories become smaller the corresponding sovereignty differentials become smaller *and* fragile.

The mutual causation between adult literacy rates and per capita income raises concerns about simultaneity biases in our estimates. Accordingly, the sovereignty differentials in the first panel of table 6.5 were re-estimated with an instrumental variable substituting for per capita income.[54] These corrections did not significantly modify the earlier results. The sovereignty differentials (for the sample of 86 lagging countries, and no control for *AFR*) between *SOV* and the four polar categories are: 49.5, 41.9, 33.9 and -2.5 percentage points; the differentials between *SOV-DEP* and the three polar categories are: 53.9, 46.9 and 19.8 percentage points; the differentials between *SOV-DEP-QC* and the two polar categories are 26.4 and 19.8 percentage points; and the differential between *SOV-DEP-QC-NIC* and *COL* is 21.3 percentage points. All the positive differentials are statistically significant at the one percent level; the only negative differential was not significant at the ten percent level.[55]

Table 6.7
Comparing Sovereignty Differentials (SD) in Years of Schooling (*YSCHOOL*): 1960

Group I	Group II	SD: I over II	*YSCHOOL* in II	$\bar{R}^2$	F
All Lagging Countries (n=64)					
SOV	COL	6.1**	1.6	0.73	12.9**
	COL- NIC	5.7**	1.7	0.72	13.5**
	COL-NIC-QC	4.7**	1.7	0.68	12.6**
	COL-NIC-QC-DEP	1.0	1.9	0.63	10.7**
SOV-DEP	COL	5.9**	1.6	0.73	14.1**
	COL- NIC	5.6**	1.7	0.72	14.8**
	COL-NIC-QC	4.6**	1.7	0.69	13.9**
SOV-DEP-QC	COL	2.4**	1.6	0.67	12.0**
	COL- NIC	2.1**	1.7	0.67	12.8**
SOV-DEP-QC-NIC	COL	1.1**	1.6	0.65	11.6**
All Lagging Countries *minus* Sub-Saharan Africa (n=46)					
SOV	COL	5.3**	2.6	0.70	8.6**
	COL- NIC	5.4**	2.4	0.71	9.5**
	COL-NIC-QC	5.0**	2.2	0.71	10.0**
	COL-NIC-QC-DEP	0.9	2.4	0.63	7.9**
SOV-DEP	COL	5.2**	2.6	0.71	9.4**
	COL- NIC	5.3**	2.4	0.72	10.5**
	COL-NIC-QC	4.9**	2.2	0.71	11.1**
SOV-DEP-QC	COL	1.5*	2.6	0.63	7.5**
	COL- NIC	1.6*	2.4	0.65	8.5**
SOV-DEP-QC-NIC	COL	0.2	2.6	0.61	7.3**

(**),(*) and (+) denote statistical significance at 1, 5 and 10 percent levels.

Years of Schooling in Labor **Force:** *1960 and 1965.* Sovereignty differentials were estimated for average years of total schooling (*YSCHOOL*) in the labor force, a more comprehensive measure of human capital than adult literacy. These estimates confirm that sovereignty had a strong positive impact on a country's educational endowments during industrial epoch *I*. As expected, the sovereignty differentials in *YSCHOOL* are quite a bit larger than the corresponding differentials in *LITERACY*.[56]

The sovereignty differentials in *YSCHOOL* (1960) were estimated for a sample of 64 lagging countries with a per capita income in 1900 equal to or less than 50 percent of the per capita income in United States in 1900.[57] The control variables employed in estimating these sovereignty differentials are identical to those used for estimating sovereignty differentials in adult literacy rates. An examination of the results in table 6.7

Table 6.8
Comparing Sovereignty Differentials (SD) in
Years of Schooling (*YSCHOOL*): 1987

Group I	Group II	SD: I over II	*YSCHOOL* in II	$\overline{R}^2$	F
SOV	COL	4.0**	4.0	0.79	17.5**
	COL- NIC	3.8**	4.3	0.78	17.8**
	COL-NIC-QC	3.3**	4.3	0.74	16.2**
	COL-NIC-QC-DEP	0.2	4.4	0.71	15.2**
SOV-DEP	COL	4.1**	4.0	0.79	19.1**
	COL- NIC	3.8**	4.3	0.78	19.5**
	COL-NIC-QC	3.4**	4.3	0.74	17.9**
SOV-DEP-QC	COL	2.4**	4.0	0.78	19.8**
	COL- NIC	2.1**	4.3	0.77	20.6**
SOV-DEP-QC-NIC	COL	1.2**	4.0	0.75	19.0**

(**),(*) and (+) denote statistical significance at 1, 5 and 10 percent levels.

shows a good fit for the regressions with adjusted R^2s ranging from 0.63 to 0.73. The sovereignty differentials are positive for all the comparisons, and all but one of them are statistically significant at the one percent level. Most of the sovereignty differentials are also quite large, in absolute as well as relative terms, with values ranging from 1.0 to 6.1 (years of schooling) compared to average values of *YSCHOOL* (1960) in group II countries ranging from 1.6 to 1.9.[58] Finally, the values of the sovereignty differentials decline, as expected, both when we extend the scope of group I and group II countries, confirming once again the validity of our taxonomy of sovereignty.[59]

Once again, controlling for the presence of Sub-Saharan countries in our sample did not substantially alter the sovereignty differentials. The results in panel two of table 6.7 show that the exclusion of Sub-Saharan countries from our sample produced only minor changes in the basic results. Most of the sovereignty differentials are now somewhat smaller, though two have higher values. Six of the ten sovereignty differentials are statistically significant at the one percent level, two at the five percent level, and only two fail the test at the ten percent level. We obtained nearly identical results, not reported here, when we estimated sovereignty differentials with a dummy variable for *AFR*. As expected, these new results show a pattern of declining values of sovereignty differentials for successive expansions in the scope of group I and group II countries.

The sovereignty differentials relating to *YSCHOOL* were estimated for an identical set of countries in 1987.[60] A comparison of these results in table 6.8 with the results in panel one of table 6.7, shows that in seven of the ten cases, group II countries had significantly narrowed their absolute lag behind group I countries in 1987; in two cases the lag remained unchanged, and in one case it had increased modestly from 1.1 to 1.2 (years of schooling). In relative terms, the sovereignty differentials in 1987 have declined across the board, significantly in most cases; the average values of *YSCHOOL* in 1987 range from 4.0 to 4.4 years, more than twice as high as before. It may be noted that the sovereignty differentials in *YSCHOOL* could not have disappeared completely in the two or three decades following decolonization in the 1960s, as they did in the case of *LITERACY*, because *YSCHOOL* is a more comprehensive measure of human capital. This ensures that advances in *YSCHOOL* will take much longer to achieve than similar changes in *LITERACY*.

The robustness of the sovereignty differentials in *YSCHOOL* (1960) was tested using Leamer's extreme bounds analysis; the set of always-included and conditioning variables are the same as those used for *LITERACY*. The sovereignty differentials between *SOV* and the first three polar categories are robust at the one percent level; the differential relative to the fourth polar category is not robust at the ten percent level. The sovereignty differentials between *SOV-DEP* and all three polar categories are robust at the one percent level. The three remaining differentials are not statistically significant at the ten percent level. As before, the sovereignty differentials with the highest values are robust to changes in specifications.

When the sovereignty differentials in *YSCHOOL* (1960) were reestimated with instrumental variables substituting for per capita income, in order to correct for any simultaneity biases in the estimates, this did not substantially alter the earlier results.[61] The new sovereignty differentials between *SOV* and the four polar categories are 4.2, 4.0, 3.1 and -0.5 years of schooling; those between *SOV-DEP* and the three polar categories are 4.9, 4.7 and 3.8 years of schooling; those between *SOV-DEP-QC* and the two polar categories are 2.2 and 2.1 years of schooling; and the differential between *SOV-DEP-QC-NIC* and *COL* is 0.71 years of schooling. All the positive differentials are statistically significant at the one percent level; the only negative differential was not statistically significant at the ten percent level.

Sovereignty differentials were also measured for an alternative estimate of average years of schooling in 1965 provided by Kyriacou (1991).[62] Despite differences in methods employed for estimating average years of schooling in Kyriacou (1991) and the earlier estimate in Nehru *et al.* (1995), as well as variations in the sample of countries for which these estimates are available, the sovereignty differentials for the two data sets are quite similar. All the sovereignty differentials in *YSCHOOL* (1965) are positive, six are significant at the one percent level, two at the five percent level, one at the ten percent level, and only one is not significant at the ten percent level.[63] Although the differentials are smaller than before, all but one of them are as large or larger than the corresponding mean *YSCHOOL* for the group II countries. The exclusion of Sub-Saharan countries from our sample or, alternatively, the addition of a dummy variable for Sub-Saharan countries, reduced the magnitude of the sovereignty differentials, but in most cases these reduced values are nearly as large as, or larger, than the average values of *YSCHOOL* in the relevant group II countries. In addition, all six of the sovereignty differentials with the largest values are still statistically significant at the one percent level.

Sovereignty Differentials in the Growth Record

Our theory of the global economy during industrial epoch *I* predicts that loss of sovereignty will have a strong adverse impact on growth rates.

The reasons for this are quickly summarized. Whenever a lagging country lost its sovereignty, this led to its forced integration with one or more advanced economies. In examining the dynamics of integration between two economies at unequal levels of development, we showed that this leads the lagging country to specialize in a narrow and shrinking range of primary products; displaces capital, indigenous enterprises and skills in the lagging country; and transfers its savings and skills to the advanced country. When the loss of sovereignty ends in colonization, it leads to two additional consequences which are detrimental to growth. Nearly always, the colonies are forced under the monopoly control of capital from a single advanced country, adversely affecting its terms of trade. More seriously, colonization exposed a country to direct appropriation of its markets and resources by capital and labor from an advanced country. A sovereign country would have avoided, or minimized, all these adverse consequences.

Thanks to the work of a generation of economic historians, whose researches have been integrated and standardized by Maddison (1995), we can now compare the historical growth record of several lagging countries with varying records of sovereignty. Table 6.9 presents data on weighted average annual growth rates of per capita income over 1870 to 1900, 1900 to 1913, 1913 to 1950, and 1950 to 1992, for three categories of lagging countries: sovereign countries, dependencies and quasi-colonies-

Table 6.9
Sovereignty and Growth Rates of Per Capita Income: 1870-1992

	1870-1900	1900-1913	1913-1950	1950-1992
Weighted Growth:				
Sovereign Countries	1.00	1.61	1.34	2.58
Dependencies	(.)	(.)	0.96	0.95
QCC	0.59	0.50	-0.27	2.96
% World Population:	1870	1900	1913	1950
Sovereign Countries	17.0	19.9	22.5	22.1
Dependencies	(.)	(.)	0.2	0.3
QCC	48	50	49	48

Growth rates are weighted averages for countries in each category: the weights are populations in initial year of growth period. Growth rates for dependencies are for 1920-1950 and 1950-1990.

cum-colonies (*QCC*).[64] A country is lagging if it had a per capita income that was 66 percent or less of the per capita income of United States in 1900. The growth rates for the sovereign countries and the *QCC* are available for each of the four periods, while growth rates for the dependencies are available only for the last two periods. In each of the first three periods, the sovereign countries grew faster than the *QCC*, and the differentials in growth rates between them increased significantly over successive periods, rising from 0.41 percent during the first period to 1.11 and 1.61 percent in the next two periods. Over 1913 to 1950, the average annual growth rates were 1.34 percent in the sovereign countries, 0.96 percent in the dependencies, and -0.27 percent in the *QCC*.[65]

One might object that these results are not representative because of the relatively small number of *QCC* in our sample: the growth rates for the *QCC* in the three periods are based on four, 12 and 13 countries respectively.[66] Although the samples of *QCC* are relatively small, they include nearly all of the largest countries in this category, so that their combined population in each of the three periods was only slightly less than three-quarters of the total population of all *QCC*, or nearly half of the world population at the beginning of each of the three periods.[67] More importantly, with the possible exception of a handful of small countries in West Africa which experienced rapid export growth during this period, it is unlikely that growth rates of the missing *QCC* were different from the reported growth rates.

A comparison of the *mean* growth rates of the sovereign countries, dependencies and *QCC* yields similar results. The average annual growth rates for the sovereign countries over the first three growth periods are

1.07, 1.67 and 1.34 percent respectively; the corresponding growth rates for the *QCC* are 0.49, 0.81 and -0.02 percent.[68] Over the first period, only one of the 14 sovereign countries grew at rates below the mean for the *QCC*; in the second period, only three of the 18 sovereign countries grew at rates below the mean for the *QCC*; in the third period, there was no sovereign country with growth rates below the mean for the *QCC*. Similarly, none of the dependencies grew at rates below the mean for the *QCC* over the relevant time period. Once again, the disparity in mean annual growth rates between sovereign countries and the *QCC* increased progressively over the three periods.

We also estimated sovereignty differentials in growth rates of per capita income over 1900 to 1950.[69] The growth rates for the dependencies are for 1920 to 1950; the growth rates for Greece, Bulgaria, South Africa, Turkey and Yugoslavia are for 1913 to 1950. The sovereignty differentials were estimated with three control variables: initial per capita income, adult literacy rates in 1930, and a dummy variable (EUR=1) for countries in Europe.[70] Both neoclassical and productivity-gap theories of growth predict an inverse correlation between growth rates and initial per capita income.[71] Adult literacy rates serve as proxies for human capital, which are important growth factors in the recent theories of endogenous growth.[72] The dummy variable for lagging countries in Europe serves to check if their 'superior' institutions or proximity to advanced countries advanced their growth.[73] Arguably, if these advantages had been material to their growth, this would be reflected *via* faster growth in higher levels of initial incomes, making it unnecessary to add a European dummy. We let the evidence sort out the facts from conjecture.

The sovereignty differentials were estimated for four samples of lagging countries obtained by varying the definition of lagging countries. The largest sample of 40 lagging countries consists of all countries with a per capita income in 1900 (1913 for some sovereign countries and 1920 for the dependencies) equal to or less than 66 percent of the per capita in United States in 1900; the earlier comparisons were based on this sample. Three additional samples were defined by moving the cutoff point successively to 50, 40 and 30 percent; this reduced the sample of lagging countries from 40 to 37, 34 and 27 respectively. It may be noted that the number of *QCC* remains unchanged across the four samples, while the number of dependencies remains unchanged for all but the last sample which includes four dependencies, down from five in the larger samples. Sovereignty differentials are reported for each of the four samples corresponding to the three alternative taxonomies of sovereignty: sovereign countries, dependencies and *QCC*; sovereign countries-*plus*-dependencies

Table 6.10
Sovereignty Differentials (SD) in Growth Rates of Per Capita Income:
1900 to 1950

Group I	Group II	SD: I over II (% points)	Growth Rates in II (%)	$\bar{R}^2$	F
(PCI<$2703 in 1900: Sample size=40)					
SOV	QCC	1.60**	0.20	0.29	4.21**
DEP	QCC	0.64*	0.20	0.29	4.21**
SOV	DEP-QCC	1.37**	0.38	0.26	4.57**
SOV-DEP	QCC	1.19**	0.20	0.23	3.89*
(PCI<$2048 in 1900: Sample size–37)					
SOV	QCC	1.80**	0.20	0.32	4.38**
DEP	QCC	0.87**	0.20	0.32	4.38**
SOV	DEP-QCC	1.45**	0.38	0.26	4.24**
SOV-DEP	QCC	1.41**	0.20	0.25	4.07**
(PCI<$1638 in 1900: Sample size=34)					
SOV	QCC	1.96**	0.20	0.36	4.71**
DEP	QCC	1.02**	0.20	0.36	4.71**
SOV	DEP-QCC	1.56**	0.38	0.28	4.28**
SOV-DEP	QCC	1.61**	0.20	0.29	4.41**
(PCI<$1229 in 1900: Sample size=27)					
SOV	QCC	2.18**	0.20	0.43	4.88**
DEP	QCC	0.83*	0.20	0.43	4.88**
SOV	DEP-QCC	1.90**	0.34	0.40	5.24**
SOV-DEP	QCC	1.69**	0.20	0.31	3.89*

(**), (*) and (+) denote statistical significance at the one, five and ten percent levels.
The samples of lagging countries are defined with respect to US PCI in 1900; the four samples have PCI in 1900 equal to, or less than, 66, 50, 40 and 30 percent of US PCI in 1900.

and *QCC*; sovereign countries and dependencies-*plus-QCC*. In order to conserve space, we only report the estimated values of the sovereignty differentials together with the corresponding adjusted R^2s, F-statistics, and mean growth rates of per capita income for the base category.

An examination of the results on sovereignty differentials in table 6.10 confirms that sovereignty had a large positive impact on growth rates in lagging countries. The sovereignty dummies for each of the three taxonomies have positive coefficients for *all* four samples, and all but two of these coefficients are statistically significant at the one percent level, with the remaining two significant at the five percent level.[74] The magnitude of these coefficients shows that sovereignty made a large difference to growth rates. Consider the results for the largest sample of lagging countries: the sovereign countries had a growth advantage of 1.60 and

1.37 percentage points over *QCC* and *DEP-QCC* respectively; *SOV-DEP* had a growth advantage of 1.19 percentage points over *QCC*; and even the dependencies grew significantly faster than *QCC*. In addition, each of the four sovereignty differentials increase as the sample size becomes more restrictive, suggesting that sovereignty had a stronger impact on growth at lower levels of development. To illustrate, the sovereignty differential in growth rates between sovereign countries and *QCC* increased from 1.60 to 1.80, 1.96 and 2.18 percentage points as the sample size was reduced successively from 40 to 37, 34 and 27 countries. The same pattern may be observed for the sovereignty differentials between *SOV* and *DEP-QCC* and *SOV-DEP* and *QCC* for every reduction in sample size. The sovereignty differentials between *DEP* and *QCC* increased over the second and third samples, but declined between the third and fourth samples.

An application of Leamer's extreme bounds analysis shows that the reported sovereignty differentials in growth rates are robust.[75] The independent variables in our regressions were disaggregated into three subsets: the *I*-variables, where *I* is a vector of always-included variables; the *M*-variables, where *M* is a vector of sovereignty dummies; the *Z*-variables, where *Z* is a vector of all other explanatory variables. In one set of tests, the *I*-variable is per capita income and the *Z*-variables are adult literacy rates and the European dummy. In order to check the sensitivity of the results in table 6.10 to changes in specifications, we re-estimated the regressions with *all* linear combinations of the *Z*-variables. These exercises were repeated with the adult literacy rates as the *I*-variable, and per capita income and the European dummy as the *Z*-variables. A comparison of the high and low estimates of the sovereignty differentials (alternatively, with per capita income and adult literacy rates as the *I*-variable) from both sets of estimations showed that the sovereignty differentials between *SOV* and *QCC*, *SOV* and *DEP-QCC*, and *SOV-DEP* and *QCC* are robust at the one percent level in all the samples, and the sovereignty differentials between *DEP* and *QCC* are robust at the one percent or five percent levels in all the samples.

At this point a skeptic might object that the sovereignty dummies are merely proxies for some missing growth factors. Only the most backward countries were colonized, so that their poor growth record as *QCC* can be explained by their prior backwardness–that is, by the factors which led to their colonization–and not by their colonial status *per se*. This argument is based on two hidden premises. The first premise equates economic backwardness–*via* military weakness–with vulnerability to colonization. The second premise maintains that the conditions which caused the backwardness of *QCC* survived colonization, ensuring their lackluster growth record as *QCC*. Both premises are seriously flawed. [76] As for the first premise, we have shown in chapter two that this is not grounded in historical facts: the *QCC* in our samples did not lag behind the sovereign countries and dependencies around 1800. There are other problems with this premise. Given that the great powers were not on missions of mercy during the nineteenth century, this makes it hard to see why they would target only the most backward countries for colonization. In addition, a country's ability to defend itself, at least in the nineteenth century, was not closely tied to the state of its economic development. A host of other factors intervened, including distance from the colonizing powers; threat of incurable diseases; barriers set up by terrain, warlike tribes, a politically cohesive population; and, most importantly, the rivalry of colonial powers. As for the second premise, it is hard to see–even if we concede that only the most backward countries were colonized–how the structural factors that held back development before colonization could have survived all the traumatic changes in governance, class structure, institutions and laws that generally attended colonization.

These concerns receive no support from the empirical evidence either. We estimated sovereignty differentials in growth rates for a later period, 1950 to 1992, but with the original country samples and taxonomies of sovereignty. Since all the *QCC* in our sample had gained sovereignty by 1950, we do not expect to find positive sovereignty differentials in growth rates for this later period. On the other hand, if the taxonomies are proxies for missing growth factors, the earlier results should be reproduced. The latter interpretation, however, receives no support from the evidence. [77] The estimation results in table 6.11 show that each of the four sovereignty differentials in growth rates over 1950 to 1992 are negative for all four samples of lagging countries. Moreover, these differentials are far from negligible. The sovereignty differentials between *SOV* and *QCC* range from -0.59 to -0.95 percentage points over the four samples; the differentials between *DEP* and *QCC* range from -1.62 to -1.79 percentage points and are statistically significant at the one percent level; the differentials between *SOV-DEP* and *QCC* range from -1.22 to -1.38 percentage points and are statistically significant at the one or five percent levels. This dramatic reversal in the sign of the sovereignty differentials after 1950 shows that the operative factor retarding growth rates in the *QCC* before 1950 was the absence of sovereignty in this period. Alternatively, we can make sense of these results only if we are willing to claim that all the long-surviving obstacles to growth–not related to colonialism–that had retarded growth in the *QCC* over the period

Table 6.11

**Sovereignty Differentials (SD) in Growth Rates of Per Capita Income:
1950 to 1992**

Group I	Group II	SD: I over II (% points)	Growth Rates in II (%)	$\bar{R}^2$	F
(PCI<$2703 in 1900: Sample size=40)					
SOV	QCC	-0.95	2.75	0.26	3.74*
DEP	QCC	-1.79**	2.75	0.26	3.74*
SOV	DEP-QCC	-0.29	2.27	0.14	2.53*
SOV-DEP	QCC	-1.38**	2.75	0.26	4.36*
(PCI<$2048 in 1900: Sample size=37)					
SOV	QCC	-0.86	2.75	0.25	3.43*
DEP	QCC	-1.77**	2.75	0.25	3.43*
SOV	DEP-QCC	-0.13	2.27	0.13	2.39+
SOV-DEP	QCC	-1.38*	2.75	0.25	3.97*
(PCI<$1638 in 1900: Sample size=34)					
SOV	QCC	-0.68	2.75	0.25	3.19*
DEP	QCC	-1.75**	2.75	0.25	3.19*
SOV	DEP-QCC	0.07	2.27	0.13	2.25
SOV-DEP	QCC	-1.31*	2.75	0.23	3.55*
(PCI<$1229 in 1900: Sample size=27)					
SOV	QCC	-0.59	2.75	0.24	2.61+
DEP	QCC	-1.62**	2.75	0.24	2.61+
SOV	DEP-QCC	-0.06	2.30	0.15	2.11
SOV-DEP	QCC	-1.22*	2.75	0.24	3.08*

(**), (*) and (+) denote statistical significance at the one, five and ten percent levels. The samples of lagging countries are defined with respect to US PCI in 1900; the four samples have PCI in 1900 equal to, or less than, 66, 50, 40 and 30 percent of US PCI in 1900.

leading up to 1950, disappeared abruptly and simultaneously in all these countries at around the time that they gained their sovereignty.

Concluding Remarks

This chapter has presented a variety of empirical results which demonstrate that erosion of sovereignty during industrial epoch *I* increased export orientation and reduced industrialization, human capital formation and growth rates.

These results are not statistical artifacts. Not only are they backed by theory, but the empirical support for the inverse connection between loss of sovereignty and economic performance has been developed at several levels. The evidence presented in chapter two showed that the lagging countries in Asia and Africa–nearly all of them quasi-colonies and colonies–were on average more integrated into the global economy than sovereign lagging countries; yet the former experienced little growth. A review of economic policies across the sovereignty categories, in chapter five, revealed systematic differences in their policies towards integration. While the sovereign lagging countries employed policies which sought to structure their integration into the world economy, the quasi-colonies and colonies fostered integration, and the colonies discriminated against the interests of indigenous factors.

Given the variations in policy regimes across sovereignty categories, we expected industrialization and human capital, all other things held constant, to increase with sovereignty. We also expected the export orientation of colonies to increase over time. These expectations are strongly confirmed by the estimated sovereignty differentials for 1960 and 1965. The sovereign lagging countries had substantially lower levels of export orientation and higher levels of industrialization and human capital compared to the quasi-colonies and colonies. Not only were these differentials statistically significant (in most cases, at the one percent level), they do not vanish with changes in the taxonomy of sovereignty, variations in the sample of lagging countries, changes in specifications of the estimating equations, and corrections for simultaneity biases. Finally, we designed statistical tests which show that the observed sovereignty differentials could not be proxies for some hidden institutional obstacles to growth, industrialization or human capital formation; these differentials vanish completely or diminish significantly when they are estimated for later periods when systematic and large differences in sovereignty across countries had disappeared.

The capstone to our empirical evidence is provided by the estimates of sovereignty differentials in growth rates of per capita income over 1900 and 1950. These differentials are large–1.60 percentage *points* between sovereign countries and *QCC*–statistically significant and robust to changes in specifications. Moreover, since these differentials vanish or are reversed for the period 1950 to 1992, this rejects, as before, concerns that the differentials in growth rates are proxies for unaccounted institutional differences between sovereign countries and the *QCC*.

These results have the potential to change the way we look at the recent evolution of the global economy. It will not do to present accounts of capitalist development, and of its propensity to produce unequal development, without explicitly taking account of the very important part that unequal states and 'unequal races' played in this process. Merely switching the status of the colonies in our sample to sovereign countries would have increased their growth rates by 1.59 percentage points per annum between 1900 and 1950. This could have produced more than a two-fold increase in their per capita income over this period. These results are also contrary to the recent headlong rush towards *laissez faire* economics. There is nothing in the evidence for our period which shows that free trade advanced economic growth in the lagging countries. On the contrary, countries which were free to structure their integration into the global economy systematically outperformed countries which were forced to maintain free or near-free trade regimes. Deliberate industrialization and growth were complementary during industrial epoch *I*, not substitutes, as suggested by classical and neoclassical theory.

Notes

1   Report submitted to British Foreign Minister, John Palmerston (Stavrianos 1981: 218).
2   The sovereignty differentials in the structural parameters are estimated for 1960; hence, the new category, *NIC*, defined as colonies which gained independence between 1940 and 1950.
3   Reporting all the sovereignty differentials would take up too much space. Also, the number of observations for the intermediate categories are often quite small.
4   The pressures towards greater accommodation emanated from four sources: the growing strength of liberation movements; the weakness of the colonial powers resulting from the war; the global tensions created by the Cold War; and graduation of the advanced economies to higher value-added manufactures (Alam 1994: 244-47).
5   There is a more voluminous empirical literature that has emanated from the theories of dependency, but this literature makes no attempt to measure sovereignty differentials. Instead, it measures dependency primarily in terms of three variables, *viz.* dependence on trade, direct foreign investments and aid flows. This literature has been reviewed in Hirsch (1986) and Bornschier and Chase-Dunn (1993).
6   See also Kleiman (1977) and Livingstone (1976).
7   Offer (1993) has pointed to several flaws in the estimates of Davis and Huttenback (1988) which undermine their reliability.
8   Per capita income was dropped from the regressions because the associated *t*-statistics were very small and statistically insignificant at the ten percent level. *RX* is expected to be higher in oil-producing countries. *LEAD* is included to accommodate concerns that Western Europe and Japan possessed institutions which promoted openness. The inclusion of *AFR* acknowledges the opposite concern, that there was something about Sub-Saharan Africa

(say, poor roads) which discouraged exports. *LEAD*=1 for Finland, Italy, Japan, Norway, Portugal, and Spain. *OIL*=1 for Algeria, Gabon, Iran, Iraq, Trinidad and Tobago, and Venezuela.

9   Lagging countries include countries which had a per capita income in 1900 equal to or less than 50 percent of per capita income in United States in 1900. These countries are listed in table 2 of the appendix.

10 The coefficients for the sovereignty dummies are -12.9, -8.0, -6.4, and -8.8 percentage points. These results were not affected when Liberia and Ethiopia were reclassified as dependencies (instead of quasi-colonies).

11 We have direct evidence on the income shares of foreign factors for several colonies. In 1958 the foreign minority in Belgian Congo, constituting one percent of the population, owned 95 percent of the total assets and received 42 percent of the national income (Peemans 1975: 181). In Indonesia, foreign factors received 23.5 percent of the net domestic product over 1921-1939. The British share in India's income was around 5 percent in the 1930s (Maddison 1990: 363). Data on export surpluses—measured as ratio of exports to imports—are available for Indonesia (2.4 for 1840-69, 1.45 for 1870-1912), India (1.72 for 1840-69, 1.48 for 1870-1912, and 1.33 for 1913-1938), and Egypt (1.55 for 1850-1869, 1.53 for 1870-1912, and 1.07 for 1913-1938) (Maddison 1990: 366). Golay (1976: 375-376) suggests that somewhat more than half of the export surpluses of several Southeast Asian countries financed net outflows of interest and dividends.

12 Additional information on the variables in our regressions, together with data sources, is available in table 1 of the appendix.

13 This amounts to $2048 in 1990 international dollars: see Maddison (1995: 23-24) for data on per capita income in 1990 international dollars. A list of the countries in our sample together with their political status may be found in table 2 of the appendix.

14 The controls in these regressions are: *PCI, POP, PCI², POP², AGECOL, DEN, OIL* and *LEAD*. The regressions were estimated using ordinary least-squares method; the estimated coefficients were corrected for heteroskedasticity using White's heteroskedasticity-consistent estimator. The results for the control variables are quickly summarized. The coefficients for *PCI* and *POP* are positive, as expected, in all the regressions and are statistically significant in all but one regression at the one percent level; their square terms appear with negative coefficients in all the regressions and are statistically significant in all but one regression at the one percent level. Interestingly, despite its crudity as a proxy for resource endowments, the coefficients for *DEN* have the expected positive sign in all the regressions, are stable across all the regressions, and are statistically significant at the five percent level in all but one regression. As expected, the oil-rich countries have lower levels of industrialization, but this relationship is not always statistically significant at the ten percent level. Surprisingly, the coefficients for *LEAD* sometimes appear with negative signs, but nearly always these coefficients had very low values, and are never statistically significant at the 10 percent level. Similarly,

in about half the regressions, *AGECOL* appears with a negative sign, but these coefficients have very low values and are never statistically significant at the ten percent level of significance.

15 The results in table 6.3 were not significantly affected when Liberia and Ethiopia were reclassified as dependencies (instead of quasi-colonies). To illustrate: the sovereignty differentials between SOV, SOV-DEP, SOV-DEP-QC, and SOV-DEP-QC-NIC, on the one hand, and the colonies, are 11.7, 6.7, 5.1 and 4.8 percentage points respectively. The first and second differentials are statistically significant at the one percent level; the third and fourth at 5 percent level.

16 The four samples had 107, 101, 90 and 88 observations respectively.

17 These results are reported in table 4 of the appendix. There are no dependencies in the subsample of large countries. There are 42 large countries and 53 small countries in our disaggregated samples.

18 The sovereignty differentials between sovereign countries, on the one hand, and *COL*, *COL-NIC* and *COL-NIC-QC*, are 19.4, 19.6 and 16.9 percentage points respectively.

19 There are 29 Sub-Saharan countries amongst the 45 colonies in our sample of 95 countries.

20 In the agrarian societies, agriculture was based on the plow and animal draft; horticultural societies used the hoe and did not use draft animals.

21 Hill (1956), Ingham (1979) and Smith (1979).

22 Amin (1972), Manning (1988: ch. 2) and Kennedy (1988).

23 In Belgian Congo, the whites, who were one percent of the population, owned 95 percent of the total assets and received 42 percent of the total income (Peemans 1975:181).

24 Dropping the Sub-Saharan countries still left us with a sample of 63 countries, of which 16 are colonies.

25 The age of the colony still has no impact on the level of industrialization in the colonies. Further, differences in initial conditions do not appear to have any impact on levels of industrialization; the coefficients of *LEAD* are negative, though none of them are significant at the 10 percent level.

26 Although the estimated sovereignty differentials relating to industrialization in 1960 are quite large, most likely these differentials were larger at an earlier date, before the softening in colonial policies that began in the 1940s.

27 Levine and Renelt (1992).

28 Kyi (1970: 30) writes: 'It is not an exaggeration to contend that the growth of Western enterprises [in trade, transportation and mining sectors in Myanmar] in fact had been promoted and their success assured by patronage and subsidies granted in their favor by the [colonial] government.' Similar policies were pursued in India by the British. By early twentieth century, Europeans had a nearly complete monopoly in external trade, shipping (ocean, coastal and inland), and the organized money markets (Bagchi 1970: 225, 229-31).

See Kennedy (1988: ch. 3) on official discrimination against indigenous enterprises in Africa.

29 Kennedy (1988: 32).

30 The entry of Indians into the higher ranks of the civil service occurred late in the colonial period. In 1912 there were only 6 Indians out of 412 higher-level officers in the Geological Survey of India, the Agriculture, Civil Veterinary, Forestry, and Railways departments (Headrick 1988: 321). Indigenization in Africa began after the second world war, and had not gone very far in most of the colonies at the time they became independent.

31 Kyi (1970: 45) has shown that in Myanmar, the proportion of indigenes employed as managers in industrial establishments in 1921 declined rapidly with the size of the firms: 70 percent (10-19), 55 percent (20-49), 38 percent (50-99), 8 percent (100-199), 0 percent (200 and above); the numbers in parentheses represent size of firm by employees. There was a similar decline in the proportion of indigenes employed in supervisory and technical positions: 49 percent (10-19), 43 percent (20-49), 42 percent (50-99), 27 percent (100-199), 5 percent (200 and above). The largest firms were almost all owned by foreigners. Similarly, according to Headrick (1988: 322), the managerial and higher technical jobs in Indian railways were held by Europeans, the mid-level skilled and supervisory positions by Anglo-Indians, and the Indians were 'at the bottom, in the unskilled jobs'. Although European locomotive drivers were paid ten times what their Indian counterparts received, it was common for express trains as late as the 1930s to be in European hands. Other industries owned and operated by Europeans 'discriminated as much as the railways'

32 The British government in India ensured that their officials spent their retirement outside India. The sight of less than athletic members of the British race threatened to undermine the mystique of their superiority.

33 This policy was reinforced by a cheap labor policy which neglected subsistence agriculture and, in South and East Africa and Southeast Asia, encouraged the immigration of cheap labor from India and China.

34 Gregory (1992: 210, 215) has remarked that in British East Africa, 'the Asian's philanthropy appeared remarkable. It far surpassed that of the local Europeans'. The per capita income of Indians in Uganda was less than a third of that enjoyed by the British expatriates.

35 The loss of tariff revenues in the colonies could scarcely be made up by levying taxes on income in the commercial sectors (which accrued mostly to expatriates), or on land (whose owners were often the only important indigenous beneficiaries of British rule). Lord Canning, British Viceroy to India, pointed out in the early 1860s: 'I would rather govern India with 40,000 British troops without an income tax than govern it with 100,000 British troops with such a tax (Tomlinson 1982: 134).'

36 Baber (1996: 187-90).

37 Headrick (1988: 310-11, 312).

38 These views have been examined in Griffin and Gurley (1985: 1106-7).

39 Behrman and Rosensweig (1994).
40 In 1990 international dollars this amounts to $2048. See Maddison (1995: 23-24) for data on per capita income in 1990 international dollars. A list of the countries in our sample together with their political status is presented in table 2 of the appendix.
41 Reclassifying Liberia as a dependency (instead of a quasi-colony) did not fundamentally alter these results. Thus, the sovereignty differentials (after the reclassification) between SOV, SOV-DEP, SOV-DEP-QC, and SOV-DEP-QC-NIC, on the one hand, and the colonies, are 44.1, 36.3, 24.2, and 16.8 percentage points. The first and third differentials are statistically significant at the one percent level; the second and fourth at the five percent level.
42 The results relating to the remaining control variables are quickly summarized. There is evidence of a strong nonlinear relationship between adult literacy rates and per capita income (*PCI*) across all the regressions; per capita income and its squared terms always appear with positive and negative coefficients respectively, and are statistically significant at the one percent level. Population density (*DEN*) appears with positive coefficients, but it is not always statistically significant at the ten percent level. Once again, the results do not uphold the presumption that initial conditions affected adult literacy in 1960; *LEAD* always appears with negative coefficients, though they are not significant at the ten percent level. The oil-rich countries show a large and persistent literacy lag across all the regressions that remains statistically significant at the one percent level. The results support a literacy lag in Muslim countries; though, there is no evidence that adult literacy rose with the proportion of Christian population. The interaction between colonialism and religion, whether Islam or Christianity, does not appear to have produced any clear or significant results for adult literacy in 1960.
43 Of the 40 colonies in our sample, 29 are in Sub-Saharan Africa.
44 Wilks (1968: 166).
45 Findlay (1989: 130).
46 Consider a sampling of primary enrollment rates in some of these countries during the nineteenth century: Portugal (1848: 1.72 percent), Bolivia (1882: 0.85 percent), Brazil (1871: 1.4 percent) and Chile (1882: 2.5 percent). Primary enrollment rates are pupils in primary schools divided by total population (Mitchell 1992, 1993).
47 Gifford and Weiskel (1971: 703).
48 Davidson (1994: 320).
49 See Headrick (1981) for an account of how Africa's topography and diseases held Europe's imperialist ambitions at bay till the last decades of the nineteenth century.
50 The sovereignty differential declined from 44.5 to 39.0, 39.5, and 20.0 percentage points as the group II category was expanded to include NIC, QC and DEP. The sovereignty differentials between SOV-DEP, on the one hand, and

COL, COL-NIC, and COL-NIC-QC are 43.4, 37.5 and 37.7 percentage points respectively.

51 These sovereignty differentials were estimated for a common sample of 72 lagging countries.

52 Thus, the sovereignty differentials for the first four comparisons in table 6.5 (those between sovereign countries and the remaining polar categories) for the larger sample of 93 countries are 59.9, 49.2, 41.9 and 17.3 percentage points respectively; for the original sample of 86 countries, these values are 60.5, 54.3, 44.1 and 11.5 percentage points; for the second sample of 82 countries, these values are 60.7, 49.5, 41.8 and 14.1 percentage points; the results for the third sample of 79 countries are 75.8, 64.3, 52.5 and 13.2 per centage points. A similar pattern holds for the remaining comparisons.

53 Levine and Renelt (1992).

54 In order to derive the instrumental variable, we regressed per capita income against the following variables: *SOV, DEP, QC, NIC, AGECOL, MUSLIM, CHRISTIAN, CL-MUSLIM, CL-CHRISTIAN, DEN, OIL, LEAD, AFR, PRICE, INVESTMENT*, and *OPEN. PRICE* is the price level across countries, derived from International Comparison Project; *INVESTMENT* is the ratio of gross domestic investment to gross domestic product; and *OPEN* is the ratio of exports to GDP. Data for the last three variables were obtained from Summers, *et al.* (1995). The adjusted R^2 for this regression is 0.70.

55 We obtained similar results when we added a control for Sub-Saharan countries. Only now, as before, the values of the sovereignty differentials are somewhat smaller.

56 The point was made earlier that the bias against the indigenous populations, resulting from the loss of sovereignty, increases as we move up the skill ladder.

57 The data on *YSCHOOL* (1960) are from Nehru, Swanson and Dubey (1995). Their estimates are constructed from time-series data on enrollment rates using the perpetual inventory method, with corrections for age-specific mortality rates, grade repetition and country-specific dropout rates for primary, secondary and tertiary students.

58 These results were not significantly affected when Ethiopia was reclassified as a dependency (instead of a quasi-colony). Thus, the new sovereignty differentials between *SOV, SOV-DEP, SOV-DEP-QC, SOV-DEP-QC-NIC*, on the one hand, and the colonies, are 4.9, 4.6, 2.5, and 2.3 years of schooling respectively; all of them statistically significant at the one percent level.

59 The results on the control variables are reviewed quickly. Per capita income (*PCI*) and PCI^2 always appear with positive and negative signs respectively, although the latter is generally not significant at the ten percent level. Population density (*DEN*) appears with mixed signs and is never significant at the ten percent level. Although age of a colony (*AGECOL*) always appears with positive coefficients that are statistically significant at the one percent level, the absolute values of these coefficients are very small, ranging in value from 0.0036 to 0.0064 years, so that the sovereignty differentials change very little

when adjusted for the age of a colony. Oil-rich countries have lower-than-normal values for *YSCHOOL*; in most cases, the coefficients for *OIL* are significant at the five percent level. The coefficients on *LEAD* are positive, ranging between 1.57 and 2.37 years, and significant at the one and five percent levels. The coefficients on *MUSLIM* and *CHRISTIAN* are almost always negative, although they are not always significant at the ten percent level. The coefficients on *CL-MUSLIM* and *CL-CHRIST* are nearly always positive; the first is not significant at the ten percent level in most cases, the second is significant at the one and five percent level in most cases. In any case, the values of these coefficients are too small to have any quantitatively significant impact on *YSCHOOL*.

60 The choice of 1987, instead of 1980 as in previous comparisons, reflects the fact that adjustments in *YSCHOOL* take longer than similar changes in *LITERACY* or *MFG*.

61 The instrumental variable for per capita income was obtained by regressing per capita income against *PRICE* (price level), *RC* (ratio of coastline to area), *AREA*, *OIL*, *AFR*, *SOV*, and *LEAD*; the adjusted R^2 for this regression was 0.67. Data on RC are from CIA (1992).

62 Kyriacou's (1991) estimates are extrapolations from estimates of average years of schooling in the mid-seventies for 42 countries in Psacharapoulos and Arriagada (1986); he regresses these estimates on lagged enrollments at the primary, secondary and higher levels and, on the assumption that this relationship remains constant, derives estimates for educational stock for other countries as well as other time periods.

63 These results are reported in table 5 of the appendix.

64 The colonies and quasi-colonies were merged into a composite category because of the small number of observations in each of the two primary categories taken individually. A list of all the lagging countries together with their growth rates of per capita income may be found in table 6 of the appendix. The weighted growth rates for the sovereign countries and the *QCC* were derived from Maddison (1995), and the growth rates for dependencies are from Bulmer-Thomas (1987: 312). The weights in all the growth rates are the populations of individual countries at the beginning of each growth period.

65 A word of explanation on why we chose 1950 as the cutoff point for our exercises. Alam (1994: 244-47, 253-55) has argued that the colonial governments, starting in the 1940s, showed greater willingness than before to accommodate indigenous interests; this was the result of several developments, including the growing strength of liberation movements, the two great wars, and the rise of communism leading up to the Cold War. This considerably narrowed the policy differences between the sovereign countries and some colonies after the second great war.

66 The growth rates for the sovereign lagging countries in the three periods are based on samples containing 14, 18 and 22 countries respectively.

67 Maddison (1995: 23-24, 226).

68 The means for the sovereign countries and *QCC*, for each of the three periods, are statistically different at the one percent level of significance.

69 The period before 1900 was excluded because of the small number of *QCC* in our sample.

70 Since per capita income for the dependencies are not available in Maddison (1995), we used 1950 per capita income from Maddison and growth rates in Bulmer-Thomas (1987) to derive the per capita income in 1920. Data on adult literacy rates for China, India, Pakistan, Bangladesh and Ghana are for 1950. Data on adult literacy rates are from Eisenstadt and Rokkan (1973: 245-47).

71 Solow (1956) and Abramovitz (1986).

72 Romer (1986) and Lucas (1988). See Van de Klundert and Smulders (1992) for a survey of this literature.

73 Morris and Adelman (1988) have presented data which show that in 1850 the *QCC* in our sample did not lag behind the sovereign countries in adult literacy rates, state of inland transportation, agricultural technology, and development of market institutions. In 1850, adult literacy rates in India and Egypt (less than 10 percent) were comparable to those in Brazil and Russia; China was in the same league as Spain, Argentina, Japan and Italy; and Myanmar was better placed than Spain, Brazil, Argentina, Japan and Italy. In the same year, India, Myanmar, China and Egypt were comparable in their inland transportation to Argentina, Brazil, Australia, Canada, Denmark, Italy, Russia, Spain, Sweden, Switzerland and Japan. Agricultural technology in China, Egypt and India in 1850 was at the same level as in Russia and Spain. Judging from the development of market institutions in 1850, Myanmar, China and Egypt were at the same level as Brazil, New Zealand and Russia; and India was at the same level as Argentina, Australia, Denmark and Japan (Morris and Adelman 1988: 391-92, 321-28, 283-89, 462).

74 The reported results are corrected using White's heteroskedasticity-consistent estimator. The results for the control variables may be quickly summarized. As expected, *PCI* always appears with a negative sign but none of the coefficients are statistically significant even at the ten percent level. The dummy for Europe also appears with a *negative* sign that is significant in three regressions at the 10 percent level. The coefficients for adult literacy rates appear with mixed signs, but none of them are significant at the ten percent level. There is little evidence that these results are due to multicollinearity between these variables and the sovereignty dummies. Dropping the sovereignty dummies did not alter these results much and, in addition, produced very low adjusted R^2s.

75 Levine and Renelt (1992).

76 We have shown earlier in chapter five how the racist biases in European norms of sovereignty determined which countries would be targeted for colonization.

77 The data in table 6.9 support the same conclusion. The *QCC* experienced not only a dramatic acceleration in growth rates after 1950, but grew faster than

the sovereign countries and the dependencies during this period. The weighted average annual growth rate for the colonies was 2.96 percent over 1950 to 1992 compared to -0.08 percent between 1900 and 1950; the growth rates of the sovereign countries and dependencies over 1950 to 1992 were 0.95 and 2.58 percent respectively.

7

Epilogue

*'The day of the oppressed against the oppressor is more severe than
the day of the oppressor against the oppressed'.*

Ali Ibn Abu Talib (7th century CE)[1]

How did industrial epoch *I* come to an end, and what are the characteristics of industrial epoch *II* that has unfolded since?

Industrial epoch *I* is set apart from what went before and after by a singular development: a growing concentration of the world's manufactures in a small number of advanced countries. Orthodox economists have explained this concentration in terms of market forces alone, a parsimonious discourse that excludes politics from the global economy. In their obsession with ideally free global markets, the orthodox economists forgot to ask *how* global markets were created, and whether they *were* really free? These questions would have led ineluctably, as we have shown, to the incorporation of states into the analysis of the global economy.

The global concentration of manufactures was produced not by market forces *per se*, nor by market forces alone. These market forces were shaped–advanced in some places and constrained in others–by the deployment of power: the kind that flows from the barrel of a gun. The advanced countries used their superior power to *re*arrange the markets of lagging countries to create the greatest advantage for their *own* capital, labor and enterprises. Their first preference was to convert the lagging countries into colonies; this would ensure direct control over policies in these countries. There were, however, limits to what the advanced countries could do with their superior power. There were several historical forces, working through racial and cultural affinities, which ensured that Latin America and Europe would remain off limits to the colonial ambitions of the great powers. Countries in Africa and Asia were less fortunate: and nearly all of them were colonized or converted into quasi-colonies. This single difference had a seminal impact on the evolution of the global economy during industrial epoch *I*.

The Changing Spatial Distribution of Manufactures

First, consider the evidence on the concentration of manufactures during industrial epoch *I* and its reversal starting in the early 1950s.

The concentration of manufactures is best examined in terms of the share of global manufactures produced by the big four advanced countries: Britain, United States, Germany and France. There is no evidence of a concentration of manufacturing output in the big four in 1750. It may be seen from table 7.1 that they produced 8.9 percent of world manufacturing output, only marginally higher than their share of 7.1 percent in world population. Over the next fifty years their share rose to 12.8 percent, but the most dramatic increase came between 1800 and 1860, when their share more than tripled to 39.9 percent. The concentration appears to have peaked at 66.5 percent in 1913, falling back modestly to 62.2 percent in 1953.[2] A reversal in this concentration is also clear, beginning in the 1950s. The decline was quite steep between 1953 and 1963, when the share of the big four went down from 62.2 percent to 51.7 percent. This was followed by a slower decline, with the share going down to 47.3 percent in 1973 and 44.1 percent in 1980.

Similar trends may be observed at a more aggregate level, *viz.* that of all developed countries.[3] In 1750, the developed countries had 23 percent of the world population and 27 percent of the world's output of manufactures, but this share had escalated to 92.5 percent in 1913, and to a slightly higher level of 93.5 percent in 1953. Since then it has declined modestly to 88.0 percent in 1980. However, concentration within the group of developed countries has declined more dramatically since 1953. The Gini coefficient of concentration was 0.43 in 1953 and 0.29 in 1980.[4]

The changing spatial distribution of manufactures may also be tracked relative to Britain, the pioneer industrial country, and its successor, United States. Britain's share in world manufacturing output increased more than twelve-fold from 1.9 percent in 1750 to a peak of 22.9 percent in 1880, after which it went into an irreversible decline, and was down to 4.0 percent in 1980. The growth in the share of United States was even more dramatic; its global share increased 40 fold between 1800 and 1913, reached a peak of 44.7 percent in 1953 but has declined steadily since then, with a share of 31.5 percent in 1980.

It may be useful to examine this process in obverse, in terms of the shares of lagging countries in world manufacturing output.[5] These countries had a share of 73 percent in 1750, roughly in keeping with their share in world population, but this had declined to 36.6 percent in 1860, 7.5 percent in 1913, and an even lower 6.5 percent in 1953. The declining trend in the share of lagging countries was reversed in the 1950s, and had slowly risen to 12 percent in 1980. This trend has persisted with significantly more rapid growth of manufactures in several large lagging countries than in the advanced countries. Between 1980 and 1990, the manu-

Table 7.1
Shares of Advanced and Lagging Countries in
World Manufacturing Output

Year	Big-Four	Britain	United States	Developed Countries	Lagging Countries
1750	8.9	1.9	0.1	27.0	73.0
1800	12.8	4.3	0.8	32.3	67.7
1860	39.9	19.9	7.2	63.4	36.6
1913	66.5	13.6	32.0	92.5	7.5
1953	62.2	8.4	44.7	93.5	6.5
1963	51.7	6.4	35.1	91.5	8.5
1973	47.3	4.9	33.0	90.1	9.9
1980	44.1	4.0	31.5	88.0	12.0

Source: Bairoch (1982: 296, 304)

facturing sector in thirteen industrial lagging countries grew at an average annual rate of 6.9 per cent, compared to a growth rate of 5.8 percent for Japan and an average growth rate of 2.0 percent for six advanced countries.[6] As a result, the share of all lagging countries in world manufacturing output, estimated in current dollars, stood at 28.1 percent in 1995.[7]

The spatial concentration was even more dramatic in some key manufactures; although the evidence for this is indirect. The gap in productivity per capita between Britain and the lagging countries in iron was already 29 to one in 1830 and had exploded to 1081.5 in 1881. United States had a lead of 897.3 in 1910, Germany of 662.3 and France of 344.3. In 1910, the productivity gap in cement was 211 to one for Britain, 587 for Germany, 448 for Belgium, and 433 for United States. The productivity differentials in 1910 were considerably smaller for cotton yarn, at 44 to one between Britain and the Third World, and 27 to one for United States.[8] These comparisons suggest that the degree of geographical concentration was much greater in the heavy industries.

We have argued in this book that the primary cause of the growing concentration of manufactures during industrial epoch *I* was unequal power amongst states which, in turn, gave rise to colonial policies which retarded industrialization in the quasi-colonies and colonies. Attention may be drawn here to factors, not considered before, which may have helped to accentuate this concentration. One such factor was lagging wages in the leading industrialized countries. Wages in capitalist manufacturing, so Lewis (1954) has taught us, are generally determined by subsistence wages, and these do not begin to rise until the pool of surplus labor begins to disappear, thus creating a tight labor market. Of course, manufacturing wages also depend upon the ability of urban workers to engage in collective action, and this too takes time to develop. The fallout of all this was that wages in the leading industrial countries during the first half of the nineteenth century rose little while productivity continued to expand, sometimes very rapidly, giving to these countries a crushing competitive advantage in several branches of manufactures.

A second conditioning factor was the relatively modest volume of world demand for manufactures during the nineteenth century. Not only was global per capita income quite low around 1800, but given the very unequal spread of economic growth, this rose very slowly throughout most of the nineteenth century. At these low levels, not much more than a tenth of family incomes is spent on manufactures, ensuring that the volume of demand for manufactures, as well as its growth, would be quite modest for a long time to come. When combined with the enormous increases in labor productivity in some of the key branches of manufacturing, this meant that much of the growth in this demand could be met by a small number of advanced countries. Thus, with two percent of the world's population in 1830, Britain used her competitive edge and access to global markets to capture 40-50 percent of the world's output in modern manufactures.[9]

A third factor that extended the spatial concentration of manufactures was the entry of United States into the industrial race. Britain and France had reached their peak shares in world manufacturing output in 1880 and Germany in 1914. But their declining shares were more than compensated by industrialization in United States whose share of manufacturing output continued to grow both because of a faster growth in productivity and a faster growth of population sustained by high levels of immigration. Between 1840 and 1914, United States admitted 24 million immigrants, more than half of them in the fifteen years before the first world war; this was more than a quarter of the natural increase in population during this period.[10] In turn, immigration increased the natural growth of population since a high proportion of immigrants were young. Between 1850 and 1950, the population of United States had increased more than six fold, from 23.3 million to 152.3 million.[11] It is doubtful that United States could have increased its share of global manufacturing from 2.4 percent in 1820 to 44.7 percent in 1953 without this extraordinary increase in its population.[12] Had population growth in United States followed the pattern of Britain or Germany, it is unlikely that so large a proportion of world manufactures could have been concentrated in a single country.

Trees do not grow up to the sky; and so the concentration of manufacturing production could not have gone on indefinitely. The growing concentration of manufactures created the conditions for its own reversal, since this concentration eventually led to a growing wage gap between the advanced and lagging countries. For some time, the growing wage gap was more than offset by a faster growth of productivity in manufacturing, so that the advanced countries' comparative advantage in manufactures continued to deepen. But as technologies in the first generation of manufactures matured and their productivity growth slowed down, the advanced countries' cost advantage in these manufactures began to shrink, helped also by the growing ability of some lagging countries to reduce their costs as a result of their growing industrial experience. By protecting their manufactures, most sovereign lagging countries succeeded in accelerating this process of catching up. With a longer lag, a few colonies, in particular India, were able to compete even under free market conditions as their relative wages sank to a point where they acquired competitive advantage in the simplest manufactures such as yarn and cloth. Thus, market forces, with or without the help of industrial policies, worked to shift the comparative advantage in some of the older branches of manufactures to the lagging countries. It was the task of imperialism *I* to delay this process.

In time, the diffusion of manufactures was helped by a growing gap between the world demand for manufactures and the industrial capacity of the advanced countries. The growth in world demand for manufactures was at first quite limited because of low initial levels of global per capita income combined with a slow growth in global population. However, this changed over time, both as economic growth spread to a growing number of sovereign lagging countries and population growth accelerated both in advanced and lagging countries. These developments, combined with a high elasticity of demand for manufactures at lower levels of income, fueled an accelerating growth in world demand for the basic consumer goods. Britain, France and Netherlands were unable to expand their industrial capacity fast enough to meet the growth in world demand, and began to lose market shares in their colonies to United States, Germany and Japan. Rather than lose markets to their rivals, this persuaded the colonial powers to selectively tolerate the emergence of manufactures in some of their colonies.

This shift in colonial policy was most visible during the second great war. Not only did the war disrupt the ability of the great powers to export manufactures, it was also destroying their industrial capacity. Under these conditions, manufacturing capital from Britain and France sought safe havens in the Americas as well as the colonies. The colonial powers did not oppose this shift of manufactures to the colonies since they expected these new industries to support their global war effort if things did not go well at home. Japan went further, and even encouraged some of her heavy industries to relocate to Taiwan, Korea and Manchuria both before and during the second great war.

Imperialism *I* too could not be sustained forever. It was plagued with two sets of contradictions, both related to the fact that it operated primarily through the instrument of colonies. The colonies were spheres of monopoly control for the great powers; they discriminated against entry of exports, capital and enterprises from all sources other than the occupying country. These barriers to trade and investments were acceptable only as long as there were new countries to be colonized, or as long as all the great powers owned a 'fair' share of colonies. These conditions had changed towards the beginning of the twentieth century. There were few territories now that remained to be colonized without serious costs. In addition, several countries had entered into the ranks of great powers, but were without substantial colonial empires.[13] These have-nots now had only one choice: grab what they could take from other colonial empires. This was a powerful underlying motive behind two devastating wars amongst the great powers within the space of three decades. Of course, these wars were good news for the lagging countries, and in particular for the quasi-colonies and colonies. The first war led to the communist takeover of Russia, the nemesis of global capitalism over the next seven decades. The second war devastated the economies of the great colonial powers. They were now superseded in the power game by United States and Soviet Union, each committed to dismantling the colonial empires.

Colonialism could not have been sustained much longer even without these wars. In most cases, colonial conquests had been easy, and the military burden of colonial rule was light because most colonized populations did not yet possess a national consciousness, making it easy for colonial armies to draw their manpower from the conquered territories. But nearly everywhere this was changing with the marginalization and racial discrimination that came in the wake of colonialism. In time, as a national consciousness emerged from the experience of deprivation and exploitation, and as an indigenous middle class was slowly reconstituted in the modern sectors of the colonies, the two coalesced to lay the foundations for movements of national liberation. The two world wars spurred these liberation movements by revealing cracks in the imperialist armor: by forcing the colonial powers to enlist large numbers of natives into their armies, and by giving them combat experience. A hundred mutinies and insurrections were now ready to erupt, as they did erupt in India, Egypt, Indonesia, Kenya, Vietnam, and Algeria. The colonial powers were quick to read the writing on the wall. They decided that discretion was the better part of valor, and made plans to shed the colonies before they exploded in their faces. By the early 1960s, imperialism *I* had been formally terminated.

It is not merely coincidental that industrial epoch *I* ended in the years immediately following the second great war. The conditions for the termination of this epoch were slowly being prepared by the deepening polarization it was creating between the advanced and the lagging countries. But its timing was determined by the second great war. While the war was in progress, it created some strong tendencies towards the diffusion of manufactures to the lagging countries. But the strongest impetus towards diffusion flowed from the decentralization of power that followed *after* the end of the war.

A Window of Opportunity

This decentralization of power would not last long, but while it lasted it created a window of opportunity during which several lagging countries succeeded in creating mostly indigenous capitalist economies.

Although the colonial powers sought to preserve their interests in the former colonies, there were limits to what they could arrange. Several countries had gained their independence at a cost, after years of struggle against colonial rule, and determinedly sought to work out an independent course. But even colonies which were granted independence before they could mount an effective struggle for liberation, came to exercise fairly wide powers over their economic policies. They were empowered by the Cold War that soon polarized the world. United States and the former colonial powers were careful not to lean too hard on the newly independent countries, lest they defected to the Soviets.

Most countries in Asia and Africa, by the early 1960s, were free to determine their economic policies, and they lost no time in instituting a variety of policies that would encourage the growth of indigenous manufactures, capital and enterprises.[14] They imposed a system of protective tariffs and overvalued currencies to encourage import substitution in the simpler manufactures; they set up banks to finance an indigenous capitalist class; they invested in roads, railways, ports, and power stations; they boosted school enrolments; they set up technical colleges and universities; they nationalized many foreign-owned firms in mining and manufactures; and they indigenized the public services. All this would have been unthinkable under colonialism.

Import substitution of simple consumer goods never failed to work; it was failproof. Given sufficiently high protection, domestic production could always be set up to displace imported manufactures. But this industrialization also quickly ran out of steam. Once the simple consumer imports had been replaced, industrialization could only be sustained by breaking into world markets for manufactures, or extending import substitution to intermediate goods, consumer durables and capital goods. A few countries in East and Southeast Asia broke into world markets; their success was spectacular because few lagging countries chose this option. The deepening of import substitution looked promising only in the larger countries which also had a base of industrial skills. Nevertheless, many lagging countries chose this option by default. If you could not break into export markets for manufactures, the alternative was to deepen import substitution, and finance the growing trade and savings deficits with official loans from the advanced countries. This would turn out to be a trap for many countries. Industrialization was easy to start; for most, it would prove harder to sustain.

Nevertheless, taken together, these efforts at industrialization were sufficient to inaugurate industrial epoch *II* which reversed the earlier trend towards concentration of manufactures in a small number of advanced countries. In time, this would change the dynamics of the global economy. During industrial epoch *I* capital from advanced countries showed little inclination to industrialize the lagging countries; they moved into lagging countries to build railways or to process bulky or perishable raw materials, motivated by the savings in transportation costs. This changed when the lagging countries began to exclude manufactured imports, persuading foreign corporations to jump the import barriers. More importantly, over time, import substitution created nascent industrial bases in several lagging countries which soon began to penetrate the markets of advanced countries with their own exports. Threatened in their home markets, many labor-intensive manufactures in advanced countries began relocating their operations to the lagging countries. This is what injected a new dynamic into the global economy.

The former colonies and quasi-colonies (*QCC*) were also asserting their sovereignty in their primary export sectors. In most colonies, the best lands, mines and oil wells belonged to foreigners. This was not always acceptable to the nationalists who replaced the colonial rulers. Their independence had to be translated quickly into economic gains for the indigenous population, lest they began to dream of more radical solutions. This resulted in waves of nationalization and expropriation, complemented by parallel waves of Indigenization and, occasionally, expulsion of ethnic minorities. The most spectacular victories were scored by a cartel of Oil Producing and Exporting Countries (*OPEC*), consisting mostly of countries in the Middle East and North Africa, who engineered a quadrupling of crude oil prices in 1973. This emboldened other countries to think that they too could get more for their raw materials. Many of the lagging countries in the United Nations banded together and began to make raucous demands for a New International Economic Order (*NIEO*).

Imperialism *II*

It was now time to close the window of opportunity on the lagging countries; it had stayed open too long. There was growing concern in the advanced countries over the challenges to their long-held positions in the global economy. challenges that emanated from the diffusion of manufactures to lagging countries, the attempts of other lagging countries to gain control over their primary exports, and a growing crescendo of demands for a more equitable international order. It was clear that the diffusion of manufactures that was already in motion was irreversible. The point was not to stop or reverse this process, but to gain control over it: to direct, appropriate and, when necessary, delay it. The concern was not so much about industrialization *per se* but the fact that this was largely in the hands of independent national bourgeoisie that had emerged under Listian strategies of growth which favored indigenous capital and enterprises.

The advanced countries' capital and labor developed three responses to the growing diffusion of manufactures to lagging countries Both tried harder to keep out manufactured exports from lagging countries; since tariffs were banned by *GATT*, invisible barriers to trade began to proliferate. They demanded higher labor and environmental standards in the lagging countries, as well as stricter enforcement of their intellectual property rights. These strategies could only buy time. Capital's long-term solution lay in relocation to lagging countries, an option that looked more attractive with the growing ability of multinationals to organize global production, facilitated by advances in communications technology and growing knowledge about labor markets in lagging countries. Capital also had the option of moving out of manufacturing and into high value-added services where they still retained a strong comparative advantage. These strategies would work only if they could move freely into and out of lagging countries. In turn, as capital began to move out of the advanced countries, organized labor redoubled their efforts to export their own labor and environmental standards to lagging countries.

In the meanwhile, the tide was turning against lagging countries on several fronts. With a quick recovery from war damages, followed by two decades of unprecedented growth, the advanced countries had acquired a stronger lead over most lagging countries than they had before the war. They now had the resources and the confidence to try to gain back the ground they had lost in the world economy. Cold war concerns were on the wane. The Chinese and Soviets were at odds. The policy of containment had worked well. The Soviets had made few significant gains since the 1950s; their economy had begun to show signs of trouble; and their occupation of Afghanistan had run into serious trouble. More ominously, the two oil crises had forced many oil-importing lagging countries to run deep foreign debts to keep their growth engines running. When the advanced countries went into recession in 1981, and interest rates escalated, many of these countries stared at bankruptcy. The *IMF*, World Bank, the United States Agency for International Development (*USAID*) and other regional agencies, rose to the occasion, offering to bail them out at a price. One after another, these debt-ridden economies would have to eat the humble pie, and accept programs of 'stabilization' and 'structural adjustment', euphemisms for smaller governments, privatization and liberalization. Without a shot being fired, imperialism *II* had arrived.

The intellectual underpinnings for imperialism *II* had been in preparation for some time. The fundamental thesis of the early development economists, that market failures are more serious in lagging countries and require government interventions, came under concerted attack during the 1970s, mostly from studies sponsored by advanced countries, and well before the lagging countries had run into any serious trouble. This began with a series of country studies funded by the Organization for Economic Cooperation and Development (*OECD*) on import substitution policies; the compendious gloss on these studies was written by Little, Scitovsky and Scott (1970). The National Bureau of Economic Research (*NBER*) followed this up with another series of country studies whose results were summarized in two separate volumes by Bhagwati (1978) and Krueger (1978). At about the same time, a third set of country studies was undertaken by the Institut fur Weltwirtschaft in West Germany.[15] Not to be left out of the loop, the World Bank sponsored its own studies under the leadership of Balassa (1982).[16] The primary thesis of these studies was that by distorting market prices, import substituting policies were retarding growth in lagging countries, and that "getting prices right" would free their economies for more rapid growth. All these studies appropriated Taiwan, South Korea, Singapore and Hong Kong as neoclassical successes: they had grown faster because they had moved away from distortionary policies.[17] These claims were seriously and, we believe, successfully contested by several economists working without the support or financial backing of institutional sponsors.[18]

Slowly but inevitably, the results of this research program were mobilized by United States, the *OECD*, and the two leading multilateral economic agencies, the World Bank and the *IMF*, to press the lagging countries for structural adjustments in exchange for loans. At first, these programs were modest, and were aimed primarily at reforming import quotas, excessive tariffs, multiple exchange rates, and direct controls on markets. However, as the successive oil crises of 1973 and 1979 and the recession in advanced countries made it increasingly difficult for many lagging countries to service their foreign debts, the World Bank and *IMF* used their growing financial leverage over the debt-ridden countries to expand the definition of structural adjustments to include the elimination of fiscal deficits, privatization of public enterprises, removal of state subsidies, removal of controls on capital accounts of the balance of payments, elimination of barriers to entry of foreign enterprises, the opening up of government contracts to foreign firms, and the reform of trade policies to bring them close to a free trade regime.[19] The emergence of a consensus on these matters amongst the major Washington players was first noted by Williamson (1994, 1996) as early as 1989 who, appropriately, dubbed it the 'Washington consensus'. Washington *et al.* were now determined to recreate the economies of lagging countries according to the mantras of one-size-fits-all economics. What was good for United States would henceforth be good for Mali, Mauritania and Madagascar.

The shift of power back to the advanced countries was sealed by the collapse of Soviet Union; it was the last nail in the coffin. This had two damaging consequences for the lagging countries. It was used as damning evidence in the case against state-ownership and economic planning. More importantly, the demise of Soviet Union had orphaned the lagging countries: they had lost the most powerful counterweight to United States. The sovereignty which they had wielded after independence was partly illusory, since it was backed by another outside power. The Gulf War signaled the arrival of the new world order without the Soviets. Power would now emanate from Washington alone.

How has imperialism *II* affected the prospects for growth in lagging countries? In the first three decades following the second great war, the lagging countries structured their economic relations with the world economy to protect their manufactures from imports and their indigenous capital from multinational corporations. Taken together, these policies gave the lagging countries a new and, in some cases, a growing leverage over foreign capital. Faced with loss of their markets abroad and at home, a growing number of producers in advanced countries were eager to relocate production to the lagging countries. This would endow some lagging countries with the power to affect the terms under which foreign capital entered their markets. They used this power to acquire technology and entry into the markets of advanced countries.

Imperialism *II* seeks to re-integrate the lagging countries into the world economy. Increasingly, lagging countries are being forced to dismantle policy regimes which gave protection to their manufactures and indigenous capital. This represents an attempt to create a global economy that will be more open than it had ever been before. During industrial epoch *I* only the quasi-colonies and colonies were fully integrated into the economies of the advanced countries; nearly all sovereign countries were free to structure their relations with the global economy. Imperialism *II* embraces all lagging countries.

It is not clear how, on balance, these changes will affect the prospects for growth in the most industrialized lagging countries. On the one hand, those industries which have already attained global competitiveness will benefit as barriers to trade are lowered both in the advanced and lagging countries. On the other hand, re-integration will dilute their ability to promote selective import substitution in the more advanced industries, and thus will delay their transition to more advanced industries. Further, when these industries are developed they are likely to be penetrated by foreign corporations, working on their own or in collaboration with indigenous firms. More importantly, foreign capital is likely to displace indigenous capital in the high value-added service activities, including finance, consultant, advertising and marketing, making it difficult for indigenous firms to reach the size and strength necessary to launch themselves in world markets. Finally, the liberalization of their financial markets makes them vulnerable to currency crises which, by devaluing their currencies and forcing bankruptcies, may lead to rapid and large-scale denationalization of their capital.

The second tier of industrializing countries, with a weaker technological and financial base, will be more vulnerable to import competition and foreign capital. Import competition will almost certainly shut down many of their inefficient industries, especially those producing intermediate and capital goods. At the same time, under the threat of competition, some of these industries may be forced to reorganize, rationalize their operations, modernize their technology, thus creating the nucleus of an efficient indigenous manufacturing sector. The prospects for economic growth in these countries will depend on their ability to attract foreign capital into their manufacturing sector. In turn, this depends on whether they can provide good governance, cheap skills, roads, communications and utilities–necessary for serving as production platforms for global capital. In their eagerness to modernize their infrastructure, they will show increasing willingness to sell their utilities, highways, ports, and telephones to foreign interests. Provided they can modernize their infrastructure, these countries are likely to be superior to the colonial economies which specialized in primary production. These economies are capable of cumulative growth; since they provide both unskilled and skilled labor, the indigenous population can increase their share in these economies. The downside to these economies is that their success may be difficult to sustain, since success will raise wages, reducing their competitiveness as production platforms. Thus, unless they can upgrade their skills they face the risk of being abandoned for cheaper production sites in lower-wage lagging countries.

The re-integration of lagging countries without an industrial base and only modest savings is likely to re-create the erstwhile colonial economies. This will shut down their few industries; their mining, large-scale farms, utilities, financial sector, and international trade will pass into foreign hands; and their debts will continue to mount. Worse, without labor skills and an appropriate infrastructure, it is unlikely that they will serve as production platforms for foreign capital; and without protection and domestic savings, they cannot create the labor skills and infrastructure that will attract foreign capital. Most likely, these economies will be locked into primary production in a global economy where primary goods are even more vulnerable than they were during industrial epoch *I* to adverse movements in terms of trade. Industrialization in these countries may have to wait until their wage advantage deepens, diverting manufactures from other lagging countries where wages have risen. Or, they may have to wait until a new crisis in global capitalism opens another window of opportunity for the lagging countries. It could be a long wait.

Notes

1   Cleary (1996: 45).
2   Most of this phenomenal growth in the share of world manufacturing output, from under a tenth to two-thirds, between 1750 and 1913 was due to growth of per capita output; the combined share of the big four in world population had risen from around 7 to 13 percent over this period (Maddison 1995: 104-107, 226-27).
3   The 'developed' countries include all of Europe, United States, Canada, Australia, New Zealand, South Africa and Japan; all others are lagging countries.
4   Bairoch (1982: 303).
5   Lagging countries include Asia *minus* Japan, Africa *minus* South Africa and the Americas *minus* United States and Canada.
6   The thirteen lagging countries are: Argentina, Brazil, Chile, China, India, Indonesia, Korea, Malaysia, Mexico, Singapore, Taiwan, Thailand and Tur-

key; the six advanced countries are Canada, France, Germany, Italy, UK and USA (Amsden 1997).

7 The 1995 estimate is derived from World Bank (1997). These numbers are not directly comparable to Bairoch's (1982) estimate of a share of 12.0 percent in 1980. Bairoch's estimates are in international dollars; the estimate for 1995 is in current dollars (using exchange rate conversions).

8 Bairoch (1991: 8, 10).

9 Crouzet (1982: 4-5).

10 Hughes (1990: 307).

11 Maddison (1995: 106-107).

12 On an alternative reading of the evidence, it would appear that United States' share increased up to 1928, when it was 39.3 percent, declining to 31.4 percent in 1938. Most likely, the dramatic rise to 44.7 percent in 1953 was due, at least in part, to the damage inflicted by war on the manufacturing capacity of Britain, Germany, Japan and France.

13 At the beginning of the twentieth century, United States, Germany, Japan and Italy had either attained, or were seeking, entry into the ranks of great powers; none of them had substantial colonial possessions.

14 Most of the sovereign lagging countries in Latin America and Europe had initiated this process at various dates during the nineteenth century; the entry of Africa and Asia was significant because these regions contained some two-thirds of the world's population.

15 Donges and Riedel (1977).

16 Other country studies were sponsored in the 1980s. See Michaely, Papageorgiou and Choksi (1991).

17 Regression analysis was also employed to demonstrate the superiority of export-oriented regimes over import-substitution regimes (Edwards 1993).

18 Amsden (1989), Alam (1989) and Wade (1990).

19 To ensure compliance with these demands, in a manner reminiscent of the nineteenth century, lagging countries were forced to accept officials from the *IMF* to ensure accurate monitoring of their financial accounts.

Appendix

Table 1
List of Variables and Data Sources

Description of Variables	Sources of Data
Dependent Variables	
Adult Literacy Rates: 1935	Eisenstadt and Rokkan (1973: 245-47).
Adult literacy rates: 1960	World Bank, *World Development Report* (1980); Norton Ginsburg, (1961).
Adult literacy rates: 1980	World Bank, *World Development Report* (1983).
Average Years of schooling: 1960, 1980	Nehru *et al.* (1995).
Average years of schooling: 1965	Kyriacou (1991).
Level of industrialization: 1960	World Bank, *World Development Report* (1980).
Level of industrialization: 1980	World Bank, *World Development Report* (1982).
Export orientation: 1960	World Bank, *World Development Report* (1980).
Growth rates of GDP	Maddison (1995: 23-24).
Independent Variables	
Description of Variables	**Sources of Data**
Per capita income	Summers *et al.*, *Penn World Table* (Mark 5.6) (1995).
Population	Summers *et al.*, *Penn World Table* (Mark 5.6) (1995).
Total area	*Oxford World Atlas* (1993)
Oil producing countries	Algeria, Gabon, Iran, Iraq, Saudi Arabia, Trinidad and Tobago and Venezuela
Percent population Christian: 1970	Barrett (1982).
Percent population Muslim: 1970	Barrett (1982)
Price level of GDP: 1960	Summers *et al.*, *Penn World Table* (Mark 5.6) (1995).

181

Table 1 (continued)
List of Variables and Data Sources

Description of Variable	Sources of Data
Investment Ratio: 1960	Summers *et al.*, *Penn world table* (Mark 5.6) (1995).
Openness [(Exports + Imports)/GDP]: 1960	Summers *et al.*, *Penn world table* (Mark 5.6) (1995).
Coastline	CIA, *The world factbook, 1992*
Dates of colonization	Kurian (1982) and *Encyclopedia Brittanica*
Dates of independence	Taylor and Hudson (1972) and CIA (1992)

Table 2
Samples Countries in Regressions

	Countries	EXP-1960	MFG-1960	LIT-1960	YS-60	YS-65
		Sovereign Countries				
1	Bolivia	*	*	*	*	*
2	Brazil	*	*	*	*	*
3	Chile	*	*	*	*	*
4	Colombia	*	*	*	*	*
5	Czechoslovakia		*	*		
6	Ecuador	*	*	*	*	*
7	Finland	*	*	*	*	
8	Greece	*	*	*	*	*
9	Italy	*	*	*	*	*
10	Japan	*	*	*	*	*
11	Mexico	*	*	*	*	
12	Norway	*	*	*	*	
13	Paraguay	*	*	*	*	*
14	Peru	*	*	*	*	*
15	Portugal	*	*	*	*	*
16	S. Africa	*	*	*		
17	Spain	*	*	*	*	*
18	Uruguay	*	*		*	*
19	USSR		*	*		
20	Venezuela	*	*	*	*	*
21	Yugoslavia	*	*	*		
	Total	19	21	20	17	15

Table 2 (continued)
Samples Countries in Regressions

	Countries	EXP-60	MFG-1960	LIT-1960	YS-60	YS-65
		Dependencies				
1	Costa Rica	*	*		*	*
2	Dominican Rep.	*	*	*		*
3	El Salvador	*	*	*	*	*
4	Guatemala	*	*	*	*	*
5	Haiti	*	*	*	*	*
6	Honduras	*	*	*	*	*
7	Nicaragua		*			*
8	Panama	*	*	*	*	*
	Total	7	8	6	6	8
		Quasi-Colonies				
1	China	*		*	*	
2	Egypt	*	*	*	*	
3	Ethiopia	*	*		*	
4	Iran	*	*	*	*	*
5	Iraq	*	*	*	*	*
6	Liberia	*	*	*		*
7	Nepal		*	*		
8	Saudi Arabia		*	*		
9	Thailand	*	*	*	*	*
10	Turkey	*	*	*	*	*
	Total	8	9	9	7	5
		NICs				
1	Bangladesh	*	*	*	*	
2	Myanmar	*	*	*	*	
3	India	*	*	*	*	*
4	Indonesia	*	*	*	*	
5	Israel	*	*	*	*	*
6	Jordan		*	*	*	*
7	Pakistan	*	*	*	*	*
8	Philippines	*	*	*	*	
9	S. Korea	*	*	*	*	*
10	Sri Lanka	*	*	*	*	
11	Syria		*	*		*
12	Taiwan	*				
	Total	9	12	11	10	6

Table 2 (continued)
Samples Countries in Regressions

	Countries	EXP-60	MFG-1960	LIT-1960	YS-60	YS-65
			Colonies			
1	Algeria	*	*	*	*	*
2	Angola	*	*	*	*	
3	Barbados	*	*	*		
4	Benin	*	*	*		
5	Botswana	*	*	*		*
6	Burkina Faso	*	*	*		
7	Burundi	*		*		
8	Cameroon			*	*	*
9	Central Afr. Rep.	*	*	*		*
10	Chad	*	*	*		*
11	Congo	*	*	*		
12	Cyprus		*			
13	Fiji	*				*
14	Gabon	*	*	*		*
15	Gambia	*	*	*		
16	Ghana	*	*	*	*	*
17	Guinea		*	*		
18	Guinea Bissau					*
19	Guyana		*			
20	Hong Kong	*	*	*		
21	Ivory Coast	*	*	*	*	*
22	Jamaica	*	*	*	*	*
23	Kenya	*	*	*	*	
24	Lesotho	*				*
25	Madagascar	*	*		*	*
26	Malawi	*	*		*	*
27	Malaysia	*	*	*	*	*
28	Mali	*	*	*	*	*
29	Malta	*	*	*		
30	Mauritania	*	*	*		
31	Mauritius		*		*	*
32	Morocco	*	*	*	*	*
33	Mozambique	*	*	*	*	*
34	Niger	*	*	*		*
35	Nigeria	*	*	*	*	*
36	Papua N. Guinea	*	*	*		
37	Rwanda	*	*	*	*	*
38	Senegal	*	*	*	*	*
39	Singapore	*	*		*	

Table 2 (continued)
Samples Countries in Regressions

		EXP-60	MFG-60	LIT-60	YS-60	YS-65
40	Somalia	*	*	*		*
41	Surinam	*	*	*		
42	Swaziland	*	*			*
43	Tanzania	*	*	*	*	*
44	Togo	*	*	*		*
45	Trin. & Tobago	*	*	*		*
46	Tunisia	*	*	*	ı	*
47	Uganda	*	*	*	*	*
4Y	Σaire	*	*	*	*	
49	Zambia	*	*	*	*	*
50	Zimbabwe		*	*	*	
	Total	43	45	40	24	31
	All Countries	86	95	86	64	65

Table 3
Sensitivity Analysis:
Sovereignty Differentials for Growth Rates of *PCI*, 1900-1950

Sov. Dummies/ Base Categories	Sovereignty Differentials			Robust/ Fragile
	High	Base	Low	
(N=40)				
SOV/QCC	1.60**	1.35**	1.43**	Robust**
DEP/QCC	0.64*	0.73*	0.64*	Robust*
SOV/DEP-QCC	1.37**	1.07**	1.15**	Robust**
SOV-DEP/QCC	1.22**	1.16**	1.15**	Robust**
(N=37)				
SOV/QCC	1.80**	1.61**	1.65**	Robust**
DEP/QCC	0.95**	0.96**	0.87**	Robust**
SOV/DEP-QCC	1.45**	1.17**	1.24**	Robust**
SOV-DEP/QCC	1.44**	1.40**	1.38**	Robust**

Table 3 (continued)
Sensitivity Analysis:
Sovereignty Differentials for Growth Rates of *PCI*, 1900-1950

Sov. Dummies/ Base Categories	Sovereignty Differentials			Robust/ Fragile
	High	Base	Low	
(N=34)				
SOV/QCC	1.97**	1.77**	1.84**	Robust**
DEP/QCC	1.17**	1.19**	1.01**	Robust**
SOV/DEP-QCC	1.56**	1.20**	1.30**	Robust**
SOV-DEP/QCC	1.63**	1.60**	1.60**	Robust**
(N=27)				
SOV/QCC	2.18**	1.87**	2.02**	Robust**
DEP/QCC	0.93*	1.03*	0.84*	Robust*
SOV/DEP-QCC	1.89**	1.42**	1.66**	Robust**
SOV-DEP/QCC	1.69**	1.66**	1.68**	Robust**

(*I*-variable = Per capita income)

Table 4
Comparing Sovereignty Differentials in Industrialization
for Large and Small Countries: 1960 and 1980

Category I	Category II	SD: I over II (*% points*)	MFG in II (% GDP)	$\bar{R}^2$	F
	Large Countries (more than 5 million; n=42)				
SOV	COL	19.4*	8.9	0.44	3.9**
	COL- NIC	19.6*	10.9	0.46	4.4**
	COL-NIC-QC	16.9*	11.2	0.46	4.9**
SOV-QC	COL	5.6	8.9	0.34	3.1**
	COL- NIC	5.8	10.9	0.36	3.6**
SOV-QC-NIC	COL	2.5	8.9	0.34	3.4**
	Small Countries (less than 5 million; n=53)				
SOV	COL	7.4**	8.5	0.67	9.9**
	COL- NIC	5.3**	9.1	0.64	9.5**
	COL-NIC-QC	5.9**	8.9	0.63	9.8**
	COL-NIC-QC-DEP	3.7*	9.7	0.57	8.6**
SOV-DEP	COL	6.6**	8.5	0.68	10.9**
	COL- NIC	4.8**	9.1	0.65	7.2**
	COL-NIC-QC	5.4**	8.9	0.64	11.1**

Table 4 (continued)
Comparing Sovereignty Differentials in Industrialization
for Large and Small Countries: 1960 and 1980

Category I	Category II	SD: I over II (% points)	MFG in II (% GDP)	R^2	F
SOV-DEP-QC	COL	7.3**	8.5	0.67	11.8**
	COL- NIC	7.1**	9.1	0.68	13.3**
SOV-DEP-QC-NIC	COL	5.0**	8.5	0.61	10.0**

(**),(*) and (+) denote statistical significance at 1, 5 and 10 percent levels.

Table 5
Comparing Sovereignty Differentials in Average Years of Schooling
(AYS) (Kyriacou): Lagging Countries in 1965

Group I	Group II	SD: I over II	AYS in II	R^2	F
All Lagging Countries (n=65)					
SOV	COL	4.4**	1.6	0.76	15.4**
	COL- NIC	3.0**	2.0	0.72	13.5**
	COL-NIC-QC	2.5**	2.1	0.72	14.5**
	COL-NIC-QC-DEP	1.0*	2.2	0.72	15.4**
SOV-DEP	COL	4.1**	1.6	0.75	15.6**
	COL- NIC	2.7**	2.0	0.71	13.9**
	COL-NIC-QC	2.3+	2.1	0.71	15.1**
SOV-DEP-QC	COL	1.9*	1.6	0.73	15.4**
	COL- NIC	1.1	2.0	0.69	14.5**
SOV-DEP-QC-NIC	COL	1.6**	1.6	0.73	17.0**
All Lagging Countries *minus* Sub-Saharan Africa (n=41)					
SOV	COL	2.7**	3.7	0.64	6.1**
	COL- NIC	2.2**	3.6	0.65	6.6**
	COL-NIC-QC	2.2**	3.4	0.66	7.4**
	COL-NIC-QC-DEP	0.8+	3.2	0.65	7.8**
SOV-DEP	COL	2.4**	3.7	0.63	6.3**
	COL- NIC	1.9**	3.6	0.63	6.3**
	COL-NIC-QC	2.0**	3.4	0.65	7.7**
SOV-DEP-QC	COL	0.6	3.7	0.61	6.2**
	COL- NIC	0.3	3.6	0.62	6.9**
SOV-DEP-QC-NIC	COL	0.5	3.7	0.62	7.0**

Table 5 (continued)
Comparing Sovereignty Differentials in Average Years of Schooling (AYS) (Kyriacou): Lagging Countries in 1965

	All Lagging Countries: New Results with Dummy for AFR				
Group I	Group II	SD: I over II	AYS in II	$\bar{R}^2$	F
SOV	COL	3.1**	1.6	0.79	17.3**
	COL- NIC	2.4**	2.0	0.79	18.3**
	COL-NIC-QC	2.1**	2.1	0.79	19.8**
	COL-NIC-QC-DEP	1.0*	2.2	0.79	21.1**
SOV-DEP	COL	2.9**	1.6	0.78	17.4**
	COL- NIC	2.2**	2.0	0.78	18.6**
	COL-NIC-QC	1.8**	2.1	0.78	20.2**
SOV-DEP-QC	COL	0.5	1.6	0.77	17.8**
	COL- NIC	0.8	2.0	0.77	19.4**
SOV-DEP-QC-NIC	COL	0.6	1.6	0.77	19.2**

(**),(*) and (+) denote statistical significance at 1, 5 and 10 percent levels.

Table 6
Average Annual Growth Rates of *Per Capita Income*: 1870-1992

	Country	1870-1900	1900-1913	1913-1950	1900-1950	1950-1992
				Sovereign		
1	Finland	1.27	1.79	1.89	1.87	3.01
2	Italy	0.5	2.78	0.84	1.35	3.70
3	Canada	1.77	3.20	1.39	1.88	2.25
4	Sweden	1.44	1.46	2.10	1.93	2.19
5	Ireland	1.14	0.70	0.68	0.69	2.86
6	Norway	1.01	1.97	2.11	2.07	3.00
7	Greece	(.)	(.)	0.05	(.)	3.96
8	Portugal	0.87	-0.30	1.23	0.83	3.93
9	Spain	1.31	0.77	0.17	0.32	3.93
10	Bulgaria	(.)	(.)	0.2	(.)	2.14
11	Czech.	1.32	1.48	1.39	1.41	1.60
12	Hungary	0.94	1.70	0.45	0.78	1.96
13	USSR	0.58	1.54	1.74	1.69	1.19
14	Yugoslavia	(.)	(.)	1.10	(.)	2.20
15	Brazil	-0.17	1.35	1.87	1.73	2.43
16	Chile	(.)	2.37	0.58	1.05	1.52
17	Columbia	(.)	2.13	1.41	1.60	2.09
18	Mexico	1.63	1.83	0.95	1.18	2.14
19	Peru	(.)	1.83	2.10	2.04	0.55

Table 6 (continued)
Average Annual Growth Rates of *Per Capita Income*: 1870-1992

Country	1870-1900	1900-1913	1913-1950	1900-1950	1950-1992
		Sovereign			
20 Venezuela	(.)	2.28	5.15	4.40	0.50
21 Japan	1.42	1.24	0.92	1.00	5.57
22 S. Africa	(.)	(.)	1.19	(.)	1.02
Wt. Average	**1.00**	**1.61**	**1.34**	**1.43**	**2.58**
% World Pop.	17.0	19.9	22.5	19.9	22.1
Dependencies			1930-1950		1950-1990
1 Costa Rica	(.)	(.)	0.90		1.72
2 El Salvador	(.)	(.)	1.70		0.63
3 Guatemala	(.)	(.)	1.07		0.96
4 Honduras	(.)	(.)	0.10		0.94
5 Nicaragua	(.)	(.)	0.40		0.90
Wt. Average			**0.96**		**0.95**
% World Pop.			0.22		0.32
Colonies & Q-Colonies	1870-1900	1900-1913	1913-1950	1900-1950	1950-1992
1 Egypt	(.)	-0.01	0.05	0.03	3.13
2 Turkey	(.)	(.)	0.76	(.)	2.92
3 Thailand	0.42	0.30	0.01	0.09	4.07
4 Ghana	(.)	2.6	1.65	1.90	-0.40
5 Bangladesh	(.)	0.46	-0.3	-0.11	0.64
6 Pakistan	(.)	0.45	-0.31	-0.11	2.21
7 India	0.38	0.45	-0.28	-0.09	1.94
8 Myanmar	(.)	-0.16	-1.30	-0.99	1.53
9 Indonesia	0.42	1.60	-0.13	0.32	2.73
10 China	0.73	0.41	-0.31	-0.12	3.85
11 Philippines	(.)	2.44	-0.25	0.45	1.28
12 South Korea	(.)	0.83	-0.21	0.06	5.80
13 Taiwan	(.)	0.34	0.40	0.39	6.03
Wt. Average	**0.59**	**0.50**	**-0.27**	**-0.08**	**2.96**
% World Pop.	48	50	49	50	48

Countries with PCI less than 66 percent of US PCI in 1900; weights in weighted averages are population in initial year of growth period. (.) denotes data not available

References

Abramovitz, Moses, "Catching up, forging ahead, and falling behind," *Journal of Economic History* 46, 2 (June 1986): 385-406.

Abu-Lughod, Janet, *Before European hegemony: The world system AD 1250-1350* (New York: Oxford University Press, 1989).

Alam, M. Shahid, "Sovereignty differentials and economic growth: 1900-1950," in: John Adams and Francesca Pigliaru, eds., *Economic growth and change: Comparative perspectives* (Aldershot: Elgar, 1999).

Alam, M. Shahid, Why isn't the whole world industrialized? The contribution of imperialism (Boston: Department of Economics, Northeastern University, mimeo, November 1996a).

Alam, M. Shahid, Sovereignty and human capital formation: An empirical study of historical links (Boston: Department of Economics, Northeastern University, mimeo, 1996b).

Alam, M. Shahid, "Colonialism, decolonization and growth rates: Theory and empirical evidence," *Cambridge Journal of Economics* 18 (June 1994): 235-257.

Alam, M. Shahid, *Governments and markets in economic development strategies: Lessons from Korea, Taiwan and Japan* (New York: Praeger, 1989).

Alam, M. Shahid, "Capital decumulation and trade expansion: A theory of colonial trade, *Bangladesh Development Studies* (Monsoon 1980): 29-38.

Amin, Samir, *Delinking: Towards a polycentric world* (London: Zed Books, 1990).

Amin, Samir, *Eurocentrism* (New York: Monthly Review Press, 1989).

Amin, Samir, "Underdevelopment and dependency in black Africa," *Journal of Modern African Studies* 10, 4 (December 1972): 503-24.

Amin, Samir, *Accumulation on a world scale* (New York: Monthly Review Press, 1970 [1974]).

Amsden, Alice, "Editorial: Bringing production back in–Understanding government's economic role in late industrialization," *World Development* 25, 4 (April 1997): 469-480.

Amsden, Alice, *Asia's next giant: South Korea and late industrialization* (New York: Oxford University Press, 1989).

Aroian, Lois A. and Richard P. Mitchell, *The modern Middle East and North Africa* (New York and London: Macmillan and Collier Macmillan, 1984).

Asad, Muhammad, *Principles of state and government in Islam* (Gibraltar: Al-Andalus, 1993).

Avineri, Shlomo, *Karl Marx on colonialism and modernization* (Garden City, NY.: Doubleday and Company, 1968).

Baber, Zaheer, *The science of empire: Scientific knowledge, civilization, and colonial rule in India* (Albany, NY.: State University of New York, 1996).

Bagchi, Amiya K., "De-industrialization in India in the nineteenth century: Some theoretical implications," *Journal of Development Studies* 12, 2 (January 1976): 135-64.

Bagchi, Amiya K., "European and Indian entrepreneurship in India, 1900-1930," in: Edmund Leach and S. N. Mukherjee, eds., *Elites in South Asia* (Cambridge: Cambridge University Press, 1970).

Bairoch, Paul, *Economics and world history* (Chicago: University of Chicago Press, 1993).

Bairoch, Paul, "How and not why? Economic inequalities between 1800 and 1913: Some background figures," in: Jean Batou, ed., *Between development and underdevelopment: The precocious attempts at industrialization of the periphery, 1800-1870* (Geneva: Librairie Droz, 1991).

Bairoch, Paul, *Cities and economic development: From the dawn of history to the present* (Chicago: University of Chicago Press, 1988a).

Bairoch, Paul, "European trade policy, 1815-1914," in: P. Mathias and S. Pollard, eds., *The Cambridge economic history of Europe*, vol. viii, *The industrial economies: The development of economic and social policies* (Cambridge: Cambridge University Press, 1988b).

Bairoch, Paul, "International industrialization levels from 1750 to 1980," *Journal of European Economic History* 11, 2 (Spring 1982): 269-333.

Bairoch, Paul, "The main trends in national economic disparities since the Industrial Revolution," in: Paul Bairoch and Maurice Lévy-Leboyer, eds., *Disparities in economic development since the Industrial Revolution* (New York: St. Martin's Press, 1981).

Bairoch, Paul, "Ecarts internationaux des niveaux de vie avant la rèvolution industrielle," *Les Annales* (January-February 1979).

Bairoch, Paul, *The economic development of the Third World since 1900*, trans., Cynthia Postan (Berkeley, CA.: University of California Press, 1975).

Balassa, Bela, *et al. Development strategies in semi-industrialized economies* (Baltimore: Johns Hopkins University Press, 1982).

Balassa, Bela, "The purchasing power parity doctrine: A reappraisal," *Journal of Political Economy* 72 (December 1964): 584-596.

Baldwin, Robert, "Patterns of development in newly settled regions," *Manchester School of Economic and Social Studies* (May 1956): 161-79.

Baran, Paul, *The political economy of growth* (New York: Monthly Review Press, 1957).

Baran, Paul, "On the political economy of backwardness," *The Manchester School of Economic and Social Studies* (January 1952): 66-84.

Bardhan, Pranab, "Economics of development and the development of economics," *Journal of Economic Perspectives* 7, 2 (Spring 1993): 129-42.

Barrett, David B., *World Christian encyclopedia* (Nairobi: Oxford University Press, 1982).

Barry, Tom, *Roots of rebellion: Land and hunger in Central America* (Boston: South End Press, 1987).

Batchelor, R. A., R. L. Major, and A. D. Morgan, *Industrialization and the basis for trade* (Cambridge: Cambridge University Press, 1980).

Batou, Jean, "Muhammad-'Ali's Egypt, 1805-1848:A command economy in the nineteenth century," in: *Between development and underdevelopment, 1800-1870* (Geneva: Librairie Droz, 1991).

Bauer, Peter T., "The economics of resentment: Colonialism and underdevelopment," *Journal of Contemporary History* 4, 1 (January 1969): 51-71.

Bayly, C. A., *Indian society and the making of the British empire* (Cambridge: Cambridge University Press, 1988).

Behrman, Jere R. and Mark R. Rosenzweig, "Caveat emptor: Cross-country data on education and the labor force," *Journal of Development Economics* 44, 1 (June 1994): 147-72.

Bernal, Martin, *Black Athena: The Afroasiatic roots of classical civilization* (New Brunswick, N. J.: Rutgers University Press, 1987).

Bhagwati, Jagdish, *Foreign trade regimes and economic development : Anatomy and consequences of exchange control regimes* (Cambridge, MA.: Ballinger for National Bureau of Economic Research, 1978).

Blaut, J. M., *The colonizer's model of the world: Geographical diffusionism and Eurocentric history* (New York and London: Guilford Press, 1993).

Bloomfield, Arthur I., "British thought on the influence of foreign trade and investment on growth, 1800-1880," *History of Political economy* 13,1 (Spring 1981): 95-120.

Bornschier, Volker and Christopher Chase-Dunn, "Transnational penetration and economic growth," in: Mitchell A. Seligson and John T. Passe-Smith, eds. *Development and underdevelopment: The political economy of inequality* (Boulder: Lynne Rienner Publishers, 1993).

Brecher, R. and C. Diaz-Alejandro, "Tariffs, foreign capital and immiserizing growth," *Journal of International Economics* 7 (1977): 317-322.

Brennan, Lance, John McDonald, and Ralph Shlomowitz, "Trends in the economic well-being of South Indians under British rule: The anthropometric evidence," *Explorations in Economic History* 31 (April 1994a): 225-260.

Brennan, Lance, John McDonald, and Ralph Shlomowitz, "The heights and economic well-being of North Indians under British rule," *Social Science History* 18, 2 (Summer 1994b): 271-307.

Brenner, Robert, "Agrarian class structure and economic development in pre-industrial Europe," *Past and Present* 70 (February 1976): 30-74.

Bukharin, N., *Imperialism and the world economy* (London: Merlin, 1917 [1972]).

Bulmer-Thomas, Victor, *The political economy of Central America since 1920* (Cambridge: Cambridge University Press, 1987).

Cain, P. J. and A. G. Hopkins, *British imperialism: Innovation and expansion, 1688-1914* (London: Longman, 1993).

Carey, Henry C., *The past, the present and the future* (New York: Augustus M. Kelly, 1847 [1967]).

Carlyle, Thomas, "Signs of the times," in : A. Shelston, ed., *Thomas Carlyle: Selected writings* (Harmondsworth: 1980).

Central Intelligence Agency, *The world factbook, 1992* (Washington: CIA, 1992).

Chaudhuri, K. N., "Foreign trade and balance of payments (1757-1947)," in: Dharma Kumar, ed., *The Cambridge economic history of India, vol. 1* (Cambridge: Cambridge University Press, 1983).

Chenery, Hollis B. and Moises Syrquin, *Patterns of development, 1950-1970* (London: Oxford University Press, 1975).

Chenery, Hollis B. and Lance J. Taylor, "Development patterns: Among countries and over time," *Review of Economics and Statistics* 50 (November 1968): 391-416.

Cherif, M. H., "New trends in the Maghrib: Algeria, Tunisia and Libya," in: J. F. Ade Ajayi, ed., *General history of Africa, VI: Africa in the nineteenth century until the 1880s* (Oxford: Heinemann, 1989).

Clark, Colin, *The conditions of economic progress* (London: Macmillan, 1957).

Cleary, Thomas, *Living and dying with grace: Counsels of Hadrat 'Ali* (Boston: Shambhala, 1996).

Clower, Robert, George Dalton, Mitchell Harwitz and A. A. Walters, *Growth without development: An economic survey of Liberia* (Evanston, IL.: Northwestern University, 1966).

Crafts, N. F. R., British economic growth during the industrial revolution (Oxford: Clarendon Press, 1985).

Crafts, N. F. R., "Patterns of development in nineteenth century Europe," *Oxford Economic Papers* 36 (November 1984): 438-458.

Crenshaw, Edward M., "Democracy and demographic inheritance: The influence of modernity and proto-modernity on political and civil rights, 1965 to 1980," *American Sociological Review* 60, 5 (October 1995): 702-18.

Crouchley, Arthur E., *The economic development of modern Egypt* (London: Longman, Green and Co., 1938).

Crouzet, Francois., *The Victorian economy,* tr. Anthony Forster (New York: Columbia University Press, 1982).

Crowder, Michael, ed., *West African resistance: The military response to colonial occupation* (New York: Africa Publishing Corporation, 1971).

Curtin, Philip D., *The image of Africa: British ideas and action, 1780-1850* (Madison: University of Wisconsin Press, 1964).

Davidson, Basil, *The search for Africa: History, culture, politics* (New York: Random House, 1994).

Davis, Lance E. and Robert A. Huttenback, *Mammon and the pursuit of empire: The economics of British imperialism* (Cambridge: Cambridge University Press, 1988).

Davis, Ralph, "English foreign trade, 1660-1700," in: W. E. Minchinton, ed., *The growth of English overseas trade in the seventeenth and eighteenth centuries* (London: Methuen, 1969).

Deane, Phyllis, *The first industrial revolution* (Cambridge: 1965).

Dixon, Chris, *South East Asia in the world economy* (Cambridge: Cambridge University Press, 1991).

Donges, Jurgen B. and James Riedel, "The expansion of manufactured exports in developing countries: An empirical assessment of supply and demand issues," *Weltwirtschaftliches Archiv* 111, 1 (1977): 58-85.

Dutt, Romesh, *The economic history of India under early British rule* (London: Kegan Paul, Trench, Trubner & Co., 1910).

Easterlin, Richard A., *Growth triumphant: The twenty-first century in historical perspective* (Ann Arbor: University of Michigan Press, 1996).

Edwards, Sebastian, "Openness, trade liberalization, and growth in developing countries," *Journal of Economic Literature* 31, 3 (September 1993): 1358-93.

Eisenstadt, S. N. and Stein Rokkan, eds., *Building nations and states: Models and data resources, Vol. 1* (Beverley Hills, CA.: Sage Publications: 1973).

Elmslie, Bruce, "The endogenous nature of technological progress and transfer in Adam Smith's thought," *History of Political Economy* 26, 4 (Winter 1994): 649-663.

Emmanuel, Arghiri, *Unequal exchange: A study of the imperialism of free trade* (London: New Left Books, 1969 [1972]).

Falk, Richard, "Sovereignty', in : *Oxford Companion to Politics of the World* (Oxford: Oxford University Press, 1993).

Ferns, H. S., *Britain and Argentina in the nineteenth century* (Oxford: Clarendon Press, 1960).

Fieldhouse, David K., *Colonialism, 1870-1945: An introduction* (New York: St. Martin's Press, 1981).

Fieldhouse, David K., *The colonial empires: A comparative survey from the eighteenth century* (New York: Delacorte Press, 1967).

Findlay, Carter Vaugh, "Knowledge and education in the modern Middle East: A comparative view," in: Georges Sabagh, eds., *The modern economic and social history of the Middle East in its world context* (Cambridge: Cambridge University Press, 1989).

Floud, Roderick, "The heights of Europeans since 1750: A new source for European economic history," in: John Komlos, ed., *Stature, living standards, and economic development: Essays in anthropometric history* (Chicago: University of Chicago Press, 1994).

Floud, Roderick, Measuring the transformation of the European economies: Income, health and welfare (CEPR Discussion Paper No. 33: 1984).

Frank, Andre Gunder, *ReOrient: Global Economy in the Asian Age* (Berkeley, CA.: University of California Press, 1998).

Frank, Andre Gunder, *Capitalism and underdevelopment in Latin America* (New York: Monthly Review Press, 1967).

Furnivall, J. S., *Colonial policy and practice* (Cambridge: Cambridge University Press, 1948).

Gallagher, John and Ronald Robinson, "The imperialism of free trade," *Economic History Review*, 2nd Series, 6, 1 (1953): 1-15, reprinted in: Alan G. L. Shaw, *Great Britain and the colonies, 1815-1865* (London: Methuen, 1970): 142-63.

Ganguly, P., "Progressive decline in stature in India: A study of sixty population groups, " in: W. A. Stini, ed., *Physiological and morphological adaptation and evolution* (The Hague: Mouton Publishers, 1979).

Gerschenkron, Alexander, *Economic backwardness in historical perspective* (Cambridge, MA.: Harvard University Press, 1962).

Gifford, Prosser and Timothy C. Weiskel, "African education in the colonial context: French and British styles," in: Prosser Gifford and Wm. Roger Louis, eds., *France and Britain in Africa: Imperial rivalry and colonial rule* (New Haven: Yale University Press, 1971).

Ginsburg, Norton, *Atlas of economic development* (Chicago: Chicago University Press, 1961).

Golay, Frank H., "Southeast Asia: The 'colonial drain' revisited," in: C. D. Cowan and O. W. Walters, eds., *Southeast Asian history and historiography* (Ithaca: Cornell University Press, 1976).

Gong, Gerrit W., *The standard of 'civilization' in international society* (Oxford: Clarendon Press, 1984).

Goody, Jack, *The East in the West* (Cambridge: Cambridge University Press, 1996).

Gregory, Robert G., *The rise and fall of philanthropy in Africa: The Asian contribution* (New Brunswick, NJ.: Transaction Publishers, 1992).

Griffin, Keith and John Gurley, "Radical analyses of imperialism, the Third World, and the transition to socialism: A survey article," *Journal of Economic Literature* 23, 3 (September 1985): 1089-1143.

Haberler, Gottfried, *International trade and economic development* (Cairo: National Bank of Egypt, Fiftieth Anniversary Lectures, 1959), reprinted in: Anthony Y. C. Koo, ed., *Selected essays of Gottfried Haberler* (Cambridge, MA.: The MIT Press, 1985).

Hamilton, Alexander, *Papers on Public Credit, Commerce and Finance,* edited by Samuel McKee, Jr. (New York: Columbia University Press, 1791 [1934]).

Hanson II, John R., *Trade in transition: Exports from the Third World, 1840-1900* (New York: Academic Press, 1980).

Harnetty, Peter, "The imperialism of free trade: Lancashire and the Indian cotton duties, 1859-1862," *Economic History Review*, 18, 2 (1965): 333-49.

Headrick, Daniel R., *The tentacles of progress: Technology transfer in the age of imperialism* (New York: Oxford University Press, 1988).

Headrick, Daniel R., *The tools of empire: Technology and European imperialism in the nineteenth century* (New York: Oxford University Press, 1981).

Heckscher, Eli, "The effect of foreign trade on the distribution of income," *Ekonomisk Tidskrift*, 21 (1919): 497-512, reprinted in: American Economic Association, *Readings in the theory of international trade* (Philadelphia. Blakiston, 1949).

Hilferding, Rudolf, *Finance capital: A study of the latest phase in capitalist development* (London: Routledge & Kegal Paul, 1910 [1981]).

Hill, Polly, *The Gold Coast cocoa farmer* (London: Oxford University Press, 1956).

Hinsley, F. H., *Sovereignty* (Cambridge, MA.: Cambridge University Press, 1986).

Hirsch, Leonard Paul, "Incorporation into the world economy: Empirical tests of dependency theory," in: Mary Ann Tetreault and Charles Frederick Abel, eds., *Dependency theory and the return of high politics* (New York: Greenwood Press, 1986).

Hirschman, Albert, "The rise and decline of development economics," in: *Essays in trespassing* (Cambridge: Cambridge University Press, 1981).

Hirschman, Albert O., *The strategy of economic development* (New Haven, CT.: Yale University Press, 1958).

Hont, Istvan, "The 'rich country-poor country' debate in the Scottish political economy," in: Istvan Hont and Michael Ignatieff, eds., *Wealth and virtue* (Cambridge: Cambridge University Press, 1983).

Hughes, Jonathan, *American economic history* (Glenview, IL.: Scott, Foresman and Co., 1990).

Hume, David, *Essays: Moral, political and literary*, eds., T. H. Green and T. H. Grose (Darmstadt: Scientia Verlag Aalen, 1742 [1964]).

Hussain, Asad, *British India's relations with the Kingdom of Nepal* (London: Allen and Unwin, 1970).

Ingham, Barbara, "Vent for surplus reconsidered with Ghanaian evidence," *Journal of Development Studies* 15, 3 (April 1979): 19-37.

Ingram, James C., *Economic change in Thailand since 1850* (Stanford, CA.: Stanford University Press, 1955).

Issawi, Charles, *An economic history of the Middle East and North Africa* (New York: Columbia University Press, 1982).

Jalal, Ferhang, *The role of government in the industrialization of Iraq* (London: Frank Cass, 1972).

James, Alan, *Sovereign statehood: The basis of international society* (London: Allen and Unwin, 1986).

Johnson, Harry G., "The possibility of income losses from increased efficiency or factor accumulation in the presence of tariffs," *Economic Journal* 77,1 (March 1967): 151-54.

Kennedy, Paul, *African capitalism: The struggle for ascendancy* (Cambridge: Cambridge University Press, 1988).

Keynes, John M., "The end of laissez faire," in: William Ebenstein and Alan O. Ebenstein, eds., *Great political thinkers: Plato to the present* (Fortworth, TX.: Holt, Rinehart and Winston, 1991).

Kilby, Peter, "African labor productivity reconsidered," *Economic Journal* 71 (June 1961): 273-91.

Kleiman, Ephraim, "Trade and the decline of colonialism," *The Economic Journal* 86 (September 1976): 459-80.

Kleiman, Ephraim, "Heirs to colonial trade," *Journal of Development Economics* 4,2 (1977): 93-103.

Kravis, Irving B., "The three faces of the international comparison project," *World Bank Research Observer* 1,1 (January 1986): 3-26.

Kravis, Irving, Alan W. Heston and Robert Summers, *World product and income* (Baltimore, MD.: Johns Hopkins University Press, 1982).

Kravis, Irving B., Zoltan Kenessey, Alan W. Heston, and Robert Summers, *A system of international comparisons of gross domestic product and purchasing power* (Baltimore, MD.: Johns Hopkins University Press, 1975).

Krueger, Anne O., *Foreign trade regimes and economic development: Liberalization attempts and consequences* (Cambridge, MA.: Ballinger for National Bureau for Economic Research, 1978).

Kurian, G. T., *Encyclopedia of the Third World* (New York: Facts on File, Inc., 1982).

Kuznets, Simon, "Quantitative aspects of the economic growth of nations: X," *Economic Development and Cultural Change* 15, 2 (part 2) (January 1967): 1-73.

Kuznets, Simon, *Economic growth and structure* (New York: Norton, 1965).

Kuznets, Simon, "Underdeveloped countries and the pre-industrial phase in the advanced countries: An attempt at comparison," in: *Proceedings of the world population conference* (Geneva: United Nations,

1954), reprinted in: A. N. Agarwala and S. P. Singh, eds., *The economics of underdevelopment* (London: Oxford University, 1958).

Kuznets, Simon, *Economic growth and structure* (New York: Norton, 1965).

Kyi, U Khin Maung, "Western enterprise and economic development," *The Journal of Burma Research Society* 53, 1 (June 1970): 25-51.

Kyriacou, George A., *Level and growth effects of human capital: A cross-country study of the convergence hypothesis* (New York: C. V. Starr Center for Applied Economics, Department of Economics, New York University, 1991).

LaFeber, Walter, *Inevitable revolutions: The United States in Central America* (New York: W. W. Norton, 1984).

Landes, David S., *The wealth and poverty of nations: Why some are so rich and some so poor* (New York: W. W. Norton, 1998).

Landes, David S., *The unbound Prometheus: Technological change and industrial development in Western Europe from 1750 to the present* (Cambridge, UK: Cambridge University Press, 1969).

Laroui, A., "Morocco from the beginning of the nineteenth century to 1880," in: J. F. Ade Ajayi, ed., *General history of Africa, vi: Africa in the nineteenth century until the 1880s* (Paris: UNESCO and Heinemann International, 1989).

Lenin, Vladimir I., *Imperialism: The highest stage of capitalism* (New York: International Publishers, 1917 [1963]).

Lenski, Gerhard and Patrick D. Nolan, "Trajectories of development: A test of ecological-evolutionary theory," *Social Forces*, 63, 1 (September 1994): 1-23.

Levin, Jonathan V., *The export economies: Their pattern of development in historical perspective* (Cambridge: Harvard University Press, 1961).

Levine, Ross and David Renelt, "A sensitivity analysis of cross-country growth regressions," *American Economic Review* 82,4 (September 1992): 942-63.

Lewis, W. Arthur, *Growth and fluctuations, 1870-1913* (London: George Allen and Unwin, 1978a).

Lewis, W. Arthur, *The evolution of the international economic order* (Princeton, NJ: Princeton University Press, 1978b).

Lewis, W. Arthur, "Economic development with unlimited supplies of labor," *Manchester School of Economic and Social Studies* 22 (May 1954): 139-91.

Lieberman, Victor, "An age of commerce in Southeast Asia? Problems of regional coherence--A review article," *The Journal of Asian Studies* 54,3 (August 1995): 796-807.

List, Friedrich, *The national system of political economy*, translated by Sampson S. Lloyd, ed., (Fairfield, N.J.: Augustus M. Kelley, 1841 [1991]).

Little, I. M. D., Tibor Scitovsky and Maurice F. G. Scott, *Industry and trade in some developing countries* (Oxford: Oxford University Press, for OECD, 1970).

Livingstone, I., "The impact of colonization and independence on export growth in Britain and France," *Oxford Bulletin of Economics and Statistics* 38, 2 (1976): 211-18.

Lockwood, William W., *The economic development of Japan* (Princeton, NJ: Princeton University Press, 1954).

Low, J. M., "An eighteenth century controversy in the theory of economic progress," *The Manchester School* 20, 3 (September 1952): 311-30.

Lucas, Robert, "On the mechanics of economic development," *Journal of Monetary Economics*, 22 (1988): 2-42.

Luxemburg, Rosa, *The accumulation of capital* (New York: Monthly Review Press, 1913 [1964]).

MacDougall, G. D. A., "British and American exports: A study suggested by the theory of comparative costs: Part I," *Economic Journal* 61(1951): 697-724.

Maddison, Angus, *Monitoring the world economy, 1820-1992* (Paris: Organization for Economic Cooperation and Development, 1995).

Maddison, Angus, "The colonial burden: A comparative perspective," in: Maurice Scott, ed., *Public policy and economic development* (Oxford: Clarendon Press, 1990).

Maddison, Angus, *The world economy in the twentieth century* (Paris: OECD Development Center, 1989).

Maddison, Angus, "A comparison of levels of GDP *per capita* in developed and developing countries, 1700-1980," *Journal of Economic History* 43, 1 (March 1983): 27-41.

Maizels, Alfred, "Commodities in crisis," in: *The economics of primary commodities: Models, analysis and policy*, eds. David Sapsford and Wyn Morgan (Aldershot: Edward Elgar, 1994).

Mandemakers, C. A. and J. L. Van Zanden, "The height of conscripts and national income: Apparent relations and misconception," *Explorations in Economic History* 30 (1993): 81-97.

Manning, Patrick, *Francophone Sub-Saharan Africa: 1880-1985* (Cambridge: Cambridge University Press, 1988).

Mansfield, Peter, *A history of the Middle East* (New York: Viking, 1991).

Marx, Karl, *A contribution to the critique of political economy* (New York: International Publishers, 1970 [1859]).

Mathew, W. M., "The imperialism of free trade: Peru, 1820-1870," *Economic History Review* 21, 3 (December 1968): 561-79.

McCulloch, J. R., *The principles of political economy* (New York: Augustus M. Kelley, 1864 [1965]).

Michael, Franz H. and George E. Taylor, *The Far East in the modern world* (New York: Holt, Rinehart and Winston, 1964).

Mill, John Stuart, *Principles of political economy* (New York: Augustus M. Kelley, 1864 [1965])

Mitchell, Brian R., *International historical statistics: The Americas, 1750-1988* (New York: Stockton Press, 1993).

Mitchell, Brian R., *International historical statistics: Europe, 1750-1988* (New York: Stockton Press, 1992).

Moosvi, Shireen, "Note on Professor Alan Heston's 'Standard of living in Akbar's time': A comment," *The Indian Economic and Social History Review* 14, 3 (1977): 397-401.

Morris, Cynthia Taft and Irma Adelman, *Comparative patterns of economic development, 1850-1914* (Baltimore, N. J.: The Johns Hopkins University Press, 1988).

Morris, Morris D., "Towards a reinterpretation of nineteenth century Indian economic history," *Journal of Economic History* 23, 4 (October 1967): 606-618.

Mundell, Robert A., "International trade and factor mobility," *American Economic Review* 47 (June 1957): 321-35.

Mullet, Charles F., *The British empire-commonwealth: A plural community in evolution* (Washington, D. C.: American Historical Association, 1966).

Myint, Hla, "Adam Smith's theory of international trade in the perspective of economic development," *Economica* 44, 175 (August 1977): 231-248.

Myint, Hla, "The 'classical theory' of international trade and the underdeveloped countries," *The Economic Journal* 68 (June 1958): 317-37, reprinted in: *Economic theory and the underdeveloped countries* (London: Oxford University Press, 1971).

Myint, Hla, "An interpretation of economic backwardness," *Oxford Economic Papers*, New Series, 6, 2 (June 1954): 132-63.

Myrdal, Gunnar, *Economic theory and underdeveloped regions* (London: University Paperbacks, 1957 [1964]).

Needham, Joseph, *Science and civilization in China* (Cambridge: Cambridge University Press, 1954).

Nehru, Vikram, Eric Swanson and Ashutosh Dubey, "A new database on human capital stock in developing countries: Sources, methodology and results," *Journal of Development Economics* 46 (1995): 379-401.

Ness, Gayl D. and William Stahl, "Western imperialist armies in Asia," *Comparative Studies in Society and History*, 19, 1 (January 1977): 2-29.

Offer, Avner, "The British empire, 1870-1914: A waste of money?" *Economic History Review*, 46, 2 (May 1993): 215-38.

Ohlin, Bertil, *Interregional and international trade* (Cambridge: Harvard University Press, 1933).

Panikkar, K. M., *Indian states and the government of India* (London: Martin Hopkinson, 1932).

Papageorgiou, Demetris, Michael Michaely and Armeane M. Choksi, *Liberalizing foreign trade* (Oxford: Basil Blackwell, 1991).

Parthasarathi, Prasannan, "Rethinking wages and competitiveness in eighteenth century India: Britain and South India," *Past and Present* 158 (February 1998): 79-109.

Peemans, Jean-Philippe, "Capital accumulation in the Congo under colonialism: The role of the state," in: Peter Duignan and L. H. Gann, eds., *Colonialism in Africa: 1870-1960* (Cambridge: Cambridge University Press, 1975).

Philpott, Daniel, "Sovereignty: An introduction and brief history", *Journal of International Affairs* 48, 2 (Winter 1995): 355-68.

Platt, D. C. M., ed., *Business imperialism, 1840-1930: An inquiry based on the British experience in Latin America* (Oxford: Clarendon Press, 1977).

Platt, D. C. M., *Latin America and British trade, 1806-1914* (London: A. and C. Black, 1972a).

Platt, D. C. M., "Economic imperialism and the businessman: Britain and Latin America before 1914," in: Roger Owen and Bob Sutcliffe, eds., *Studies in the theory of imperialism* (Harlow, Essex: Longman, 1972b).

Platt, D. C. M., *Finance, trade and politics in British foreign policy, 1815-1914* (Oxford: Clarendon Press, 1968).

Potash, Robert A., *Mexican government and industrial development in the early republic* (Amherst, MA.: University of Massachusetts Press, 1983).

Prebisch, Raul, "Five stages in my thinking on development," in: Gerald M. Meier and Dudley Seers, eds., *Pioneers in Development* (New York: Oxford University Press, 1984).

Prebisch, Raul, *The economic development of Latin America and its principal problems* (New York: United Nations, 1950a).

Prebisch, Raul, *Economic survey of Latin America, 1949* (New York: United Nations, 1950b).

Psacharopoulos, G., and A-M, Arriagada, "The educational attainment of the labor force: An international comparison," *International Labor Review*, 125, 5 (September-October 1986): 561-74.

Rae, John, *New principles of political economy* (New York: Augustus M. Kelly, 1834 [1964]).

Ranger, Terence, "African attempts to control education in East and Central Africa, 1900-1939," *Past and Present* 32 (December 1965): 57-85.

Reid, Anthony, *Southeast Asia in the age of commerce, 1450-1680, Vol. 1: The lands below the winds* (New Haven, CT.: Yale University Press, 1988).

Ricardo, David, *The principles of political economy and taxation* (London: Dent, 1817 [1965])

Robinson, Ronald, "Non-European foundations of European imperialism: Sketch for a theory of collaboration," in: Roger Owen and Bob Sutcliffe, eds., *Studies in the theory of imperialism* (Burnt Mill, UK: Longman, 1972).

Romer, Paul, "Increasing returns and long-run growth," *Journal of Political Economy* 94 (1986): 1002-37.

Ronning, C. Neale, ed., *Intervention in Latin America* (New York: Knopf, 1970).

Rosenberg, Nathan, "Neglected dimensions in analysis of economic change," *Oxford Bulletin of Economics and Statistics* 26, 1 (1964): 59-77.

Rostow, W. W., *The world economy: History and prospect* (Austin, TX.: University of Texas, 1978).

Rostow, W. W., *How it all began: Origins of the modern economy* (New York: McGraw-Hill, 1975).

Sachau, Edward, *Albiruni's India* (New York: W. W. Norton, 1971).

Said, Edward, *Orientalism* (New York: Random House, 1978).

Samuelson, Paul, "Theoretical notes on trade problems," *Review of Economics and Statistics* 46 (May 1964): 145-154.

Samuelson, Paul A., "International trade and the equalization of factor prices," *Economic Journal* 58, 2 (1948): 181-97.

Schoonover, Thomas D., *United States in Central America: 1860-1911* (Durham: Duke University Press, 1991).

Schwartz, Herman M., *States and markets: History, geography, and the development of the international political economy* (New York: St. Martin's Press, 1994).

Smith, Adam, *An inquiry into the nature and causes of the wealth of nations* (New York: The Modern Library, 1776 [1965]).

Smith, Adam, *Lectures on jurisprudence*, ed., R. L. Meek, D. D. Raphael and P. G. Stein (Oxford: Clarendon Press, 1762-3, 1766 [1978]).

Smith, Sheila, "Colonialism in economic theory: The experience of Nigeria," *Journal of Development Studies* 15, 3 (April 1979): 38-59.

Solow, Robert, "A contribution to the theory of economic growth," *Quarterly Journal of Economics* 70, 1 (February 1956): 65-94.

Stavrianos, L. S., *Global rift: The Third World comes of age* (New York: William Morrow, 1981).

Stein, Stanley J., *The Brazilian cotton manufacture: Textile enterprise in an underdeveloped area, 1850-1950* (Cambridge, MA.: Harvard University Press, 1957).

Strang, David, "The social construction of state sovereignty," in: Thomas J. Biersteker and Cynthia Weber, eds., *State sovereignty as social construct* (Cambridge, MA.: Cambridge University Press, 1996).

Stryker, J. Dirck, *Trade, exchange rate, and agricultural pricing policies in Ghana* (Washington D. C.: The World Bank, 1990).

Sugiyama, Shinya, *Japan's industrialization in the world economy* (London: The Athlone Press, 1988).

Summers, Robert, Alan Heston, Betina Aten and Daniel Nuxoll, *Penn World Table* (Mark 5.6) (Boston: National Bureau of Economic Research, 1995).

Svedberg, Peter, "The profitability of UK foreign direct investment under colonialism, *Journal of Development Economics*, 11 (December 1982): 273-86.

Svedberg, Peter, "Colonial enforcement of foreign direct investment," *The Manchester School*, 49, 1 (March 1981): 21-38.

Taylor, Charles L. and Michael Hudson, *World handbook of political and social indicators* (New Haven, CT.: Yale University Press, 1972).

Tomlinson, B. R., "The political economy of the Raj: The decline of colonialism," *Journal of Economic History* 42,1 (March 1982): 133-37.

Toutain, J. -C., "Le produit intérieur brut de la France de 1789 à 1982," *Economies et Sociétés-Cahiers de l'I.S.M.E.A.*, Série A.F. 15 (1987).

Trebilcock, Clive, *The industrialization of the continental powers, 1780-1914* (London: Longman, 1981).

Van de Klundert, Theo. C. M. J., and S. Smulders, "Reconstructing growth theory: A survey," *De Economist*, 140, 2 (1992): 177-203.

Wade, Robert, *Governing the market: Economic policy and the role of the government in East Asian industrialization* (Princeton, NJ.: Princeton University Press, 1990).

Wallerstein, Immanuel, *The capitalist world economy* (Cambridge: Cambridge University Press, 1979).

Wallerstein, Immanuel, *The modern world-system: Capitalist agriculture and the origins of European world-economy in the sixteenth century* (New York: Academic Press, 1974).

Waltz, Kenneth, *Theory of international politics* (Reading, MA.: Addison-Wesley, 1979).

Warren, Bill, "Imperialism and capitalist industrialization," *New Left Review* 81 (1973): 3-44.

Warren, Bill, *Imperialism: Pioneer of capitalism* (London: New Left Books, 1980).

Washbrook, David, "Land and labor in late eighteenth-century South India: The Golden Age of the Pariah," in: Peter Robb, ed., *Dalit movements and the meanings of labor in India* (Delhi: 1993).

Wilks, Ivor, "The transition of Islamic learning in the Western Sudan," in Jack Goody, ed., *Literacy in traditional societies* (New York: Oxford University Press, 1968).

Williamson, John, "Lowest common denominator or neoliberal manifesto: The polemics of the Washington consensus," in: Richard M. Auty and John Toye, eds., *Challenging orthodoxies* (New York: St. Martin's Press, 1996).

Williamson, John, ed., *The political economy of policy reform* (Washington, D. C.: Institute for International Economics, 1994).

World Bank, *World development report, 1997* (New York: Oxford University Press for World Bank, 1997).

World Bank, *World development report, 1996* (New York: Oxford University Press for World Bank, 1996).

World Bank, *World development report, 1986* (New York: Oxford University Press for World Bank, 1986).

World Bank, *World tables, 1976* (Baltimore, MD.: Johns Hopkins University Press for World Bank, 1976).

Wrigley, E. Anthony, "Urban growth and agricultural change: England and the continent in the early modern period," *Journal of Interdisciplinary History* 25, 4 (Spring 1985): 683-728.

Yates, P. Lamartine, *Forty years of trade* (London: George Allen and Unwin, 1959).

Zewde, Bahru, *A history of modern Ethiopia, 1855-1974* (London: James Currey, 1991).

Zimmerman, L. J., "The distribution of world income, 1860-1960," in: Egbert de Vries, ed., *Essays on unbalanced growth* (The Hague: Mouton, 1962).

Author Index

Subject Index